D0233112

Claud
Cockburn
The Devil's
Decade

Claud Cockburn
The Devil's Decade

Sidgwick & Jackson

First published in Great Britain in 1973
by Sidgwick and Jackson Limited

Copyright © 1973 by Claud Cockburn

I.S.B.N. 0.283.97883.X

Designed by Paul Watkins

Picture research by Anne-Marie Ehrlich

ACKNOWLEDGEMENTS

We are grateful to the following publishers for permission to
reproduce extracts from the works listed below:
Cassell and Co. Ltd for Winston S. Churchill's *The Second
World War*; Eyre and Spottiswoode (Publishers) Ltd for
Hugh Thomas's *The Spanish Civil War*; the Hamlyn
Publishing Group Ltd for Alan Bullock's *Hitler: A Study
in Tyranny*; Martin Secker & Warburg Ltd for William L.
Shirer's *The Rise and Fall of the Third Reich*; the Clarendon
Press, Oxford, for A. J. P. Taylor's *English History 1914-1945*;
Weidenfeld & Nicolson Ltd for Robert James's (ed.) *The
Diaries of Sir Henry Channon*.

Printed photolitho in Great Britain
by Ebenezer Baylis and Son Ltd
The Trinity Press, Worcester, and London
for Sidgwick and Jackson Limited
1 Tavistock Chambers, Bloomsbury Way
London WC1A 2SG

Contents

1 After the Crash
1929-31 *A lethal sickness*

'**G**entlemen, in the little moment that remains to us between the crisis and the catastrophe, we may well drink a glass of champagne.'

The words fell icily into what was supposed to be a celebration, a thanksgiving for deliverance. The time was the mid-summer of 1931, the place Washington. Paul Claudel, French Ambassador and poet, was addressing statesmen and diplomats gathered at the Embassy to hail a new era. Those present felt, or claimed to feel, that as a result of a great American economic and political initiative, the western world had turned a decisive corner out of Queer Street on to the highway leading to a bright future.

The initiative thus greeted was called the Hoover Moratorium, suspending all payments of inter-governmental war debts. Described at the time as 'momentous', 'an historic act', the great Hoover Moratorium proved historic only in the sense that it is remembered only by historians. It was an enormous non-event. Yet the bleak blankness of its negative effect did have historic importance. The giant opens his mouth to roar, the throat muscles twitch and strain. No sound comes. It is seen that the giant has been struck dumb.

Claudel's words, shocking to the euphoric, were preview and epitaph of the 1930s. The 'little moment' of that decade ticked between the New York stock-market crash of later 1929, and the outbreak of the Second World War.

With the resources of the French Intelligence Service at his disposal, and his own qualities as poet and seer, Claudel was well equipped to see and even foresee. He could see, and soon everyone could see, that the Very Important People, the leading figures drinking champagne in the Embassy that day, were figures only, leading nothing. The power to take effective initiatives had visibly passed from their hands. As the banks crashed in Austria and the financial structure of central Europe shook, it was hideously revealed that the initiative, if it could be so called, lay with the unemployed millions on the streets of Vienna, Berlin, and the cities of the Ruhr Valley. Their existence, their state of mind, the direction of their activity, was determining the policies of governments, bankers, industrialists. Every government justified its actions as being essential to curb, appease and possibly reduce the number of unemployed. Every political leader fought primarily to rescue the support, or at least avert the hostility, of the unemployed.

Less than two million were registered unemployed in Germany in 1929, and the number was to rise fast to more than six million in March 1932. Three political directorates struggled to control and conduct them. The Social Democrats, so long allied with the middle class against the Left to maintain the Weimar Republic, were compromised and paralysed by the collapse, at the end of 1929, of the prosperity which Weimar, materially and spiritually nourished by Wall Street, had displayed as its aim and its justification. They had become a defensive force. Their support in the middle class increased. But now Weimar and its supporters were identified with ruinous unemployment. The mass of the unemployed were beyond Social Democratic control.

The Communist vote in the Reichstag elections had risen from 3,265,000 in 1928 to 4,592,000 in September 1930. But the Communists had no allies outside the working class. And their lines of communication with a great mass of the working class, particularly the older men and the most securely

9

employed, were blocked by the solid power of the Social Democrats. Though the Communists were publicly portrayed by the Right everywhere from Berlin to London to New York as threatening imminent revolution, neither the Central Committee of the Communist International, nor the French Foreign Office observers in Berlin believed it.

The Nazi vote in 1928 had been 810,000. In September 1930 it was 6,400,000. With his huge unemployed following as leverage, Hitler had by-passed the Social Democrats to negotiate with the middle-class leadership, and to make, early in 1931, a kind of non-aggression pact with the Army High Command. By the spring of that year he was strong enough to raise enormous subsidies from the chiefs of the coal, iron and steel industries, and the banks. They saw him as a means to rationalize the rickety German capitalist system in the fullest sense. He would break the power of the trade unions. He would repudiate Versailles and reparations. He would channel multi-millions of money into rearmament. He would make them the industrial masters of Europe. Otto Dietrich, his press chief, wrote: 'In the summer of 1931, our Führer suddenly decided to concentrate on cultivating the influential economic magnates . . . In the following months he traversed Germany from end to end, holding private interviews with prominent personalities. Any rendezvous was chosen, either in Berlin or in the provinces, in the Hotel Kaiserhof or in some lonely forest glade. Privacy was absolutely imperative.'

Complete privacy for the togetherness with the tycoons in the forest glades was not preserved. Colonel Chapouilly, French Military Attaché in Berlin, was informed of such matters, and reported to the Foreign Office. These facts were known to Claudel as his guests drank their champagne. Destination Catastrophe was no secret either. Many thousands of people, with less detailed information, were out chalking and stencilling the words 'Fascism Means War' on walls and pavements all over Europe.

France, too, had lost the power of initiative. In the early summer of 1931 France had taken positive action to prevent a projected Customs Union of Germany with Austria. Over a period of months the Banque de France had executed a strategic withdrawal of its balances from the Austrian banks. This operation, known as the March of the Golden Soldiers, was an attempted continuance by other means of the policies of the First World War, the Treaty of Versailles, and the occupation of the Ruhr. It was the last such attempt. It gained its objective. The Customs Union was wrecked. But so was the biggest bank in Austria. The intention had been to neutralize Germany by a sanitary enfeeblement. The consequences outran the intention. By mid-summer the situation was beyond the control of the Banque de France. And in Paris, not to mention lonely forest glades available for secret meetings, representatives—unavowed and unavowable—of the French Foreign Office had begun in privacy with representatives of the Kremlin to probe the possibilities of a Franco-Soviet defence pact against Germany which, if publicly mooted in 1931, would have been denounced by both prospective partners as 'unthinkable'.

The policies of the Kremlin were less mysteriously enigmatic than Winston Churchill had proclaimed them to be. Or they were enigmatic only in the sense that they were obliquely affected by the uncertain struggles for power to direct the expanding forces of the domestic revolutionary economy. On this matter the French and German Intelligence Services were better informed than others. Only in France and Germany was it assumed that for the relevant Services not to have some understanding of Marxism was to understand nothing. Elsewhere in the West such education was deemed irrelevant. British and American Intelligence reports from the Soviet Union were thus weighted and distorted by the assumption that policies counter productive in a capitalist system must be so in the Soviet Union too.

Whatever might be said for public consumption, among informed observers one fact of life in 1931 was axiomatic, absolute: the Union needed a long, long peace. It remained axiomatic throughout the decade. As could be seen by Claudel, with his immense experience of East Asia, and by others calculating the probable length of the 'little moment', the fact of the Russian need for peace was both a positive and negative factor. It maintained in the world one large element of calculable stability. It implied, further, that in the event of a rationalized and armed Germany now emerging, the U.S.S.R. would prove less isolationist than the U.S.A.; it would be prepared to concert practical measures of defence with capitalist allies. Negatively, this need of the Soviet Union for peace was a standing invitation to aggressors to take advantage of the weaknesses which it inevitably implied. Hitler had emphatically and repeatedly assured both his German financial backers and western governments, particularly the British Government, that he had no desire to risk any confrontation with the West: his aim, as stated years earlier in *Mein Kampf* (published in 1925, and completed in 1926) was domination of Europe from the Rhineland to the Urals. Nobody needed to be convinced that such was his objective. But the vulnerability of the Soviet Union gave the objective a practical credibility. That fact produced the fatal flaw in the calculations, the poisonous bug in the bloodstream of the West throughout the 1930s. For political reasons it was desirable, for economic and military reasons it seemed logical, that Hitler's Germany should make its peace in the West and its war in the East. The combination of these assumptions was Hitler's greatest and indispensable source of strength, nationally and internationally, particularly in London. Thus the youth and comparative weakness of the Soviet state speeded the passing of the 'little moment'. The course of events was regulated by the pace at which the socialist state, in the teenage of its revolution, could build up its strength. As is known, the pace was not fast enough to avert the catastrophe.

To observers such as Claudel, the general course of events, the way, as they say, things were going, was grimly plain. Nobody could predict or pinpoint the details. The eyes of the most dolorous seer could not have envisaged, say, the streets of Addis Ababa and Harar full of men blinded on the mountain fronts by Italian mustard gas. But even superficial knowledge of the nature and aims of Italian Fascism provided a certainty that a colonial war would be attempted. Nobody could give precise advance notice of General Franco's revolt and the resultant Spanish War. But everyone, after the abdication of Alfonso XIII in 1931, could be sure that the Republic would not be permitted to develop without armed attack.

Some who drank Claudel's champagne that day, and had been exposed all week to the optimism of President Hoover and his entourage, boggled uneasily at the gap between what the United States claimed to be able to do to 'bring about world recovery', and the realities of its situation.

Following the collapse of the stock-market in 1929 the pace of the economic decline had become as important as its extent. Whatever the figures told about the fall in production, the number of bankruptcies, the drop in industrial freight loadings, the rise in the number unemployed; however truthfully or judiciously such figures could be used to show that the situation was by no means catastrophic, the suddenness and violence of the big jolt of 1929 had largely nullified the potential effect of such sober considerations. The statistics were droned out over the radio, the economists said their impeccable pieces. To the majority of listeners the situation was more truthfully and convincingly summed up in vulgar colloquialisms. The country was on the skids. The situation was all screwed up.

It was thought not unreasonable to suppose that Red revolution rather than prosperity was what was really just around the corner. The facts of the situation did not justify such fears or expectations. The unemployed numbered millions, and the number rose sickeningly every week. But, despite long-ago sectional triumphs of the I.W.W. (the Wobblies), notably in the north-western states, and partly just because of the glamour of the Wobblie tradition, the American unemployed in the crucial industrial centres were almost wholly unorganized. They were not a force adapted to anything beyond production of local anarchy. That being so, their existence exercised an enfeebling pressure on the still relatively weak trade union organizations of the employed. Far from thinking in terms of revolutionary political and economic action, the employed—organized or not—were paralysed by the fear of imminent unemployment. The American system was constructed so as to produce just that effect. No dole, no national insurance system existed to keep the unemployed a little above starvation point, and thus diminish the fear of unemployment and the effect of that fear in eroding resistance to wage cuts. (Contemporary American critics described the British system of Unemployment Insurance as simply 'buying off revolution'.) Despite riotous outbreaks here and there, violently contained by the police, the army, or para-military company guards, no danger from that quarter was seriously apprehended by serious people.

But the general weakening of the economy, the collapse of credit, the drying up of investment and of buying power, the nearly lethal sickness of the banking system, added up to a situation in which the operating power of the United States on the world scene was reduced to a wretchedly low level.

Initiatives could be offered, supported by all available financial inducements and resources. The inducements and the pressures that could be exerted were still numerous. But they were not enough. They could not impose policies. All that type of operation was hamstrung.

It was evident that the crucial area was, for the time being, England. Given the nearly chaotic condition of central Europe, England was now the front line of the struggle to save the system. England, too, was in crisis. But in England it might still be possible not only to avert disaster, but actually to control and turn the crisis to positive advantage.

2 Britain 1931

The dogs bark and the caravan moves on

Britain was in the front line of economic defence and the potential base for any possible counter attack. But the base, too, was insecure, though not so spectacularly as in Wall Street—the seismographs were quivering.

As was twice to happen again (in 1945 and 1964), in at least nominal charge of the political apparatus was a newly elected Labour Government. In the general election of 1929, Labour had won the greatest number of seats but, without a clear parliamentary majority, had to rely on Liberal support to carry on the government.

The arrival in office of the Labour Government under the leadership of Ramsay MacDonald had been regarded by the upper and middle classes in Britain and abroad with mixed feelings.

The politically naïve supposed it to be the ominous prelude to an alarming advance of proletarian power. They made loose but scarifying references to Kerensky.

At the other extreme, the Smart-Alecs, the fly-boys of political punditry, saw MacDonald and his colleagues as cushions or safety-valves: in time of dangerous social crisis, better to have a Labour Government to guide and where necessary moderate the excitements of the working class. The workers would submit, under a trusted Labour Government, to sacrifices which they would resist if demanded by Tories.

A third school of thought, which in the event prevailed, held that while the Smart-Alecs might be right in theory, things were moving too fast to allow the theory to be fully tested. Ramsay MacDonald himself might remain useful as a Labourist symbol. A Labour Government was not up to the demands of the job.

For people with even moderately long memories the state of affairs at the British base presented disquieting aspects. It was less than twenty years since the working class, with miners, railwaymen and dockers in the front ranks, had passed over from the defensive to the offensive and surged forward in a series of industrial strike actions which visibly threatened to topple the British social structure in syndicalist revolution.

It was barely ten years since the Government, in a defensive and offensive action against the loose 'triple alliance' of the miners, railway workers and transport workers had found it necessary to introduce an Emergency Powers Act (1920) which in peacetime gave it dictatorial authority previously regarded as tolerable by British citizens only in war. The menace from the working-class forces had been checked partly by the Emergency Powers Act, partly by the growth of vast unemployment. In June 1921 the unemployed numbered over two million. Unorganized, and almost destitute, their existence enfeebled the forces of the employed; blunting the strike weapon and frightening men and their families with the prospect of themselves falling into the wretched condition of the unemployed.

But for the leaders of finance and industry, for the middle class in general and for the huge mandarinate of the official class, there had been some exceedingly *mauvais quart d'heure* periods when the stability of the social structure seemed precarious indeed.

It was just five years since the carefully prepared showdown with the

16   *Previous pages: Dancing on a volcano—debutante's ball, 1931*

working class, culminating in the General Strike, had been successfully achieved with the total and in many respects ignominious defeat of the trade unions. The victory had been determinedly pushed home by the amendment of the Trade Disputes Act in 1927. This in 1927 struck at the whole organization of the working class by making sympathetic strikes illegal and paralysing the use of trade union funds for political purposes.

This victory did not remove the fears of people with memories more than twenty years long. But it did suggest to realistic thinkers that a further major thrust might be made without recklessly risking successful resistance.

On the other side fear, particularly fear of a repetition of the immediate past, was pervasive and debilitating. Crudely and often subconsciously it took the form of a fear that almost any form of organized resistance that could be devised might result in just such another defeat as that of the General Strike. The principal trade union and political leaders had done all they could to prevent the strike occurring. By activity or passivity they had done their best to soften its impact and to drain it of revolutionary political force. They had almost scrambled to abandon an enterprise which they had only reluctantly supported in the first place. They were sincere in the belief that they had acted correctly throughout. They could claim that only a revolutionary direction and conduct of the strike could have succeeded. And they argued, more tortuously, that the failure of the strike proved that the British working class was 'not ready' to adopt revolutionary means to revolutionary ends, and that in any case the development of the modern industrial state had somehow invalidated all syndicalist theories.

But however correct the leaders may have felt themselves to be, they had to accept that in the eyes of large numbers of the union membership, including many of the most valuable activists, the strikers had been vilely betrayed.

For the leaders, therefore, there were some chilling spectres on their left.

Looking in the other direction they were scared by the suddenly revealed vigour and determination of the opposing forces led by the Government. With money running low and manpower partially disintegrating as 500,000 disillusioned men quit the unions, they were, as they saw it, likely to have to submit to being savaged by some very ugly customers.

They were hag-ridden too by the fear of what was termed alienating public opinion, losing the sympathy of the community and forfeiting the respect of the nation. In the years before 1914 the compelling myth of the Community had lost much credibility. The visible divisions of the nation were so deep that the notion of the Nation as some kind of superhuman entity in which it could be assumed that everyone effectively believed, had to be argued about rather than taken for granted. To groups of Englishmen who regarded groups of other Englishmen as more perniciously dangerous than any other enemies in sight, the idea of the Nation as one and indivisible seemed at least as complex and esoteric, if not entirely incomprehensible, as the doctrine of the Trinity. With the outbreak of the First World War that notion, that idea, became once again comprehensible and realistic. It corresponded, by and large, to the facts.

In Britain the international war really had averted civil war. It was natural that in the years of industrial battle that followed, the slogans which had been powerful morale-raisers during the war should be adapted to new uses. Because they had become familiar in a context where they had a genuine base in reality they remained persuasive. The semantic shuffle was concealed. The Nation or Community became an amorphous creature capable of quick and extensive contractions and expansions. It was a Humpty-Dumpty word, capable of meaning whatever anyone temporarily in charge of the mass media chose it to mean. Thus one week the Community was proud to include so and so many million workers. But if next week they went on strike then they were not simply dissatisfied members of the Community, they had abruptly excluded themselves from the Community altogether. Not only had they jumped clean out of it, but were now seen as a separate creature altogether, in some cases actually holding a pistol to the head of the body from which they had separated.

These verbal devices were intended chiefly for use in influencing the people in the middle; those who without being directly involved on either side of the strike suffered inconvenience and often considerable material loss. Such people were as numerous in the seventies as in the thirties. But there are noticeable differences in the degrees of awareness and sophistication in the two periods. A reader comparing newspapers of the late twenties and the thirties with those of today must often be astonished by the extent of public ignorance which it was evidently possible in that earlier period to take for granted. It was during the 1930s that *The Times*, without fear of ridicule, one day announced that 'the strikes are still spreading, but the whole nation is behind the Government'.

The leadership and vast sections of the rank and file were in varying degrees obsessed and almost hypnotized by fears of 'forfeiting' public sympathy or esteem. The situation was reached in which policies were shaped or adapted not so much in accordance with the practical needs and demands of the people concerned but with an eye to modifying, appeasing and cajoling that public opinion which was itself mainly the invention or creation of the anti-Labour press.

This policy of modification and appeasement was a natural component of the orthodox thinking in the trade unions following the defeat of 1926. This is not to say that the defeat gave birth to a new philosophy. Almost all its life the British Labour Party had devoted a great deal of thought and energy to the task of demonstrating first that the socialism it preached was nothing for respectable British men and women to be afraid of, secondly that Labour was in its own humble phrase 'fit to govern'. The inferiority complex of the British Labour and trade union leadership thus expressed is deep-seated and long enduring.

The terrors of the 1926 collapse confirmed and so to speak petrified into dogma the tenets of the orthodox and silenced many of their critics. The defeat showed them the things to be frightened of, the powers to be exorcized. Extra-parliamentary action was to be feared. It had been proved a failure; worse than a non-starter for it had been among the runners and failed to finish, thus losing its backers their stake. Nothing must be done, nothing must even be suggested in terms of future policy which could seriously shock the traditional British community, the general public. By spectacular, even

Ramsay MacDonald, Britain's Prime Minister, and Sir John Simon   19

flamboyant moderation, its ostentatious freedom from socialist theoretical bigotry, by eye-catching eagerness to put the interests of 'the nation as a whole' before the sectional interests of the working class, the Labour Government when it took over in 1929 must show 'the nation as a whole' that it was indeed fit to govern.

It follows that all those within the ranks of the Labour Party or among the trade union activists who opposed or deviated from this general line of policy, all who by word or action threatened to disfigure the image the leaders were trying to establish, must be disowned: more than that, the Labour movement must be seen by the general public not only to disown them but to treat them as enemies possibly more dangerous than non-socialists or anti-socialists. The official Labour leadership must run no risk of being found guilty by association with extremists repugnant to the feelings of the community.

For practical political purposes the community was taken to mean what could be described in political shorthand as the middle class. In the mid-thirties the wooing of the middle-class vote, under the inspiration and direction of Herbert Morrison, became the central enterprise of the Labour leadership.

Though vulnerable to the lampoons of the left and disturbed by the croaking of many toads beneath the harrow, the official strategy was not ridiculous. Socialists could legitimately claim that it involved the abandonment for practical purposes of socialism. But it was not made ridiculous by that fact. For it could be seen as a stealthy and ingenious attempt to follow in the footsteps not of the more or less revolutionary industrial masses in the immediate pre-war years, but in those of the Liberal Party whose tracks had at that time petered out. The calculation was that it could be possible to mobilize the support of huge numbers of the electorate who had never since the pre-war elections found any recruiting offices open for a political army which they could join with hope rather than with resignation, and brigade them with citizens who would vote for liberalism today on the understanding that it was going to mean socialism tomorrow.

The enthusiasts for this policy could assert, and did loudly so assert, that the results of the 1929 election showed that they were on a winner. Labour formed the government. On the other hand, critics and pessimists viewed with sour alarm the fact that Labour was very far from having a majority of the House of Commons and more importantly still, that almost 300,000 more votes had been cast for the Conservatives than for Labour. The figures indicated among other things that the Tory Working Man was still voting Tory. For the appeasement policy worked two ways. It might seduce some liberally minded or 'leftish' voters of the middle class. But equally the more the Labour Party defused its socialism and emphasized its traditionally English character the less reason there seemed to be for anyone to give up his voting traditions in favour of this nondescript, if harmless, political organization. Labour had tried hard and with partial success to counter Tory allegations that it was after all a wolf in sheep's clothing. So Ramsay MacDonald was a sheep in sheep's clothing. Why leave the familiar Tories to follow this woolly animal? At least, so ran the thinking of the Tory Working Man; the Tory leaders, however beastly, knew their way about the jungle. Their education at the public schools and universities had taught them how to get along with or to maul other jungle beasts whether foreigners or city financiers. The mild-faced sheep had not even proved itself fit to govern.

The City

It was only six years since Winston Churchill as Chancellor of the Exchequer had brought Britain back to the gold standard. The ends to which that was a means had been achieved perhaps even more successfully than had been anticipated in 1925. The position of the City of London as the proved financial centre of the capitalist world had been re-established and strengthened. The wealth and power of the London banks, insurance companies and other institutions, and the principal holders of the national debt, had been mightily multiplied. World prices had fallen first gradually, then faster and faster. It could be shown that the share of the national income received by creditors, notably the institutions just mentioned and the *rentier* class in general, had risen from one quarter to one third during the period since the return to the gold standard. Because of the rise in the value of money the creditors of the State were being repaid ten, twenty or even thirty per cent more than they had lent. To protect the gold standard and enhance the magnetic security of the City, high interest rates were essential. The cost of the national debt was thus also maintained and increased and had to be paid for by a system of taxation which fell heavily on, in particular, industries of medium size. The high valuation of the pound partially strangled the export trade, heavily reduced employment in those industries largely concerned with exports, and sped the decline of industries which had previously and erroneously been seen as the permanent bases and motive power of British activity in the world. There was no need for the City to ask with the psalmist 'Why do the nations so furiously rage together, why have the people imagined a vain thing?' The City knew why. A true appreciation of the situation was written by A. P. Herbert in the lines:

> Steel's gone to glory, cotton's in the shade
> But we've still got the money-lending trade.

The money-lending trade was richly lucrative. It could be shown, too, to be not only patriotic and good for the nation, but basically a form of national business without which all other forms of patriotic initiative and enterprise could be seen as puny, short-sighted, sectional in their benefits, and doomed in the long run to futility.

'The dogs bark, the caravan moves on.' It was a favourite quotation of Montagu Norman, Governor of the Bank of England, when the policies of the City were under criticism. The dogs included in their heterogeneous pack the expansionists among the directors and management of industry who found themselves choked by high interest rates and the nearly lethal grip of the gold standard upon exports; trade union leaders from the suffering industries; and the distempered, flea-bitten, and wormy hordes of the unemployed. Their common, though far from united discontent, found a mouthpiece in John Maynard Keynes whose pamphlet *The Economic Consequences of Mr Churchill* seemed to translate into civilized and compelling language many furious growls. The dogs had barked loudly in 1925. Keynes and others had virtually predicted the miners' strike and all that that implied. As the caravan moved into the 1930s the barking became more tumultuous and outraged. In the House of Commons debate of February 1931 when the appointment of the May Committee was agreed, the fury of the dogs was expressed not only by Sir Norman Angel, the economist, and W. J. Brown, the Labour Member for Wolverhampton. (It was, said Brown, 'The plainest possible intonation that we have reached the position that some of us anticipated we would reach, of becoming the humble custodians of the capitalist interest we were sent here to destroy.') Robert Boothby, Conservative, was loudly heard. He took the view that since the crisis was a crisis of the capitalist system, it was better for capitalists to try their hand at solving it than for socialists to tinker with the works. At the same time he discerned a clear identity of interests between the industrial capitalists, the entrepreneurs, and the productive workers in industry who could see themselves united in common adversity against the banks.

The caravan moved on. As we shall see, the May Committee met, deliberated and pronounced.

Nostalgia and the ruling classes

The caravan drivers were charged then, and have been charged ever since, with stupidity, ignorance of economic laws, and a befuddled nostalgia for the past. The charges are ill-founded.

As to nostalgia, it was not an emotion likely to affect very seriously the minds of the leading men at the Treasury, the Bank of England or the Prudential Assurance Company. It was suggested that this toughened and disciplined brigade of guards was motivated by wistful dreams of a half-forgotten youth in halcyon days before the outbreak of the First World War. They were supposed to be so forgetful of recent history or so unversed in its realities that they imagined that period to have been one of capitalist stability unrocked by earthquakes, and capitalist prosperity unthreatened by revolutionary upheaval. They were alleged to believe in hallucinated fashion that conditions prevailing in the first decade and a half of the century had constituted a state of affairs which was not only desirable but essentially normal; a return to such a state of imaginary normality was to be seen as an objective both entrancing and well within the reach of determined men.

These assumptions, made then and still made, confuse the brigade of guards with quite different and less influential groups of people. The confusion was then and still is of importance because it did much to obscure the motives and misrepresent the actions of those concerned; often it attributed to stupidity and ignorance behaviour which was in fact directed by the most keen and intelligent appreciation of realities and strategic possibilities. There was audacity; there was ambition; an addiction to power and a craving for it. There was small place left for nostalgia.

It was true that nostalgia existed. It pervaded the thinking of very many of the middle-aged middle class, and suffused much of the literature that they bought or borrowed and the drama they saw or discussed. In their imagination the years before 1914 took on the semblance of a cosy womb from which they had been untimely ripped. This deliberate, or more often subconscious, misremembrance of things past affected in particular the mandarinate: most notably the huge army of members of that official class who were retired, at leisure, vociferous and articulate. To invent a carefree past softened memories of how harried and uncertain that past had really been, and, paradoxically but naturally, made more bearable the equally harassing pressures and worries of the present. It was more agreeable to pretend to oneself and one's children that one had come down in the world than to reflect that the world had always been a harsh and menacing environment, with 'normal conditions', then as now, including powerful elements of frustration and anxiety.

Sometimes this yearning for a never-never land of the past, which yet loomed as a future Shangri-la, was uttered in more tragic terms. There were historians and sociological assessors who made the point that the young men possessing the finest intellects and noblest characters in the nation had been killed off in the first quarter or half of the 1914-18 war. The survivors were hypothetically inferior in intelligence and moral fibre. It was a melancholy folly to suppose that these second-raters, this reserve team, could deal successfully with the affairs of the post-war world. If they had let the country and particularly its middle class down they were hardly to be censured. It was not their fault that they occupied the position they did. It was this generation gap which accounted for the lapse in the material and moral standards of living which had occurred. It was only by emulating the supposed thinking and behaviour of these dead that men of the present could create a future as bright as the past had been.

Evidence of nostalgia was mistakenly detected in the behaviour of the richest section of the hereditary upper class. But their behaviour or life pattern was not so much nostalgic as a realistic exploitation of existing possibilities. They tried sometimes quite consciously and deliberately to recreate the life patterns of their class or sub-class as they had existed in late Edwardian and early Georgian days. But this was no whimsy or fantasy.

It had been a richly enjoyable and stimulating way of life. It had cost a great deal of money. In 1930 it cost a great deal of money too. But they had the money. In September 1935, Henry Channon, Conservative M.P. for Southend, wrote in his diary: 'It is very difficult to spend less than £200 a morning when one goes out shopping.' They believed they knew how to spend it to their best advantage. And looking back over the years they could reasonably conclude that it would be hard to improve on the patterns set by themselves when young or by their immediate seniors. Their style was not at all that of the 1920s. For many it was a deliberate reaction against the 1920s' style. Of that style they had many opprobrious criticisms, some outspoken, some tacit. For example, it was cheap in both senses of the word. No really heavy money was needed to achieve the notoriety of a Bright Young Person. The real grandees had never admitted that the Bright Young People were in any sense representative of the upper echelons of the real upper class. They were the product of vulgar collusion between themselves and the mass media of the press. They were newsworthy because they were deemed to belong to, or be connected with, the aristocracy or at least the titled rich.

But they lacked the essentials of an aristocracy old or new. One of those essentials must be the existence of subtle but inexorable laws of exclusivity based on equally subtle but equally decisive considerations of wealth and birth and the relative weight to be given to each factor. The Bright Young were thus vulgarly and perniciously democratic: vulgarly, because they blurred the outlines of a real aristocracy based partly on wealth and partly on birth. They eroded the power of the aristocracy to exclude. Perniciously, because although they might win the gaping or giggling admiration of witless and hence negligible elements of the lower orders, they tended to bring the upper class into the hatred or contempt of thoughtful and hence potentially dangerous proletarians whether working or unemployed. Any public activity of the very rich may of course incur that hatred and contempt. For the aristocracy of wealth and birth it is an occupational hazard; it is a risk, but a calculated risk. It must be assumed that the description of a reception at Londonderry House, the evidence of the enormous wealth and power of the coal-owning Londonderrys, the estimates of what the jewels worn must have cost or would fetch, the imaginable size of the drink bill alone, could contribute, however slightly, to discontent and disaffection in the coalfields or among the unemployed parents of nearly starving children. But against this must be set the fact that to very large numbers of citizens,

including the literally numberless Tory Working Men, such a spectacle was uplifting and reassuring. It was a sign of solid stability. It showed to the eyes of many that foreign tales about old England being on the rocks were a pack of lies. There was plenty of cash about, and the men who had kept it or made it were brilliantly there at the top, comfortably and comfortingly in charge. Those men knew the facts about the real state of the nation. That they so richly carry on, whatever the supposed economic weather, their great houses, their splendidly accoutred servants, their enormously expensive women, can all, rightly viewed, be seen as public advertisements that basically things are all right. They are a glittering display of confidence in the rightness of the course being shaped for the nation, and proof that the course has been plotted by experts.

It was one of the weaknesses, ultimately fatal, of the then Prince of Wales that he had acquired the life style of the 1920s and imported it into the next decade. Feather-pated and ill-educated he lacked appreciation of political and social nuances. Henry Channon noted his appearance at a Court Ball where he 'seemed in a very bad temper, but looked about twelve'. The aristocracy was aware that the Prince was often in a bad temper at traditional social functions because he saw them only as tedious, old-fashioned, irrelevant and, as he sometimes suggested in thoughtful moments, provocative. Such an attitude might indeed be natural in a boy 'about twelve'. But it showed a dangerously imperceptive unawareness of the true function and importance of such functions in maintaining those myths which are essential

to the maintenance of any social structure. His crudely emotional assessments were superficial to the point where he imagined that an ostentatiously informal style of life, taking over the drums at the Kit Kat Club, even the high jinks of the Bright Young People, would endear him, and the upper classes along with him, to the masses.

The aristocracy had a better understanding. Foreign visitors from Europe or the United States at that time noted censoriously or admiringly that the British aristocracy had deliberately created an ambience which, as a Russian émigré remarked, was reminiscent not so much of the fast, partially liberalized looseness of pre-war Moscow society, as of the more grandiose and rigid splendours of St Petersburg. The analogy seemed obvious, but the answer was impeccable; if war were really just round the corner, if the expensive dancing were in fact being performed on the slopes of a volcano about to erupt, then to stop dancing, send the jewels permanently to the bank for safe keeping, go shopping in Oxford Street rather than Bond Street, go boating on the Broads rather than yachting at Cowes or Cannes, would provide no solution to present problems nor would it exorcize whatever dangers might be lurking in things to come.

The unemployed

The existence of what was generally called a pool of unemployment had been the decisive factor in the maintenance of Britain's social and economic structure throughout the 1920s. At no time between 1921 and 1929 had it fallen more than fractionally below the million mark. During that decade, as at the beginning of the 1970s when it rose slightly above the million, the existence of mass unemployment was seen as the essential part of the machinery required to resist wage demands from the organized working class and for curbing or weakening the power of the trade unions. Full employment was doubly menacing. It emboldened the militancy of the working class and could lead to an inflation damaging to the interests of the *rentier* class in general and of the City of London in particular. Only in periods of international war, when the products of labour and capital were destined to be literally exploded, could the contradiction of interests be seen as at least temporarily and partially solved.

Between the moment of the return to the gold standard in 1925 and the beginning of 1931 the number of the unemployed had risen from just under a million to a total of 2,500,000. By June 1933 nearly half a million had been added to the figure, but for the correct or optimum use of unemployment, qualitative as well as quantitative factors had to be taken into consideration. By July 1935 unemployment had fallen below two million. But it was not until the end of 1935 that a revival of world trade began to exercise even a marginal effect on the employment situation. In 1937 the trade and financial indices indicated that the revival was beginning to end, rapidly. A new slump appeared to be alarmingly on the way. It was averted chiefly by the start of rearmament, with its immediately beneficial boost to the engineering and metal industries. Also narrowly political as well as economic and financial assessments had to be made. There was a point beyond which the mere quantitative rise in unemployment could from the City's viewpoint be

26 *Previous page: Gaiety for some: Henley Regatta, 1931*

regarded as counter-productive in the sense that it would bring inimical political forces undesirably into play. In Germany this development had already occurred. The political potential of the Nazis on the one hand and the Communists on the other was vastly increasing and the outcome not easily calculable. But it was already disagreeably clear that Hitler, unquestionably commanding the support of many hundreds of thousands of the unemployed, had taken on some of the aspects of Frankenstein's monster. He had been discovered, trained, groomed and richly nurtured as an ultimate defender of the interests of the leading German capitalists against Communist attacks. But now Nazism had achieved a partial, if temporary, independence of action. It could be claimed too that Nazism was at that time not monolithic. It had a large and genuinely radical wing composed of what were colloquially called 'the Beefsteak Nazis'—brown outside and red within. If the capitalists sought to drive hard bargains with Hitler, to impose conditions upon him in his advance to political power, then the thin exterior of that lightly barbecued steak would disappear and hordes of radical Nazis would join the Communists overnight. Hitler had been able to promote himself from the rank of puppet to that of ally.

There was certainly no analogy between the positions in Germany and in Great Britain. But the course of events in Germany was important as a warning that the rise of unemployment above a certain (though admittedly unforseeable point) can release forces impossible to estimate accurately in advance and perhaps uncontrollable in the end.

But if the advantages of a quantitative rise in unemployment were thus limited, there was wide scope for effective action in qualitative terms. It was obvious that all supports or benefits which could be said to ease the life of the unemployed to that extent blunted the cutting edge of unemployment as a weapon against militancy, organized defence of real wage levels— which had risen slightly as a result of the fall in prices—and inflation. Any lessening of the gap between what a man would have to live on if unemployed and what he would have to live on if he accepted a low wage offer to that extent inhibited wage cuts.

It was true that the large majority of the unemployed were living in conditions of stagnant misery. Four years earlier Neville Chamberlain, then Conservative Minister of Health, had described those in the minefields as living in 'such conditions of destitution as are without parallel in the memory of living persons'. By 1931 more than six million people were living on the dole—on the shadowy borderline between malnutrition and slow starvation. Numerous dietary surveys and Ministry of Health investigations produced results which would have been disastrously startling and subversive in a less disciplined society than that of England. They are summarized by Professor Drummond of University College, London, and Anne Wilbraham in their book entitled *The Englishman's Food* (Jonathan Cape, 1958). The facts officially gathered cast sharp light on a situation which was particularly worrying to those who may have been inclined to place exaggerated reliance on the high level of unemployment as an adequate buttress of the social edifice. For they showed that the gap between the living standards of the unemployed and the lowest paid of the employed was dangerously narrow.

'Whole zones of the industrial areas were reduced to poverty and desolation and their inhabitants to misery and despair. We have records of a number of dietary surveys made at this time which all establish the same grim facts. The lowest wage earners and the unemployed were just able to purchase sufficient calories to keep body and soul alive; in other words, by eating large amounts of bread they could just succeed in staving off actual starvation.

'A report to the Ministry of Health in 1929 described the terrible food conditions in the Welsh coalfields, but the same distressing details were true of a thousand other areas in the country. The diets of the poor working people had become almost as bad as they had been in the worst years of Queen Victoria's reign: white bread, margarine, jam, sugar, tea and fried

Misery for many: unemployed women on hunger march

fish. Meat was seldom eaten more than once a week, while fresh vegetables, other than potatoes, were rarely bought. Fresh milk was hardly ever seen.'

Official and semi-official investigations had shown that the minimum weekly expenditure on foodstuffs which was necessary to maintain health and working capacity was somewhere between five shillings and six shillings per person per week. 'Such estimates,' writes Professor Drummond, 'made it abundantly clear why there was so much malnourishment among the poorer classes. There were thousands upon thousands of families in which nothing like so high a proportion of the weekly income could be spared for food. In Hammersmith, for example, there were many families affected by unemployment where there was as little as one shilling and seven pence per head to spend on a week's food, while even many of those who were fortunate enough to be in work were restricted to sums below four shillings.'

Again it was the fact mentioned in the final line of that statement showing the equality in poverty of the lowest paid employed with the unemployed which was to demonstrate to those in charge of operations the urgent need for a further cut in unemployment benefits. The same problem obtruded itself in ugly fashion into the Commons debate on the Army Estimates for 1931. The figures for 1 October 1930 to 30 September 1931 show army recruitment to have been 34,458, an increase of about 8,000 from the previous year; the year ending 30 September 1932, however, showed a drop to 27,500. The rate of entry had fallen so low as to be almost alarming. Very varied explanations of this phenomenon were offered. A Conservative Member suggested

that it was the policy of the Labour Secretary of State for War to discourage by cheese-paring economies the holding of spectacular military tattoos and pageants in the great provincial centres of the country. Such colourful performances must, he thought, be a great encouragement to recruiting. Others following a similar line held that the abolition (for reasons of economy) of the wearing of full dress uniforms by off-duty soldiers had reduced the attractions of the army for many citizens. Commander Kenworthy believed that the Public School Officers Training Corps, designed as a helpful kind of nursery for future officers, were really acting as deterrents to recruitment. By compulsory square-bashing and bull they were causing the finest specimens of the nation's manhood to become sick of the thought of army life before they were out of their teens. There was a consensus on the Opposition benches that the Labour Party's anti-militarist, if not positively pacifist, propaganda over the years had damaged the appeal of the army and dissuaded many who would otherwise have been recruited. After this it was a shock for Members to learn from the Secretary of State for War that the situation was otherwise than they supposed. There had not in fact been any shortage of men, employed and unemployed alike, presenting themselves at the recruiting offices. If all of them had been accepted there would have been a large rise instead of a fall in recruitment. But the fact was that of the total wanting to join the army sixty per cent had to be rejected on medical grounds. Of these a very large number failed to gain entry because they did not measure up to the minimum requirements of height of 5′ 2″. Equally large numbers were found to be stunted in their chest measurements. It seemed that conditions in the country were producing the material for an army of runts. Some might doubt whether the low stature and puny chest measurements of the would-be recruits was the result of their living conditions in general and of malnutrition in particular. These doubts were dispelled when the Secretary of State pointed out that men who were fractionally above these measurements and thus admitted to the army, after eighteen months of barrack room food and army housing conditions developed spectacularly in both these respects to a stature far above the minimal requirements. Nobody claimed that army rations were lavish. And it was generally agreed that in many areas army housing conditions were inferior to those of the best paid civilian workers. The sudden growth under army conditions of previously undersized workers was simply an indication of what their conditions in civilian life had been like. And these recruits came not only from among the despairing unemployed but about equally from men already in work or youths with the prospect of immediate employment in industry.

Self-reliance or socialism?

Active belief in the Marxist alternative, expressed in revolutionary action, had already prevailed in one-sixth of the world. Marxist ideology and Marxist actions were all over the world eroding what had once seemed the ultimate defence and the ultimate justification of the capitalist system, namely that modern humanity had no choice but to live with and in it. It was in fact not properly to be called a system at all: it was human life as determined by unchangeable human nature. But in the early 1930s the British middle class was more ignorant of Marxism than was any other middle class in the western world. Only a couple of years earlier that would have been true of the middle class in the United States. But the suddenness, speed and extent of the catastrophe which had seemed to overtake the existing system in the United States following the stock-market crash of 1929 had jolted and more or less violently propelled significant sections of the American middle class into a political awareness which they might otherwise have taken years to acquire. This is not to say that they had 'turned Red' or embraced Marxist-Leninist philosophy overnight. On the contrary, many of them becoming suddenly aware of the reality of Communism became equally suddenly terrified of it. Their alarm differed in character from the 'Red scares' of the early 1920s. Except for a couple of years immediately after the end of the war when the revolutionary successes of the Industrial Workers of the World in the north-west could be seen as a genuine challenge to the system, the American middle class as a whole did not think in terms of any alternative either desirable or repugnant. The 'Red scares' were accepted as convenient instruments in the manipulation of domestic politics. They were an occasionally convenient manoeuvre executed by financial and commercial leaders against political groupings or industrial organizations (in particular militant trade unions) who might obstruct them on the domestic front.

In Britain the impact and influence of Marxism on the middle class was miniscule. Keynesianism, often fused with theories of non-Marxist social democracy, substituted itself in the role of Alternatives. Keynesian expansionist doctrines were accepted as the general guideline for the domestic economic policies of the Labour Government of 1929. The extent to which they were put into practice was meagre and could be regarded by Keynesians as an unfortunate travesty of their ideas, leaving in the public mind a general impression of futility. Keynesianism did however provide an armoury of well-tooled weapons for those liberal elements who, in their genuine distress at the condition of the working class in general and the unemployed in particular, might otherwise have found themselves facing the City with only the cardboard and derisory swords of sentiment, humanitarianism, and a claim to some vague sense of decency. The Social Democrats, also appreciating the need for an Alternative, and offering 'socialism', consciously and outspokenly based their appeal to the electors on the ground that their socialism was of a specifically English kind. For in their effort to allay these fears which they alleged had been artificially produced by what they called 'bankers' ramp' they had to protect themselves against the other fears which they supposed would be aroused by suggestions that they were socialists of a foreign, continental, let alone revolutionary type.

It had long been recognized that notions of humanitarianism, fair play, common decency, and so on could blur the issue and impede advance. They were notions that must be taken into account. It was not very long since they had, when co-ordinated with the armed resistance of the Irish, played a notable part in first hampering and then defeating the purposes of British occupation and coercion of Ireland. It was important that this exercise should not be allowed to repeat itself in the context of the British economic struggle. For some years the greater part of the press, daily and periodical, had been at work on an image of the unemployed and their situation, their relation to the rest of the community, designed to counteract humanitarian sentiments. That there were 'deserving' unemployed, victims of causes beyond their control, was admitted. But it was suggested, sometimes broadly sometimes subtly, that essentially the unemployed were closer to parasitism. Quite simply they were living on the charity of the hard-working taxpayer. They existed, were housed and fed at the expense of the rest of the community. The houses might be barely fit for human occupation, and the rations restricted, but to improve either would ruin the rest of the community, or at least place intolerable burdens upon it. This being established certain conclusions must follow: by doing even as much as it was doing to alleviate the condition of the unemployed the rest of the community ran the risk of actually encouraging parasitism by protecting the unemployed from the worst and final consequences of current economic trends. Also, human nature being what it was, huge numbers of people who thus found means to live just above the starvation line without working would prefer such an existence to work. Lower paid workers would be encouraged to refuse wages and join the parasites. It was supremely important particularly for humanitarians to realize that this process (regardless of its effects on the wage structure and the labour market), could be very deleterious to the moral character of the individuals affected. And what was true of state expenditure on the unemployed was true too of money spent on housing and education.

The lessons which had to be learned were fully and influentially set out in the New Year's message to the nation, published by *The Times* on 1 January 1930, in its leading article entitled 'Looking Forward':

'After all, what matters most for the only basis of true prosperity, whether for a nation or an individual, is character. Perhaps we can form no better New Year's wish than that in the coming months the transcendent importance of character be more generally discerned in our public life. It is a commonplace of history that national greatness has never been conserved by material advantages only, and moral debasement is inevitably the prelude of downfall. Yet there are politicians still who argue as though recovery from the results of the war depend solely on financial ingenuity.

'Since the resources of the world are deplorably strained, the best thing we can do, they suggest, is to act as though they were unlimited, and to drift through life with what ease we may until better times return. That doctrine finds a warm welcome. Do no more than we must and be highly paid for doing it, to obtain ease and amusement at the public expense, to replace effort and discipline by slovenliness and self-indulgence, is an ideal which is almost encouraged by some of our modern legislation. It is too often forgotten that no social measures, however specious in themselves, whatever their attractiveness to a section of the community, can really be appraised without regard to their reaction on character. Amiable sentimentalism was not the foundation on which the greatness of Britain was built, nor for that matter was it the kind of quality encouraged by the Founder of our religion.

'There can be little hope of escape from the difficulties in this or any other year simply by adroit finance, or by measures offering increased comfort at the price of weakened character. To regain self discipline and self reliance, an honest pride in work and a clean patriotism, and to relate all such qualities directly with our religion, is the road back to a prosperity worth having.

'It is often said that the future must settle its own problems . . .

32

'What they [the younger generation] will do depends upon what we of the present generation make them. In some respects we recognize our responsibilities. We are lavishing our resources on educational work with unexampled freedom. Yet unhappily we sometimes seem to be more concerned with the setting and machinery of education than with its first purpose of shaping character. While our great public schools are faithful in the main to their social tradition, it is demonstrably proved that a large proportion of boys and girls in these days are almost being trained to lounge through life, averse from work and impatient of control, taking no more than a tepid interest in anything beyond the spectacles of the football ground and the cinema . . . a large share of the blame must rest with the parents. Many of them have come to believe themselves entitled to delegate the tasks which are essentially their own. It is not without justification that the Archbishop of Canterbury confessed in his address last Sunday that "we have tended to look to others or to the State for help rather than to ourselves." In fact the survival of home influence in building sound character is almost our greatest want today, and the need of homes is more urgent than the need of houses.'

The essential purpose of the message is not greatly different from many such messages delivered since against the inception and existence of the Welfare State. But in its formulations, crude or naïve to the eye of a reader in the seventies, it is a characteristic and illuminating document of the 1930s. The contradiction between good character and reliance upon the state is posed as a fact and is clearly applicable to the position and the demands of the unemployed. To do no more than we must and to be highly paid for doing it, is obviously not right and obviously it confirms an employer in his low opinion of the character of his higher paid workers. Expenditure of money on a school building or the improvement of school buildings is seen as irrelevant or even harmful to the true purposes of education. It is in fact on all fours with the excessive building of houses for the irresponsible parents of a low-grade younger generation.

The religious note is of particular interest as a barometer reading of the atmosphere at the period. The Archbishop of Canterbury is shown as demonstrably supporting the general views of the times. With less direct evidence but no less confidence Jesus Christ is declared to have held a similarly sound opinion.

Even in the relatively pagan England of today the blessing of archbishops and bishops upon this or that course of action is still considered worthwhile invoking. Correctly or not publicists still think it just worthwhile to apply the epithet 'un-Christian' to actions or policies they disapprove of. It is true that Christian is a chameleon word turning blue or pink according to the paper it is written on. But it is still considered to count for something. It is most often brought into action when some notable section of the clergy shows signs of supporting views inimical to the designs of those visibly or invisibly in power.

At such times it is still necessary that exertions be made to show that the preachers of such doctrine are temporarily unworthy of exercising spiritual authority over fellow Christians, having misread or distorted the Sermon on the Mount. But this ought not to obscure the fact that there really is a vast difference in this respect between the seventies and the thirties.

The difference can be blurred by the fact that alarm was so constantly expressed at the decline in church observances, empty pews, neglect of

Sundays. But these laments disclosed more than the facts of increasing paganism. They showed that the trend was still regarded as having profound national and political importance. The question of Sunday observance, for instance, twice during the early 1930s engaged the House of Commons in long and occasionally furious debates.

An outward and visible sign of the inward and spiritual grip which the Christian religion still had upon England was embodied by Sir John Reith, boss supreme of the B.B.C. Because in later decades his views and actions, and the public acceptance of them, began to appear as fantastic and nearly incredible, he began in later times to assume the attributes of a mythical and essentially eccentric figure. It seemed in retrospect that he had been a somewhat fanatic dictator imposing his idiosyncratic missions upon a reluctant or quite apathetic public. This was not so. During a great part of the thirties Sir John Reith's views were regarded by most of those who did

The Establishment: left: Montagu Norman, Governor of the Bank of England; centre: the Archbishop of Canterbury; right: John Reith, Director-General of the B.B.C.

not share them or openly disagreed with them as being nevertheless normal, and roughly representative of general public opinion except in times of the most acute controversy and strife. Sir John Reith considered that Britain was essentially Christian and should be confirmed and encouraged in that way of opinion. The doctrine pervaded every area of B.B.C. programmes.

In a quite intelligible paradox, the Sunday School tone and general prudery of the B.B.C. were simultaneously a national joke, and nationally accepted as more or less appropriate to a national institution of the kind. Fiddling Tom, lecherous Dick and even atheistic Harry might have their own ways of thinking and carrying on. But somebody up there ought to be thinking about God and Jesus Christ and the meaning of Easter and that entire class of caper. It was the proper business of the B.B.C. to keep up a front to and for the nation. Keeping up national appearances was what it was for, like the Monarchy. Also it was often good for a laugh. Laughable

35

reports of Sir John's efforts to impose upon the personnel of the B.B.C. what he considered to be Christian standards of sexual behaviour were common knowledge. But for every one person who wondered whether it mattered that after announcing the nine o'clock news the announcer was going off to have sexual intercourse with one or more of his secretaries, there were probably nine who felt, more or less vaguely, that a man in that position ought somehow to behave more respectably than others. Reith insisted that the B.B.C. in its programmes treat Sunday as a very special day. Though there was an intermittent trickle of demands for something brighter, the radio audience as a whole seems to have taken for granted that this was the way things ought to be. Sir John was thorough. He noted that the tone of a religious programme could be affected by the environment from which it was emitted. He observed that the religious studio looked very like any other studio. He gave instructions that it was to be fitted up with a more religious atmosphere. The executives and technicians concerned were at first nonplussed. Then someone saw that what could be done was to re-arrange the lighting. The customarily parallel light tubes around the top of the walls could be changed without much difficulty so that each pair of tubes assumed the form of a cross. This was done. And the electrician who had worked on the job probably expressed a general opinion when he said 'It was sort of crazy but you could see what the poor bastard meant.' A project of Sir John's to consecrate the studio was less successful. Shortly before the Bishop of London was due to perform the ceremony an ecclesiastical expert authoritatively declared that consecration works vertically downwards. If the religious studio were consecrated no power could prevent the simultaneous consecration of a vaudeville studio, the women's lavatories and, according to alarmists, several yards of the underground railway.

The undeserving poor

The purpose of that *Times* editorial message was to stiffen the morale of potential waverers among the people of the upper sort, in several sectors of the line. Liberal thinkers apt to be seduced by Keynesian propositions, were reminded that the Keynesians were displaying nothing more substantial than 'financial ingenuity'. Unreconstructed humanitarians were shown that mere material prosperity could be a snag, fatal to the character. This was the risk to be considered when demands were made for better wages or more assistance for the unemployed. To yield to such demands was to give way to a sentimentality which Jesus Christ would have condemned. It was also bad for the character of the workers and unemployed concerned and thus not a true humanitarianism at all. By their attitudes the working class in general and the younger generation in particular were chipping at 'the foundation on which the greatness of Britain was built'. From this it must be concluded that to call them unpatriotic might be emotive but was fully justified. They were well on their way to earning a well worn epithet of the First World War: they were slackers.

Nobody supposed that *The Times* alone could stop the rot or produce the climate of opinion in which Keynesianism, sentimentality, humanitarianism, and devious dissenting misinterpretations of truer Christian doctrine, were all suffocated or dispersed to make way for the overwhelming triumph of the May Committee's campaign at the August general election of 1931. But *The Times* was not alone. Its axioms, themes and suggestions were repeated as though by orchestration by all the instruments in the band. In the quality section of the press statistics were always available to prove to the level-headed that the extent of unemployment relief was not only financially disastrous but could be usefully correlated with selected rises in crime and delinquency. Elsewhere in the press impressions of misery existing among unemployed and poorly paid workers were as far as possible obliterated by instances in which the supposedly miserable were being positively coddled. Some were viciously parasitical. Others were not having anything like so bad a time as was pretended by sentimentalists. In fact the sentimentalists were insulting the British working man by their suggestions. On the contrary he and his wife were showing just that characteristically British adaptability and ability to make the best of things with a smile which had stood our lads in such good stead in the trenches where, it should never be forgotten, hundreds and thousands had suffered and died for our country under conditions demonstrably more disagreeable than those which the unemployed and the underpaid were temporarily asked to face without this incessant grumbling.

The ever-ready first-aid kit for consciences prone to worrying about the state of the unemployed and the underpaid, was developed nearly to perfection by the British press of the 1930s. Possibly that was a tribute to the existence of a conscience capable of being irked even in the heat of that battle. The kit had never before been so extensively used nor so successful in healing tender parts. And naturally it remains in regular use today at times when it is essential to demonstrate that this or that group of workers not only is better off than it might appear, not only cannot for profound national economic reasons get any more money, but possibly does not deserve to get it. It is interesting to see the same techniques in operation in New York during the forties. A. J. Liebling, the most expert commentator on the American press wrote in the *New Yorker*:

'There is no concept more generally cherished by publishers than that of the Undeserving Poor. The governing factor in most newspapers' attitude towards the mass of people out of luck is the Tax Rate. One way to rationalize the inadequacy of public aid is to blame it on the poor by saying that they have concealed assets, or bad characters or both.

'Obviously one of the most effective ways of keeping relief costs from rising is to shout that the people on relief don't deserve to be there and to imply that the officials of the Welfare Department are Communists who are packing the relief rolls to run down free enterprise.'

The effects upon British attitudes of this type of propaganda, the success of this form of what now would be called brain-washing, were not limited by the achievements of its immediate objectives in 1931. Very numerous observers have noted the 'bad conscience' of Britain in the thirties. The vast, sometimes hysterical, participation in the Peace Ballot, the verbal and emotional support of the Spanish Republic, were seen as being partially a penance done for the silence of the British conscience in the crises of 1931.

3 Offensive
1931 *The Ides of May*

When Sir George May came from the Prudential Assurance Company to save the country, the country had not heard of him; and when Lord May of Weybridge died, it had forgotten him. Yet he deserved remembrance. For he did more than any other single man to make the 1930s in Britain what they were.

The May Committee Report of July 1931 destroyed one government and laid the course for the two that followed. It drew up the programme behind the programmes. Physically it was a Blue Book like others, obtainable at H.M. Stationery Office, its title: Report of Committee on National Expenditure cmd 3920. Readers saw in it God's economic gospel, or the mumbo-jumbo of the Devil. In the House of Commons every oppositional argument, every criticism of policy, was considered quashed if it could be shown to run counter to the pronouncements of the May Committee. Editorial writers daily and weekly took their stand on it: this policy might seem desirable, that course of action alluring, but both had been condemned by the Majority Report of the May Committee and were therefore unworthy of serious consideration. On hundreds of platforms political orators brandished it: the document which must be seen as conferring absolute authority upon the views of the speaker, and routing hecklers in confusion. Forming and permeating policies, its basic tenets and directives accepted by authority in every sphere and at every level, it set the style for the life and labour of the people; rich life and poor life, profit and loss.

The Messiah from the Pru
There was a curse invoked by mandarins of Old China, particularly when tumult and upheaval threatened. It said, 'May you live in interesting times.' In 1931, comfortable people in Britain felt the times into which they had been thrust were indeed damnably interesting. Far from humdrum were developments in the Soviet Union, the Punjab and Shanghai. Not dull by any standard was the partial collapse of supposedly solid social and economic structures in the United States. At home the rise of the numbers unemployed rose to over 2,500,000, with the curve still going up with hideous interest. So had signs, supported by evidence of many churchmen, that ethical values were on the slide. In its New Year's greetings to the nation on 1 January 1930, *The Times* had warned that 'moral debasement is inevitably the prelude of downfall'.

The Prime Minister had said the country was experiencing 'an earthquake'. The Chancellor of the Exchequer called it 'an economic blizzard', and also 'the deluge'. Such metaphors suggested, were often meant to suggest, that the painfully interesting social phenomena were produced by Acts of God rather than of men. Nobody could be identified as having been in charge at the time of the accident, so nobody could be held responsible or justifiably called upon to assist the police with their inquiries. To blame that vast *Société Anonyme,* the System, was dangerous because it implied that under some other system things might have been different. It was better to think in terms of Acts of God, familiar to all holders of insurance policies as apt to cause a person heavy damage and leave him without coverage.

When things were at their worst, they sent for Sir George May. In the

Previous pages: The National Government: MacDonald (centre) flanked by Baldwin (left) and Samuel (right)

light of what was really going to happen his coming was almost stealthy. When, in February 1931, the House of Commons debated what was best to be done about 'the deluge', the Liberals proposed the appointment of an all-Party 'independent' committee to estimate the situation and make recommendations. Philip Snowden, Chancellor of the Exchequer, said there had been many committees. (There was also a special government committee, described reassuringly by government spokesmen as their 'thinking brain'. It was thinking continuously about the deluge, blizzard or earthquake.) Snowden said he saw no harm in having another committee, though he doubted it could do much good. In fact, he added, he believed he could probably write its report in advance. On this note of apparent scepticism he appointed the committee as requested.

After the mine exploded, people looked back to that February day and wondered aloud whether there had been more in Snowden's seemingly casual acceptance of the Liberal proposal than was meant to meet the public eye. By hindsight it seemed probable, and a bit more than probable, that the thing had been a put-up job. Perhaps there had been collusion between the Labour Chancellor and the Liberals: the Liberals would get the committee in exchange for God only knew what promises of continued support on some other issue. But given the gravity of the business in hand, that could be only a partial and superficial explanation. In the bitter clarity of hindsight it seemed more likely that the initiative had really come secretly from the Labour Government. The Liberals had been asked to call for such a committee. The Government leaders foresaw, some only in vague outline, what action they were going to take, what side they would fight on, in the coming battle. This quietly, casually appointed committee could become the crucial factor in the situation. It would be open to the Government suddenly to upgrade the committee, to invest it with authority, reverence and awe. Not the Government would have spoken, but the independent committee. It would be a committee 'of all the talents', political and financial, guided by the Superman from the Pru. Who dared disregard such guidance? In February hardly anyone noticed, or if they noticed they kept their mouths shut, that if the committee was supposed to lay down in general and in detail just what must be done to save the country, and if the Government was going to accept the committee's findings, then the committee was in effect an unelected parallel Government or super-Government with Sir George May as its Prime Minister. Whether, or at what precise stage, such notions and stratagems were present to the conscious minds of MacDonald and Snowden, that is what in fact happened. The National Government which came to power with such *sturm und drang,* such hullabaloo and heart-searching in August had effectively been created nearly six months earlier. It included two representatives of the Labour Party, Lord Plender (an accountant), the Chairman of the Hudson Bay Company and the Chairman of the Cunard Steam Ship Company.

When, and to what extent, some of those in all parties who ultimately acclaimed the committee realized just what it meant and was going to mean, cannot be determined. There is no way now of distinguishing the myopic from the keen-sighted. They included many sorts and conditions of men.

Some were scared almost witless. Some were sick in heart and head. Some already looked down vistas of unavowable hopes and ambitions. All agreed that Sir George May was the man for the job.

It is nonsense, and a cruel insult to the public intelligence to say that 'every country gets the government it deserves'. Not all burdens are self-imposed, nor all wounds self-inflicted. But it is true to say that, in calm weather and storm a group or class does promote to leadership a person who seems almost uncannily to embody the characteristics, the style and idiom of the group: he is their Average Man. Sir George May was such a man.

If people of the upper sort in Britain had been set to putting together an Identikit of Their Man, the assembled features would have produced a recognizable likeness of Sir George May. The Identikit, however helpful, has always a slightly non-human, or possibly super-human quality. From it can be seen that the man they are looking for is a person of a certain type, the type more important than the person. In Plato's sense of the word, May was the Ideal Englishman of the ruling class, including among his attributes the fact of having been born on a level a long way below the ruling class.

He was born in 1871, son of a small grocer in the small Home Counties town of Cheshunt. Under-informed foreign diplomats and newspapermen, hurriedly briefing themselves in 1931 on the subject of Sir George May, were surprised by disclosure of this origin. They had accepted the stereotype of the English structure as one in which a man in Sir George's position would inevitably have been educated at one of the leading public schools, and either at Oxford or Cambridge. May went to Cranleigh, one of many minor public schools whose function was to provide stepping stones for the crossing of social streams. He did not stay there long; and when he left school at the age of sixteen it was not to go to any university but to join the Prudential Assurance Company at the bottom, as a clerk in the cashier's department. Again breaking the stereotype, that period of late-Victorian England offered a very able and industrious boy such as George May a hundred-to-one chance to rise from the humble, laborious and ill-paid position in which he started, to higher and higher levels. British industry, domestic and imperial, was expanding. The insurance business as a whole expanded with it. Also hundreds of thousands of individuals, acquiring more goods, acquired new habits of protection for those goods. Against the corrupting moth and rust of economic vicissitudes, booms and slumps and Acts of God, against thieves with jemmies, and thieves using ruinously unfair competition, Heaven might be the best place of all to lay up one's small treasure, but next best was a good-class insurance company. When George May joined the Prudential it was no older than himself. And it was on the way up. Hard-working and of capacious intellect, May was the boy to take full advantage of the opportunities that opened wider and wider. Many other Englishmen had started at the same level, had found a *carriere ouverte aux talents,* and employed their talents to such purpose that in middle life they had their hands on the levers of power in numberless board rooms. Several of them besides George May might have been spotted by students of the Identikit.

Ibis, the Prudential's house organ, wrote of him when he left the Secretary-ship of the Company to head his mighty committee, with all that that implied:

'From his earliest days with the Company he has revealed himself as one of those men who are born to succeed, attaining qualifications and stepping from position to position with an ease which can only come from the possession of exceptional gifts and qualities. There must have been a good muster of the proverbial fairy godmothers at the cradle of the Company's future secretary.

'Looking back on his activities, one can safely say of Sir George that he has exemplified the force of the old maxim: "Know something of everything and every-thing of something." Any who have known him at all intimately would probably suggest the charm of versatility as among the first of his gifts.

'When he was younger it was a common saying that anything "George" took up, he did well.

'Lacrosse, tennis, and other forms of athletics took his attention and he had a natural aptitude for any ball game. He enjoyed an athletic lissomness of physique, and although he did not take up golf until comparatively late in life, he speedily reduced his handicap to somewhere near the scratch mark.

'He was sociability itself and seems to have gone everywhere and even to have found time to read Shakespeare.

'High finance, however, was destined to be in his sphere, but his acumen and grasp in all matters relating to investment are too well known and appreciated to call for any need of praise from us . . . Although Sir George May has retired from our Pruden-tial world, his activities in other directions are beginning anew. He has been appointed Chairman of the Government Economy Committee, and the Press is already rumour-ing his name in connection with prominent commercial concerns.'

Friendly but less subordinate contemporaries than the editor of *Ibis* noted his 'air of aloofness' and 'a slightly supercilious courtesy that was empha-sized by a single eye-glass'. (He was, in fact, blind in one eye.) It was agreed that he had an impressive capacity to sum up the character and motives of his fellow men, and to manage them with skill and with firmness when necessary. The Committee, according to a friend of Sir George, had not been quite easy to manage. It was composed of prominent businessmen, having very various political affiliations; men with minds of their own. It was laid to the credit of Sir George that of the seven other members of the Committee only two insisted on signing a minority report which could thus be deemed the work of opinionated cranks and as such almost totally disregarded.

The May Report was described by Keynes as 'the most foolish document I have ever had the misfortune to read'. And at a much later date historian A. J. P. Taylor called it 'a report compounded of prejudice, ignorance and panic'.

That was, and still is, the interpretation of the Report preferred by the orthodox Keynesians, and the intellectuals of the Labour Party. Academi-cally, the criticisms can be easily justified. But they signify, too, an arro-gantly wistful underestimate of the capacities of the Higher Management which was dangerous at the time and is perhaps dangerous still. Throughout the thirties it was a characteristic of the intellectual Left to accuse the Right of stupidity. It may be said to be stupid of the Tiger not to perceive that however many goats and villagers it may kill in its ignorant lust for food, its panicky fear of starvation, in the long run the hunters will draw their

Higher Management: Head office of Prudential Assurance Co; inset: toadying cartoon in Prudential house magazine, praising the cost-cutting Messiah from the Pru

"The Man From The Prudential."

cordon about it and destroy it. But, as Keynes himself said in another connection, 'In the long run we are all dead'. All the Tiger wants is to nourish itself at the expense of the goats and the villagers for a forseeable period. And he employs much sagacity and cunning to that end. It does not worry him that just as he springs, the villager is remarking what a poor fool of a Tiger he is.

It is, indeed, one of the most notable, and peculiarly British, characteristics of the British upper class that it positively prefers to be regarded as stupid, ignorant and blundering. It is a form of camouflage. The figure of the damn-fool Englishman who, beneath his frivolous or dropsical manner, conceals an iron will and razor-sharp intelligence is familiar in British sensational fiction.

Had the May Committee been trying to do what Keynes thought it ought to be trying to do, its proposals would have been foolish indeed. That was the nub of the matter, and the rub too. Keynes's objectives were not May's.

Montagu Norman, commenting succinctly on some aspect of Keynes's monetary theories, said: 'There is no problem about money except who has it.'

Coarse perhaps: but not foolish.

The May Report

The principle of the May Report was simple. The budget had to be balanced, which meant finding approximately £120,000,000. £24,000,000 was to come from increased taxation, but £96,000,000 was derived from cuts in government expenditure, two-thirds of that sum being at the expense of the unemployed. The unemployment benefit was seventeen shillings a week. May proposed to reduce it by twenty per cent.

Apart from this a few millions could be saved here and there by cuts in the pay of the armed forces and the police, all supposed immune to disaffection. (It was a decision that alarmed less confident men than Sir George.) Eleven million pounds could be saved by reducing expenditure on education. Briefly and coolly explaining the advantages to be gained by this reduction, the Report boldly unveiled, so to speak, an attitude of mind which previously it had not been thought prudent to disclose so fully and so officially. It made explicit the kind of hints and murmurs in, for instance, *The Times*'s message of New Year 1930:

'We fear that a tendency has developed to regard expenditure on education as good in itself without much consideration of the results that are being obtained from it and of the limits to which it can be carried without danger to other, no less vital, national interests.

'Since the standard of education, elementary and secondary, that is being given to the child of poor parents is already in very many cases superior to that which the middle-class parent is providing for his own child, we felt it is time to pause in the policy of expansion, to consolidate the ground gained, to endeavour to reduce the cost of holding it, and to reorganize the existing machine before making a fresh general advance.'

The passage exactly expressed the alarm and jealousy which any improvement of working-class education aroused in wide sections of the lower

46

middle class from which Sir George had come and of the middle class through which he had passed.

The £66 million to be taken from the unemployed was the amount by which expenditure on the unemployed insurance fund was to be cut. With unprecedented frankness the Committee explained why these cuts were necessary and who was to benefit from them. They were necessary because the country faced a deficit of £120 million. Fifty million of this was to be paid to the holders of the national debt. Given the fall in prices and the rise in the purchasing power of money the *rentier*, the creditor class, the banks and insurance companies and other very large holders of the national debt were to be paid back at a rate of ten, twenty and in some cases nearly thirty per cent above the value of the money they had originally lent. Not since the return to the gold standard six years before had there been such a bonanza.

The Report was a stupendous declaration of intent. A few months earlier hardly anyone would have believed that a man could be found bold enough to propose in the same document such an attack upon the standards of the working class, such a hand-out to the rich. The Minority Report did not worry Sir George and his associates. Their calculations of the balance of forces had shown that such views could safely be disregarded. The Minority Report, for what it was worth, noted that the majority intended to impose 'unfair measures of sacrifice upon certain large sections of the Community many of whom are already feeling with constant and growing severity the effects of the economic situation'.

The minority also stated that the policy of the majority 'would fail to lay any comparable contribution upon others more favourably situated, many of whom are enjoying to the extent of their fixed incomes effortless benefits from the increased value of money due to falling prices'. It referred not only to the holders of the national debt but to holders of post-war issues of municipal loans, debenture holders and others. It alleged that 'the present financial difficulties of the country and of industry do not result from any pursuit of wasteful public expenditure or lack of responsible control but are much more closely related to the policy of deflation followed since the war and confirmed by the return to the gold standard'.

Commenting editorially on the two reports, *The Times* stated that 'the majority consider Social Services a tempting but impossible extravagance while the minority consider these services to be a wise investment'. Acidly it added that the minority 'apparently contends' that money spent on the social services such as the relief of the unemployed was 'not bribery but wisdom'.

The National Government

Like a well-placed terrorist bomb, the May Committee Report was loosed off at a moment chosen when it would have not only maximum explosive force, but would make a maximum terrorizing noise, and when the chances of speedy interference by any fire brigade that might be within reach would be reduced to a minimum. The only fire brigade that might possibly have been troublesome was the House of Commons. The Report could have been issued at any time after the middle of June. But it had been shown particularly during the February debate that the final document was likely to be more than a little mauled, or at least howled at, by a lot of the parliamentary dogs, some of them even on the Conservative benches. The House had approved the setting up of the May Committee. But only a minority of Members, which included the Labour Chancellor of the Exchequer, had at that time any clear notion of what the Committee was going to propose. And fewer still realized that what they were doing was to set up a junta whose *pronunciamentos* would have dictatorial power over political leaders and force enough to unmake a government and make another. It was true that by the end of July it could be reckoned that the poisons of fear would have paralysed many of the critics, infecting them with political lock-jaw. Even so it was decided to take no chances. At the end of July Parliament recessed for the summer and the Committee Report was published on 31 July. It was necessary only that Parliament should go into recess. By hindsight it may seem extraordinary that in such a situation it should have seemed normal for Parliament to take its normal summer recess at the normal time. Some traditionalist democrats did protest. But it was pointed out that Parliament could always be recalled if, as they say, anything special were to happen.

It did not meet again until 8 September. The special things happening in the interlude included the overthrow of the Labour Government and the formation of a new National Government pledged to further to the limit of its political capacity the objectives mapped by the May Committee.

Eleven days after the Report was published MacDonald was hastily summoned back to London to be informed that there was a run on the pound, and that the only way to restore confidence was to cut government expenditure, thus balancing the budget.

Years later *The Times*'s obituary of Sir George May, summing up other defects of the Report, wrote:

'Abroad the effect of the May Report was equally electric. Foreigners who had balances in London were more than ever eager to withdraw them, and in spite of credits totalling 130 million pounds advanced to the Bank of England and the Treasury by Paris and New York the run on England continued and finally drove the country off the Gold Standard. May, having shown the Government the way to balance the budget, the Government when they decided to tackle the restoration of the British balance of payments by means of a tariff appointed him chairman of the Import Duties Advisory Committee.'

It is interesting to see thus perpetuated the legend popular at the time that the French bankers had been suddenly awakened by the Report to a realization of the state of British finances. In fact nobody in the City seriously supposed that the French bankers could not do simple sums just as accurately as Sir George, or that their informants had not kept them accurately advised as to the trend of the Report's impending recommendations. The French had many short-term domestic and technical reasons for withdrawing funds from London at that time, and indeed had been withdrawing them for some time before the actual publication of the findings of the Committee. More importantly they could, looking at the long-term, see just as well as Sir George that the gold standard would shortly become a liability rather than an asset and would be abandoned. Smaller French investors certainly

48

panicked. They thought they had good reason to do so because many French commentators and financial advisers, misunderstanding the real balance of forces in Britain, could not believe that the City would really achieve its objectives. Some of them took the Report as a cry of despair: an announcement that the country would be ruined unless certain things were done, without real expectation of their being done. They seriously underestimated the strength, shrewdness and accuracy in attack of the organizers of the whole campaign.

Thus in supposedly informed circles in Paris at the time there circulated persistent prediction that if the British Government attempted to implement the May Report there would be such a resistance from the British working class that the possibility of civil war could not be ruled out.

Regardless of the mixed motives for the withdrawals they served a generally useful purpose. They fuelled panic fears in England thus facilitating the coup d'état and giving an air of inevitability to the existence and behaviour of the governing junta, only two or three of whose members such as Norman, Governor of the Bank of England, and May himself were immediately recognizable by the public. Sir George added something to his human interest when on 3 September he was fined fifteen shillings at Bow Street for driving along Constitution Hill, Green Park, at thirty miles an hour. The offence had occurred on 21 July, ten days before publication of the Report. In the circumstances his illegal haste could readily be condoned.

The call of $8\frac{1}{2}$ per cent

The run on the pound, during which political leaders repeatedly invoked the spectre of the German inflation in the early twenties, was popularly seen as calling for immediate, spectacular counter-measures. With no solution of their own, the majority of the Labour leadership and of the Parliamentary Party were passionately and with a true instinct opposed to the cuts as they affected the unemployed. The Party split, leaving MacDonald, Snowden and J. H. Thomas to co-operate in the formation of the National Government: a government containing Liberals, too, and dominated by the Conservatives.

The calculations of the junta were fully justified by the ensuing general election. Partly in fear, partly confused by the absence of any clearly defined alternative, and partly rendered savagely cynical by what was seen as the treacherous or imbecile defection of the Labour leadership, the electorate voted overwhelmingly for the candidate of the National Government who campaigned on the simple slogan of a call for 'a Doctor's Mandate'.

The Higher Management had won a great battle. The war continued.

4 Counter-offensive
1932-5 *Marching men*

J ust when the caravan seemed to have accomplished the first stage of its onward journey without a hitch, a terribly startling thing happened.

The Atlantic fleet mutinied.

Just after Parliament had been successfully nullified during the crucial weeks of change, the coup was answered from the other side by vigorous extra-parliamentary action at the most dangerous level.

Continental and American observers and commentators had settled down to the conclusion that the calculations of the Higher Management in Britain had been faultless, that through mental and physical inertia, disorganization and demoralization, and perhaps by reason of some atavistic docility peculiar to England, the British working class could be relied on to offer no serious resistance. Then came the news from the naval base at Invergordon.

In the early part of September 1931 the Government had fully and openly accepted the demands of the May Committee as superior orders. The supremacy of the junta and the urgency of its requirements were acknowledged. Emergency Powers were assumed and orders in Council promulgated in an assumption of a dictatorial authority equalling, and perhaps surpassing, in extent even such measures as it had been thought possible to take at the height of the First World War. The incomes of the unemployed, of the teachers, of the civil servants, of the police, and of the armed forces were all dealt with by quick strokes of the pen. It was a triumph of managerial efficiency in overcoming the flimsy impedimenta of democracy. The triumph was interrupted by the messages from Invergordon.

The news of the cuts had reached the lower decks during the morning of Sunday 13 September. The basic pay of a naval rating was to go down from four shillings to three shillings per day. That was a loss of twenty-five per cent. When some additional allowances were calculated the loss in most cases would, however, be considerably less.

The crews of modern warships were, in terms of skills, trained intelligence, and powers of organization, among the most highly developed of industrial workers. Their responses were quick and they were accustomed to collective action. In the evening they went ashore. They gathered in the naval canteen. They debated. They organized. They agreed as a first step to test the state of opinion throughout the fleet. That there would be general indignation, verbal imprecations, lurid declarations of intent to resist, could be assumed. That the majority of men would be prepared to translate words into actions not precedented since the end of the eighteenth century could not be thus taken for granted. Volunteers were chosen to canvass ship by ship. They would have until Monday evening to get the answers to questions. On the ships they talked and listened, and in the evening went ashore with their reports. The men would act. They would go on strike.

(Some government men and others in London thought the men's use of the word 'strike' was less hair-raising than would have been a declaration of intent to 'mutiny'. Others thought 'strike' the more ominous of the two terms. It could suggest that the naval ratings saw themselves as a section of the industrial working class with the same terms applicable to their actions.)

52   *Previous pages: The Jarrow hunger march—still remembered with bitterness*

The fleet was under orders to put to sea the following morning, Tuesday. The men decided it should not put to sea. But once aboard their several ships the crews would be separated. There might be changes of heart in the night. Or the men in one ship might fall to wondering whether the others would go through with the business. There must be a last minute means of communication. The means was chosen. When the crew of the battleship *Rodney* went on strike they would start cheering. And then the men on each ship would cheer as they followed the example.

As things turned out it was the crew of the battleship *Valiant* who first took action. The *Valiant* was the first of the ships in the harbour due to leave. When, a little before 7 a.m., the order was given to raise anchor, the crew refused. Those in command had barely time to realize what was happening before a great noise of cheering came across the water from the *Rodney* lying out in the Firth. Then all the men on all the ships burst out cheering. Twelve thousand sailors were on strike. The last time cheering had been used to announce such action on British warships was during the mutinies at Spithead and the Nore in 1797.

The editors of the national press did not have to be told what to do. Their natural reflexes told them that this was news more potentially explosive than any of them had ever handled. It was played down and suffocated. But the oppositional *Daily Herald* published an eye-witness account:

'The scene in the Firth has to be seen to be believed. At the gates between the mountain peaks the *Repulse* stands like a sleeping sentry, not a whisp of smoke from her mighty funnels and her crew below deck. Behind her in the line stretching along the whole Firth lie *Valiant, Malaya, Warspite, Nelson, Frobisher, Barham, Norfolk, Hood, York, Exeter, Rodney.* From the shore I can see the meetings on the fore-decks, with the leaders addressing the men from the gun turrets and I can hear the cheers and shouts that are picked up and passed on from ship to ship till they fade into the distance.'

'We the loyal subjects . . .'

Between the cheering which marked each refusal of the men in a ship to obey orders to return to work—cheers answered by cheers from the rest of the fleet on each occasion—there were vigorous discussions, arguments, speeches and singing. Mostly they sang songs from the popular musicals, old music hall songs and familiar ballads. Occasionally they sang the Red Flag and on one or two ships the Internationale. The crew of the cruiser *Norfolk* drafted a petition which was smuggled around the fleet and endorsed by the other crews. It said:

'We, the loyal subjects of His Majesty the King, do hereby present to My Lords Commissioners of the Admiralty representative, to implore them to amend the drastic cuts in pay which had been inflicted on the lowest paid men of the lower deck. It is evident to all concerned that this cut is the forerunner of tragedy, misery and immorality amongst the families of the lower deck, and unless a guaranteed written agreement is received from the Admiralty and confirmed by Parliament stating that our pay will be revised, we are resolved to remain as one unit refusing to sail under the new rate of pay. The men are quite agreeable to accept a cut which they consider reasonable.'

It took less than thirty-six hours for the Government to assess the strength of the forces facing it.

In the face of resistance so bold, so well organized and so united they decided to retreat from this sector of the front. And if the retreat were to be made it must be made quickly. On the afternoon of Wednesday 16 September it was announced that the exercise for which the fleet had been ordered to sea was cancelled. The ships were to be dispersed immediately to their home ports. A full investigation of the proposed cuts would be made and there would be no victimization.

Some among the mutineers feared a trick. They assumed that the promises from the Admiralty were designed simply to break up the fleet into manageable units and proceed with the attack. The majority argued that the retreat of the other side and their own victory were genuine. They were right. The amount of the pay cuts ordered was cut in half. In no case were they to exceed ten per cent. Even the degree to which the promise of non-victimization could be dishonoured was limited. Thirty-six of those deemed to have been among the leaders of the strike were later dismissed from the Navy. In this the Admiralty had chosen the worst of both options. The breaking of its pledge not to victimize the strikers lowered its credibility and fuelled resentment. On the other hand a mere dismissal was so notably milder than the normal penalties for mutiny that it was seen as further proof of the extent of the victory and of its startling impact on those in charge.

For some time after the end of the mutiny the events at Invergordon were still being presented to the public as of relatively minor, certainly not of sensational, importance. 'Evidence of unrest' was the descriptive phrase found most useful. Even so, two themes luminously characteristic of the thinking of the thirties obtruded themselves at once, and increasingly so as fuller discussion of the mutiny could be ventured.

The muted mutiny—press headlines
play down the Invergordon crisis;
also: Rodney, *battleship that went*
on strike

FLEET UNREST OVER PAY CUTS.

"HARDSHIP" FOR LOWER DECK.

All Leave Stopped.

THE cuts in Naval pay proposed in the national economies have led to some unrest among lower ratings in a section of the Fleet.

The Admiralty issued the following announcement last night:—

The Senior Officer, Atlantic Fleet, has reported that the promulgation of the reduced rates of naval pay has led to unrest among a proportion of the lower ratings.

In consequence of this he has deemed it desirable to suspend the programme of exercises of the Fleet and to recall the ships to ̶ ̶ ̶ ̶ ̶ ̶ ̶ ̶ ̶ ̶ ̶ ̶ ̶ ̶ ̶ ̶ ̶ ̶ **are**

FLEET ON WAY HOME.

"ALLEVIATION" OF HARDSHIPS.

GOVERNMENT'S PROMISE.

FOLLOWING the lower-deck dissatisfaction over the Government's economy cuts in naval pay, which led on Tuesday to the suspension of the autumn exercises of the Atlantic Fleet, orders were received at Invergordon yesterday for the vessels of the Fleet to return to their home ports.

The following announcement was issued by the Admiralty

Onc was the question of the role in the affair to be assigned to the Communist Party. That there were Communists among the leadership was well established. That others became Communists during the strike and under the inspiration of its success, was equally known. At that period it was a central tenet of the politically orthodox in Britain that conditions in Britain were not such as to foster any form of indigenous Communism. This tenet was not so absurd as a study of the economic situation and the living standards of the working class could lead a person to suppose. Writing the English section of his *Inside Europe* in the mid-thirties the American journalist John Gunther noted that 'visitors from abroad to the Tyneside and Durham are incredulous that poverty of such miserable proportions does not produce revolution'. The facts of Here and Now, considered in purely economic terms, certainly did not seem to support the contention that Communism in England must be something un-English. And to that extent the contention was false.

But when economic factors potentially making for revolution are discussed it is equally false to separate them from the political and social factors engaged. Put otherwise, the climate and temperature of the greenhouse had to be seen as equally important with the soil of the seed beds. During many decades the climate inside the greenhouse had been modified by the glass roof of colonial empire. It was a climate favourable to gradualism. With the beginning of imperial decline the change in the basic economic position of Britain altered more rapidly than British thinking. Yet already in the first years of the century nobody could successfully have pretended that revolutionary thinking and revolutionary behaviour were alien to Britain or incapable of natural growth in British soil.

The First World War checked that growth and the defeat of the General Strike blasted it. In the years since then, and partly as a consequence of that defeat, the theory, teachings, and leadership of the British Labour Movement had been principally devoted to the development of orthodox parliamentary policies, against all furtherance of political aims by direct action, and as a logical consequence against Communism and Communist activity. The orthodox teaching had been pervasively successful.

To that extent and in that context, it was possible genuinely to state that Communism, like syndicalism, had become alien to British thinking, to the British way of life. From this starting point it was easy to proceed to the declaration, and even the conviction, that if Communism nevertheless existed at all in England it must be the direct creation of the Russian Bolsheviks.

When, as at Invergordon, things came to a notable crunch, they produced a dilemma, a form of national schizophrenia. To suggest that Russian agents and their English tools or dupes were in a position to infiltrate and subvert the British fleet to the point of mutiny must be counter-productive, giving the affair a most undesirably sensational aspect. On the other hand, if the Russians in particular and 'alien doctrines' in general had not been responsible, then it could seem that conditions in Britain and the British fleet were such as naturally to produce Communistic ideas and throw up native Communists as leaders. The solution most generally proffered was that

56

essentially minor and particular grievances had been exploited by agitators who in no way represented the mass opinion of the British personnel concerned. Although this explanation was widely accepted the dilemma and the schizophrenia persisted more or less jaggedly throughout the thirties and beyond.

A question of morality?
The second theme forced upon public attention by the Invergordon mutiny concerned the state of affairs and of opinion exemplified by that passage of the mutineers' petition stating that 'it is evident to all concerned that this cut is the forerunner of tragedy, misery and immorality amongst the families of the lower deck'. Officers familiar with feeling on the lower deck were not at all surprised by the emphasis laid on the danger of 'immorality' in the sailors' families. At the best of times and in the best conditions, men inevitably separated from their wives by long periods of duty at sea had special reasons for worry as to what their wives or girl-friends might feel impelled to get up to without them.

At such times and in such conditions the worry was simply and naturally lest temporarily deserted and sexually deprived women might, also simply and naturally, have to find sexual satisfaction with more available men. For sailors that was an occupational risk. Men of all classes could sympathize with the sailors' apprehensions.

But now a new element was introduced. It was not a matter of sexual urges but of economics. It had to do not with ill-satisfied sexual needs but with cash and food and clothing and the lack of all of them. Bluntly among themselves, more delicately in their petition to the Lords Commissioners of the Admiralty, the men were saying that if those cuts went through their wives would be forced to make up the difference by selling themselves to keep themselves and the children fed, clothed, and together. This was no bogey invented to frighten puritans and shock the non-conformist conscience. The men knew this was going to be a fact of life, like having to pawn the clock. Being a close-knit community and a little isolated from the prevailing influence ashore, they were in general a little less inhibited in their thinking and judgements than some of their fellow workers. Everyone who was not either cocooned in ignorance or determined to look the other way knew that the wives of the unemployed and of very poorly paid workers were regularly or irregularly forced into some form of prostitution to help keep the home together.

It was a matter of bitter and festering grievance. But it was one which the spokesmen of the unemployed hardly ever raised. Many contemporary investigators found that the unemployed were often actually ashamed of their situation. Brought up on axioms applauding self-reliance and pointing to the rewards of industrious virtue, they subconsciously believed that unemployment and its miseries must somehow be their own fault—that if useful work and a living wage were the rewards of virtue and good sense, then their present wretched situation must be to some degree the consequence of their own weaknesses or stupidities. (The same line of thought is often found among poorly educated victims of tuberculosis.)

It was hard enough for such men to admit even to themselves that the prostitution of their womenfolk, whether wives or adolescent daughters, was often a feature of that situation. It was harder still to discuss the fact communally. As for publicizing it, making it known to better placed people such as parsons and politicians, the results would be drearily predictable. Some such would be genuinely shocked, genuinely sympathetic. But they were liable to give warning that to make public use of such facts would be to insult their own womenfolk and perhaps to cause those who already believed the unemployed to be somehow feckless to give them up as hopelessly sunk in sexual immorality as well. Others would declare that these were but isolated instances and irrelevant to the general position. The attitude of all concerned was reminiscent of the period when the large-scale and open organization of proper official measures to deal with venereal disease in the army were delayed and impeded because it was thought that this kind of official recognition of that kind of fact would be shocking to Queen Victoria, suggesting to her that sexual irregularity was rife among her soldiers. To this extent the unemployed may be said to have collaborated in the concealment of their own grievous afflictions. The men at Invergordon let in some light upon the realities of life on or near the poverty line.

The impact of Invergordon upon British opinion was softened by that voluntary press censorship which in Britain is often more effective than censorship imposed by government. It was not even necessary for all proprietors to impose it on their editors. These were for the most part men either belonging by origin to the upper sort or thoroughly imbued with that kind of thinking, reacting immediately and automatically to any threat, or even a breath of a threat, to the established order. The image of the cynical editor knowing well what is really going on and deliberately distorting the facts before presenting them to the public is romantically misleading. (It is true that editors reminiscing in the glow of hindsight sometimes furbish the image. They were not, they claim, led up the garden path. They had judged it irresponsible to lay before the ill-educated and ill-informed public facts which might dangerously if not fatally enflame its alimentary canal.)

The noise made by Invergordon in the outside world could not be thus muffled. British statesmen and leader-writers viewed reactions on the Continent and particularly in the United States with dismay and contempt. The dismay was intelligible, the contempt partially justified. For the Europeans and Americans displayed in this instance an ignorance of the factors in the British situation which was nearly crass. In the United States Liberals and Radicals and embryonic New Dealers took the view that the British Higher Management, being hide-bound, pig-headed, and myopic, had been clumsily blundering right through the crisis. With some intellectual arrogance, the campaign in which the first major move was publication of the May Report was supposed to be the ill-judged floundering of old men in a panic. Now the ill-informed incompetence of these old men had been exposed: they had bitten off more than they could chew.

With optimism on the Left and pessimism on the Right it was assumed that the Invergordon mutiny was evidence that the British working class was going to react to the attack in a manner conforming with the copybook maxims of Radicals and pseudo-Marxists. The catastrophe supposed to be impending in Britain could be used in the arguments of almost every side. It proved that bankers and reactionary statesmen were stupid in trying to halt the march of progress and the working class. It also proved that the Red Menace was real indeed and called for the sternest repression of subversive or radical activities everywhere.

It was said at the time, and often taken for granted since, that the news of the Invergordon mutiny had 'driven Britain off the gold standard'. This was true only in the most limited sense. The maintenance of the gold standard under all conditions had never been a major objective of the City strategists. It was just as apparent to them as to their critics that changing conditions of world trade were likely at an early though undetermined date to render efforts to maintain it stale and unprofitable. The American and French bankers were not foolishly ignorant of the situation either. Nobody had put a ring round a date in late September to mark the day on which Britain would go off gold. And there is at least a probability that the Invergordon mutiny accelerated the coming of that day. Yet it is certain that at least a fortnight before Invergordon important American institutions and investment groups had taken up bear positions and were selling the pound short. The principal effect of Invergordon was to create panic among less shrewd or informed holders of London funds who, on the cabled news of imminent civil war or revolution, made haste to get their money home.

Though the facts and the success of the Invergordon mutiny were blurred by the voluntary censorship, and the mass media did everything possible to explain the affair as an isolated episode occurring in a vacuum without general causes or general consequences, its effects upon the strategists of the other side were immediate and serious. With characteristic flexibility and alertness the warnings were noted as recurring but necessary adjustments made to the optimum plan of campaign. Invergordon had shown that important rectifications of the line were essential. There was fright about the police, too. The *Police Review*, official organ of the Police Federation, refered to 'discontent and dissatisfaction rampant throughout the services caused by unfair and unjust treatment meted out to members of the Police Service'. In the Commons on 22 September the Prime Minister was asked whether he was now in a position to make a statement in regard to the classes of persons involved by economies whose cases were of peculiarly great hardship. The question had been pre-arranged with a supporter to give MacDonald an opportunity to give news of the rectification in his own words. He replied: 'The Government have been examining details of the proposed scheme of reduction. There are undoubtedly classes of persons who are unfairly affected, and the Government have, in view of all the circumstances, come to the conclusion that the simplest way of removing just grievances is to limit reductions, as regards teachers, police and the three Defence Services, to not more than ten per cent.'

The Welsh mining M.P., Aneurin Bevan, at once asked: 'In the event of the unemployed taking the same steps to attract the attention of His Majesty's Government as those which the Royal Navy took, will the right honourable gentleman give the same consideration to the unemployed?'

The question was a natural agitational exercise. But it remained not only hypothetical but strictly rhetorical. In fact it drew attention to the realities of the power situation. In the nature of things there were no circumstances under which the unemployed could take 'the same steps to attract the attention of the Government as those which the Royal Navy took'. They could certainly not mutiny. They could not even go on strike. It was both rhetorically useful and absurd to denounce the May Committee and the Government for their attack upon 'the weakest members of the community'. It was because they were weak they were attacked. The entire design depended upon using their weakness as the means by which a general reduction of wages and enfeeblement of the trade unions could be achieved. The only means by which the attack could be contained and perhaps repelled was by the organization of the unemployed. They must be capable of exerting not only parliamentary but extra-parliamentary pressure. By organization and the nature of their demands they must nullify the powers of leverage or blackmail which unemployment offered to the other side in its every movement to reduce wage levels and weaken the trade union.

For ten years intelligent men on both sides had seen this as the crucial area of conflict. During those ten years since 1921 millions upon millions of words had been written and spoken about the problem of unemployment and of how to 'cure' it. Most of them were otiose. The men who wrote them were not ultimately powerful. They were rendered nugatory by the fact that the operators of power had sound reason for their belief that to cure unemployment was not only impossible, but undesirable.

For them it went without saying many words about it that if it could be done at all, which they doubted, it could be done only at the cost of overturning the entire system. And talk about curing unemployment became realistic only when it was not in fact concerned with a cure but with finding out what was the best level of unemployment at any given time. This involved totting up and balancing out the optimum potential of unemployment as a means of lowering wages, the figure at which loss of purchasing power must be regarded as important, and the figure at which the unemployed could be socially and politically menacing.

This last factor could not be measured in figures alone. Its importance depended on the degree of organization and leadership existing among the unemployed at one time or another. There could be four million unemployed without organization or leadership, and they would remain negligible as a factor in the calculation. One million organized men with good leadership could force their opponents to a choice between a retreat and a possibly disastrous encounter.

It was almost exactly ten years since a National Conference of local unemployed organizations at Gorton Town Hall, Manchester, had created the first National Unemployed Workers' Movement. The basic demand of the Movement's programme went to the heart of the matter. 'Work at trade union rates or full maintenance' was the demand. No one pretended that either alternative could be accepted by the other side without a catastrophic and wholly unacceptable surrender of power. As National Organizer of the Movement the Conference elected W. Hannington.

Hunger marches in Brighton: Hannington (centre) with trade unionist Abbot confront policeman

For ten years the conflict had developed in an uproar of victories and defeats, of skirmishes and battles, of struggles organizational, political and physical, tussles and confrontations in committee rooms and lobbies, marching and fighting in the streets. The unemployed were sometimes isolated, but sometimes in active co-ordination with employed trade unionists, sometimes in alliance with authorities elected at the ballot box, borough councillors who resisted the directives of the Central Government. There were some months when reports coming in to headquarters of the N.U.W.M. showed a map of England where no day had passed without baton charges and arrests somewhere. By the thirties the N.U.W.M. had given reality to the often gaseous phrase 'a force to be reckoned with'.

Its existence entered all the reckonings of the other side.

Through the British mass media it was denounced.

Internationally it was appraised as a vital element in determining the present and future direction of Great Britain. The figure of Wal Hannington was seen counterposed to that of Sir George May. Typical was an article published in the New York *Evening Post* of 3 October 1931. Headed 'Wal Hannington, Dole Riot Leader, New British Force', it outlined the resistance to the programme of the May Committee and the Government being conducted at all levels, from the parliamentary lobbies to the streets, by the N.U.W.M. Hannington had just come out of Winchester Jail where he had been imprisoned for a month as 'a disturber of the peace and an inciter of others to commit diverse crimes and misdemeanours'.

The New York *Evening Post* report from London said:

'At the N.U.W.M. Headquarters in Bloomsbury sits a man who claims the responsibility for the recent violent mass demonstrations throughout Britain, and who is planning more of them. He is the redoubtable Wal Hannington, organizer of the National Unemployed Workers' Movement.

'The recent demonstrations are the first step in a big militant movement. Hannington said, "They are new developments. Our immediate job is to hold back operation of unemployment benefit cuts. If we do not succeed we will intensify the struggle in localities throughout Britain."

'Commands go out from Hannington's Bloomsbury office daily. Demonstrations are prepared partly by the massive chalking system by which a group of insiders in the movement chalk the sidewalks of the entire city with instructions to the workers to meet at a certain time and place. This was the system in the Manchester demonstration the other day, in Birmingham in the week of September 23, when twenty thousand paraded in Liverpool a week ago, and when the same number came out in Dundee where, according to Hannington, there has been street fighting every day this week and where the irate Lord Provost has imposed a nine o'clock curfew.

'Rumours concerning the personality of Hannington lead one to expect a craggy-jawed Neanderthal ruffian, wallowing in an atmosphere of truculent violence.

'Actually he is a soft-spoken, smiling young man of thirty-five, clean-shaven, neatly dressed and wearing tortoise-shell spectacles. His shoulder muscles bulge prominently under a well-fitting coat. His wrists are powerful, and his glance direct and friendly.'

Sir George May it will be recalled had been described as 'lissom'. The bulging shoulder muscles and powerful wrists which impressed the man from the *Evening Post* were not very surprising in this skilled engineer who was the son of a bricklayer. Had Hannington been, say, a young sergeant leading British troops in time of war, he could have served the media very well as an Identikit of the British Working Man. The well-fitting overcoat would also have suited the picture. By personal inclination, pride of class, and sound political instinct, Hannington liked to present as smart an appearance as was possible in his circumstances. All these attributes could be, and had been used for years, to present quite a different image. The bulging muscles and the powerful wrists, not to mention the powerful jaw and full sensual lips, showed kinship with Neanderthal man; were indications of brutish violence, insignia of an anti-social Caliban. The good cut of the overcoat showed something else as well. It demonstrated the falsity of the man's claim to represent the poorest of the poor. It was a gift to any good caricaturist. Properly depicted it suggested that its wearer like other Red leaders improperly enjoyed good things when he could get them. The coat with Hannington inside it could be eloquently displayed against a background of honest men, pitiably misled, and in rags.

As a very young man in his early twenties Hannington had already held important positions as a shop steward in several engineering works. He was dismissed for agitational activities and black-listed. He was a founder member of the Amalgamated Engineering Union formed in 1920. With its base among the skilled workers of a skilled and crucial industry it was among the most powerful of the unions. Hannington retained his membership all his life. He was also a foundation member of the Communist Party of Great Britain formed in 1920 and later a member of the Central Committee. Both these affiliations helped to complete the Hannington Identikit.

A simultaneous membership of the Amalgamated Engineering Union and the National Unemployed Workers' Movement signalized the intimate community of interests between the unemployed and the best-paid and best-organized workers. Membership of the Communist Party provided constant awareness of an ultimate political goal, and continuous relation of practice to theory and application of theory to practice. It is impossible to see Sir George May as acting and thinking in some kind of individual vacuum. His thoughts and actions were inseparable from those of others in the Higher Management at the Treasury, the Bank of England, the merchant banks and the insurance companies. As a member of the leadership of the Communist Party Hannington, too, existed in no political vacuum. Like Sir George May he both helped to form thinking and policy, and to reflect them: he too had his expert and dedicated advisers.

Official spokesmen naturally, and from their point of view correctly, saw the fact that the leader of the unemployed was also a leading Communist as peculiarly ominous: sinister both in the etymological and colloquial senses of the word. It was a fact which also presented certain difficulties to official public relations men and to the mass media. How explain that the Communists were a feeble clique of witless and power-hungry crooks and cranks, and simultaneously leaders of a dangerous kind patently assured of the support of millions? There was a limit to the number of dupes and fools who could credibly be supposed to exist among the unemployed.

In the early winter of 1931 when the Means Test came into operation as the principal instrument for the realization of government policy, huge protest demonstrations all over the country were contained only with difficulty and violence. The smallest of these organized outbursts of protest brought between fifteen thousand and twenty thousand demonstrators into the streets. The largest of them involved as many as a hundred thousand. The list of places where they occurred reads like a guide to industrial Britain. They marched in London, Glasgow, Manchester and Liverpool. Tens of thousands were out in Blackburn, Bolton, Derby, Nottingham, Wolverhampton, Newcastle-on-Tyne, Leeds, Wigan; in Fife, in Yorkshire and South Wales. All through 1932, the resistance movements organized by the N.U.W.M. grew. For their part government supporters in the Commons, on platforms and through the press kept urging for stronger and more effective repression.

Attack at Birkenhead

Ill-advisedly, as some of their own experts thought, the authorities decided that these pleas were justified and took the risk of notably sharpening their action against the unemployed. In September 1932 the new policy was demonstrated in Birkenhead. There a crowd of several thousand had marched to the hall where the Public Assistance Committee was meeting and forced the Committee to send a telegram to the Government asking for abolition of the Means Test. The crowd, satisfied to await the outcome of this request, began to withdraw. As they did so, the police charged them with drawn batons, and bludgeoned many. The action served notice of intent not simply to protect such bodies as the Public Assistance Committee but to punish the protestors. The novelty of the police tactics had taken the demonstrators by surprise, and many of them had brought their womenfolk on what they supposed would be an entirely peaceful gathering in support of their deputation to the Committee. To protest against the police action, employed and unemployed gathered in a huge evening demonstration at the Park Gates. This gathering, too, was charged by the police with batons, at first successfully. Then, to arm themselves, the demonstrators tore down the park railings and fought back. Between thirty and forty police were taken to hospital. Police reinforcements were drafted in from Liverpool and throughout the next day fighting continued in the streets with varying results. At nightfall the police, following out the new line of tactics, were sent into the working-class quarters, smashing ground floor windows and breaking into houses with what could be hoped would be pacificatory violence. This aim was not achieved. Sporadic fighting continued by day and police incursions by night, these now being often resisted with sticks and iron bars and heavy showers of stones. The encounter culminated on the fourth night when police moved against the thickly populated tenement blocks. A Mrs Davis, mother of five children aged between five and nineteen, her husband being an ex-service man invalided out of the army with his lungs affected by poison gas, described the scene:

'The worst night of all was Sunday. We were all in bed at Morpeth Buildings and were suddenly awakened by the sound of heavy motor vehicles. Hordes of police came rushing up the stairs of the Buildings and commenced smashing the doors. The screams of women and children were terrible, we could hear the thuds of the blows from the batons and the terrific struggles in the rooms below, on the landing and on the stairs. Presently our door was forced open by the police. Twelve police rushed into the room and immediately knocked down my husband, splitting open his head and kicking him as he lay on the floor. The language of the police was terrible. The children were screaming and the police shouted "shut up you Parish fed bastards!" My eldest daughter aged nineteen tried to protect me and her father. She too was batoned. They flung my husband down the stairs and put him into the Black Maria with other injured workers. A picture of my husband in army uniform taken in India was in a large frame hanging on the wall and before the police left they smashed this to smithereens with their batons. After taking my husband to the police station and charging him he was taken to the General Hospital where it was found that he had six open head wounds, one over the eye, and injuries to the body.'

Among government advisers argument continued as to whether the new intensification of intimidatory tactics had or had not been successful. The argument was sharpened by the course and outcome of events in Belfast.

There the N.U.W.M. had organized for 11 October a demonstration to demand an increase in the relief payments to the unemployed. The demonstration was prohibited. The prohibition was defied. Armoured cars were moved in. Barricades were erected. The *News Chronicle* reported: 'Charge after charge was made by police upon the bands of men but the charges had only a temporary effect. Even women took part in the terrific onslaught of stones and other missiles and at times it looked as if the police would be overpowered. With the assistance of the armoured cars the rioters were forced back into the side streets and alleys. This hide-and-seek warfare continued throughout the day, with men and women shouting "we must have bread".'

In further battles the police opened fire with revolvers. Thirty-seven men were taken to hospital with bullet wounds. The next day the Royal Inniskilling Fusiliers were drafted in with machine guns. Fighting nevertheless continued. Two workers were shot dead and fifty more severely injured by gun fire. In the evening the Belfast Trade Council called for a general strike. The Mayor of Belfast and members of the Stormont Government then agreed to a consultation with union representatives. The funeral march of the dead was attended by tens of thousands. The police and military did not interfere. On the same day the Northern Ireland Government decided to grant very large concessions to the unemployed. The relief scale for man and wife was raised from eight shillings to twenty shillings per week. It could be, and was, argued by many government supporters that had the concessions been made a few days earlier bloodshed would have been avoided and, more importantly, that the N.U.W.M. and its supporters would not have been presented with proof that concessions could be secured by violent resistance and by no other means.

The marchers in London

During the following fortnight contingents of a national hunger march which was to present a petition against the Means Test to the House of Commons were converging on London from all parts of the country. Almost everywhere along their routes they had been greeted either with sympathy or in predominantly working-class areas with enthusiasm and the stirring of new hopes. On the evening of 26 October the eighteen contingents had reached their overnight halting places all around the edge of London. The regular police were withdrawn from all traffic control and patrol duty and replaced by special constables. All leave was stopped for the Coldstream Guards at Wellington Barracks. More than three thousand regular police with auxiliary special constables were stationed in and around Hyde Park where the demonstration was to be held to welcome the marchers on 27 October. The enormous crowd of London unemployed and trade unionists who had come to welcome the marchers was swelled by many thousands of curious onlookers. All but one contingent of the highly disciplined marchers had arrived punctually in the park when a force of the special constables, inexperienced and naturally nervous, tried to halt the movement of the London crowd near Marble Arch, and threatened a baton charge. The crowd responded by overpowering the special constables and disarming them.

C

Hyde Park, 1932: police disperse unemployed demonstration

The regular police came to the help of the specials. Serious fighting spread from Marble Arch into Oxford Street and up Edgware Road one way and into Hyde Park the other. The mounted police were heavily engaged.

Meantime the main body of the crowd was gathered round the platform set up for the speakers and was more or less unaware of what was going on in the direction of Marble Arch. But presently demonstrators from that direction broke through the police and moved across the park to the area where the meetings were being held. As they did so mounted and foot police charged the crowds round the platforms themselves. These charges were repeatedly thrown back and the police withdrew from that area of Hyde Park. At the gates and first outside the park fighting had continued through-out the afternoon. But the meetings proceeded undisturbed, the bugle sounded to announce the end of the proceedings and the contingents marched away to their night quarters.

On the Sunday following there was to be a demonstration in Trafalgar Square where employed workers who had not been able to take time off to get to Hyde Park would have an opportunity of welcoming the marchers. On the Saturday morning the *Daily Telegraph* expressed the indignation that was general among the upper sort over the march, and in particular over the fact that the Government was not apparently acting with sufficient vigour. The *Daily Telegraph* editorial said:

'**Loot and Pillage**
'London may infer from the account given by the Home Secretary of the serious rioting near Marble Arch what is intended to occur at some later date if chance should offer. The abolition of the Means Test is a pretext. The presentation of a petition to Parliament is a blind. Hannington, the professional organizer of these marches, is conceited indeed if he supposes that his Communist riff-raff could make revolution, but that they could do incalculable damage by loot and pillage in an hour or two of mob excitement is undeniable and that bloodshed will ensue is certain.

'We urge the authorities not merely to take precautions to deal with the marchers but to put an end to the marches themselves. That can deal not with the dupes but with the organizers.

'A year ago this man Hannington was convicted at Bow Street for inciting the unemployed to riot. It is his professional occupation, and the occupation is unlawful. He is responsible not only for the behaviour of the marchers, but for attracting the crowds, which are certain to include the most dangerous elements in London, bent on the chance of mischief and riot. It is foolish to take such unnecessary risks. These Communist Organizers should be laid by the heels. What took place round Marble Arch on Thursday will certainly take place again. It is quite likely to be repeated on Tuesday. [Tuesday was the day when the petition was to be presented to the Commons.]

'Tomorrow Trafalgar Square is to be the locale of a "tremendous expression of the unity of the employed and unemployed". We trust that the Home Secretary will see that the reserve forces of law and order are in adequate attendance . . . senti-mental weakness in handling this situation will only issue in more disturbances and a longer list of casualties. These marchers are a public nuisance and a public danger.'

The events which so dramatically followed brilliantly characterize the states of mind and the state of forces in the early thirties, and are also enlightening in a general way.

More than a hundred and twenty thousand Londoners attended the demonstration in Trafalgar Square. The crowds extended far back into Charing Cross Road, the Strand, and Northumberland Avenue. Both sides regarded the enormous attendance (a record for Trafalgar Square) as especially significant because the entire meeting was designed as a demonstration of the essential unity between employed and unemployed. The meeting proceeded without much disturbance from sporadic fighting with the police on the edge of the crowd. As the principal speaker from the plinth of the Nelson memorial Hannington thought fit to address a few words to the ranks of police within hearing. He told them: 'You were drawn from the ranks of the working class and your pay has been cut under the economy measures. We marched for the abolition of the Means Test and the restoration of the economy cuts; that means the cuts in the pay of sailors, soldiers and police as well as the unemployed.' Appealing to them not to use their truncheons against the workers he added that 'the working class in uniform and out of uniform stand together in defiance of their condition'. He observed that detectives at the front of the meeting were taking shorthand notes of this speech.

On the morning of 1 November, the day when the petition was to be presented at the Bar of the House of Commons, the *Daily Telegraph* again called for action:

'How long is London to be subjected to the indignity of having its police forces— regular and special—mobilized to deal with the Communist Hannington and his Marchers but in reality Hannington and the revolutionary riff-raff of London? Ninety per cent of the Marchers may well be dupes, pawns in a Communist game directed by the master intrigues of Moscow . . . Once more therefore the London police will stand to attention tonight in anticipation of what Hannington may elect to do after he has harangued his Marchers on Camberwell Green.

'How long, we repeat, is this playing with revolution to be tolerated? These Communists are boasting that for every Hannington who is arrested twenty new leaders will come forward! Safe accommodation could easily be found for all.'

Hannington arrested
Hannington recalls how, that evening:

'the Central Marchers Council was meeting in a small hall in the vicinity of Kings Cross. A member of the Council arrived two minutes late as I was starting to submit a report. He passed up to me a sealed envelope addressed to me and marked "by hand". Fortunately I did not put it into my pocket, otherwise I might have left it there and the consequences would undoubtedly have been very serious. I opened it when I finished my report and to my astonishment found that it contained an incriminatory document intended to discredit the Marchers Council, particularly myself and McShane. It was worded in such a manner as to imply clearly that we were agreed parties to the carrying out of a terrorist campaign which included way-laying Cabinet Ministers and injuring them with violent assault, and committing acts of incendiarism against government buildings.

'I immediately stopped the proceedings of the Council and enquired how our member had obtained this document. I knew him to be a very reliable chap and he explained to me that as he was entering the hall he'd been approached by a stranger who asked if he was attending the meeting at which I would be present. He replied that he was and the man then gave the envelope and asked him to deliver it to me personally. He asked the stranger if he would be waiting for a reply and he answered "No, Hannington knows all about it".'

The document, planted obviously by an *agent provocateur*, was so worded that had it been discovered by the press or the police the N.U.W.M. leaders would have found it difficult to convince even the general public, let alone a magistrate, that it was a frame-up. Some members of the Council were for taking the document to their solicitors to add evidence of a *provocateur* being at work. Hannington pointed out that every minute that the document was in their possession was dangerous. The police might act the moment they were sure that it had been delivered to Hannington. Members of the Council certainly could not afford to wait to see the solicitors on the following morning since they could be arrested in the night with the document in their possession. They burned it on the spot and puffed away the ashes.

Next morning twenty plain-clothes police raided the N.U.W.M. headquarters in Great Russell Street, arrested Hannington and seized large quantities of documents. Hannington was taken to Bow Street police court and charged with 'attempting to cause disaffection among members of the Metropolitan Police contrary to the Police Act 1919'. (It was in 1918 that the Metropolitan Police had mutinied.) Hannington was remanded in custody and thus removed from the leadership of the deputation to the House. The enormous bundles containing the signatures to the petition had been deposited in the cloakroom at Charing Cross station. When the marchers arrived to collect them the police locked the gates of Charing Cross station yard, overpowered the marchers and seized the bundles. Meantime huge crowds had assembled outside the House of Commons chanting 'release Hannington' and later demanded to know what had happened to the petition. Fighting with the foot and mounted police broke out and lasted until after midnight. The newspapers devoted pages to pictures of the struggle. It was disclosed that the King had kept in close touch with the situation. Lord Trenchard, then Chief Commissioner of the Metropolitan Police, was at Scotland Yard until midnight and was in constant communication with Buckingham Palace.

Trade union branches, trades councils and other organizations throughout the country paid the cost of special trains and coaches to transport the marchers back to their home district. Thirty thousand people greeted the Scottish marchers at the railway terminus in Glasgow. Headlines in the *Sunday Dispatch* stated 'Hunger march backed by Red gold—£5,000 in hard cash smuggled from Moscow into Britain—"ferment hate!" command— Bolshevik agents plot to coerce unemployed—secret payroll.'

At the opening of his trial on the following Tuesday Hannington asked what action the magistrate intended to take against the *Sunday Dispatch* for publishing an article prejudicial to his trial while the case was still sub judice. The magistrate replied that he had not read the *Sunday Dispatch* and was therefore not prejudiced.

Hannington's defence against the charge of 'attempting to cause disaffection among the police' was that he could not have caused the disaffection because disaffection about the pay cuts had existed before he made his speech.

Questioned by Hannington, who dispensed with Counsel, Detective Sergeant Oliver declared that he had no knowledge of any disaffection.

Hannington then read aloud a letter published in the 21 October issue of the *Police Review* saying, 'Does the Home Office not know that there is considerable dissatisfaction in the service today as a result of continual interference with pay and Federation matters?' The *Police Review* was the organ of the official Police Federation. The detective sergeant said he had not read it. Hannington then read aloud an article from the 14 October issue which began, 'In view of the very serious discontent that prevails throughout the service upon the introduction of supplementary pay deductions...' Another article in the same magazine stated, 'The pay cuts have very naturally been the cause of much soreness . . . there were men leaving the service today—men of high rank—sick to death of the treatment they have received.' Finally Hannington quoted from the issue of 4 November where it was stated that 'the government turned a deaf ear to the definite statement that discontent and dissatisfaction was rampant throughout the service caused by the unfair and unjust treatment meted out to members of the police service'.

He was sentenced to three months' imprisonment in Pentonville.

The Higher Management understood the import of the organization of the unemployed and the strategy and tactics of the N.U.W.M. By the beginning of 1933 it was already envisaging possible checks to its own campaign and changes in its own strategy. Supposed experts had declared that its genuine concern must be translated into jabberwocky terms to be intelligible by the general public. Moscow gold, slavering looters, hundreds of thousands of zombie dupes marching the highways, were supposed to be the only images the public could understand.

It was a mistake.

To make it showed the weakest side of those in power. It was a mistake particularly characteristic of the powerful in, specifically, England.

The eternal Captain Grimes

The British public school system as developed after the middle of the nineteenth century was explicitly designed to produce a master class. It had done so. In bizarre fashion it had justified the attitudes of the Tory Working Man. Since the master class had made the rules of the game its members on the whole, and with the necessary exceptions made, were able to play it better than anyone else. Important among their many great skills was their ability to cover up and compensate for one another's mistakes. Evelyn Waugh's Captain Grimes, while 'singularly in tune with the primitive promptings of humanity', had also a singularly clear understanding of the power of the public school system. In the context of the late twenties and the thirties it was proper to see the great Captain as perpetual and deathless. Shrewd, resilient, boozy and corrupt, he fully understood the contours of the English landscape. He was a suitable captain in the infantry of the ruling powers. He was the Superman in the Saloon Bar. And in the thirties the loud voices of the men in the Saloon Bar were often taken by informers from on high as true indices of public opinion. By injecting into its bloodstream elements of alien class origin such as Sir George May the traditional ruling class sustained and mightily revivified itself. One of its notable sources of strength was its ability to perform such injections. But their own success in the upward climb had often deeply tinged these elements with a contempt, almost ethical or religious in nature, for the working class and those of the lower middle class who had failed to make the grade. This contempt naturally fused with the separately conditioned thinking of men from the older public schools and the universities of Oxford or Cambridge. Thus the coolly far-sighted, thoughtfully conceived, often brilliantly executed strategies of those in power were persistently flawed by underestimation of the intelli-gence of the enemy and his potential allies. This kind of miscalculation, and the conditioning which caused it, was an evidently important political and social factor of life in the thirties. At the time it was not often fully appraised as such. It became more obtrusive early in the war when understanding of the working class in or out of uniform became evidently essential. The inade-quacies in this respect which during the thirties had deepened the division between the Two Nations, spectacularly disclosed themselves in the over-

throw, so astonishing to so many, of Winston Churchill and the Conservatives in the General Election of 1945.

How credible?

The failure of the press campaigns of the early thirties was of wide significance. In the immediate short term it failed to help the Government to press home successfully its campaign on the industrial front. Sages and elder journalistic statesmen, particularly the owners of 'quality' journals of opinion with relatively small circulations, giving ear to the thudding flops of Lord Beaverbrook's Empire Free Trade campaign were glad to state that this showed how little irresponsible press propaganda influenced the voters. Enthralled by the impotence in this instance of the Beaverbrook press, they paid little attention to a more important aspect of the relationship between the press and the public. Literally millions of people, among them very many of the most thoughtful and keenly interested citizens in their own communities, had seen with their own eyes that the picture of the hunger marchers presented by the greater part of the national press was so crude in its falsifications as to be insulting to the intelligence of readers. Purporting to describe hunger marchers on their way from Chippenham to Swindon, the *Daily Mail* had described 'men falling by the roadside exhausted', 'marchers straggling along anyhow . . . being forced by self-seeking Red politicians to make a hardship march to London' and as a discreditable clincher declared that Hannington, complaining of foot trouble, had ridden comfortably in the sidecar of a motor cycle instead of marching. There was no motor cycle or sidecar, the men were not straggling along anyhow but advancing in an orderly column, and nobody but a company of police or troops could have 'forced' them to march anywhere. In the presence of a large crowd of local inhabitants the marchers burned the *Daily Mail* outside Swindon town hall. The paper had lost a lot of credibility in Swindon. As townspeople and villagers from one end of Britain to the other viewed the realities of the march, saw and listened to the marchers, the campaigning newspapers lost credibility everywhere. The repeated discrepancies between what really happened during and after the great demonstrations and other protest actions of the unemployed and what the newspapers said had happened widened the credibility gap. When the police, as in Birkenhead, spectacularly assumed the offensive it would have been possible, it might even have been politic, for the newspapers to explain to the public that this was a necessary change in tactics without which the economic policies of the Government, recently supported at the polls by multi-millions of the citizenry, could not successfully be carried through. It could have been declared that the intransigence of the unemployed now required sterner measures if the will of the people was to prevail. By choosing instead to pretend that the police had acted otherwise than they had, the newspapers displayed a contempt for the citizens' powers of observation and an equally contemptuous fear lest the readers who had supported government policies at the polls might be too queasy to support them in action.

Big sections of the working class had always regarded with sensible suspicion newspapers owned by people whose interests were contradictory

The Two Nations: spectators at football match between Eton and Durham unemployed

73

to their own. But in 1932, 1933 and on into 1934, the activities of the N.U.W.M. aroused and focused wider and wider attention upon the problem of the unemployed, the incredibility of the press became increasingly apparent to very numerous members of the middle class too. All this amounted to a major and decisive factor in producing a qualitative change in the attitude of the British public to the British press. Even in the thirties the image of a free press, an independent press, a neutral press, a press at least trying to be truthful, was still vivid and credible to many minds. The behaviour of the press during the unemployment crisis of the thirties battered that image. Newspaper proprietors, insulated by their conditioning, may have known the newspapers had been hit, but neither knew nor cared just what had hit them. Most of them confused credibility with circulation. Only one or two understood that while circulation rose, credibility and authority could yet be falling.

It was during this period, and at this juncture of affairs, that the mass circulation newspapers first more or less consciously acknowledged that they were essentially neither more nor less than a part of show business. And the mass of their readership increasingly accepted that as a definition and function of the newspapers. The American press, often as black a pot as the British kettle, from this time on constantly censured and shook its head at the shameless irresponsibility, triviality, and frivolity of British newspapers. To which the British could justifiably reply that they were mainly engaged in the entertainment business and that in that business frivolity was by no means out of place.

The mood changes

For a long time the newspapers seemed not to notice that the events of late 1932 had brought about a serious change in the social climate. They had constructed a distorting mirror and could see the world only in its reflection there.

If the National Unemployed Workers' Movement were a relatively insignificant and basically un-English Red rabble, then it was inconceivable that they should gain the sympathy, support, or alliance of large numbers of trade union officials, trades councillors, freely elected borough councillors, clergymen, doctors, lawyers, and influential writers. But then came 1933, and it was actually happening.

Revolt of local authorities against government policy had started as early as February 1932. It took the form of a refusal by Public Assistance Committees appointed by Labour controlled local councils to put the Means Test into effect. They either refused to employ the Means Test at all or automatically handed out the maximum permitted allowances without regard to family circumstances. Among the locally controlled authorities who received threatening letters from the Central Government were those in Durham County, Glamorgan County, Monmouth County and Northumberland County, and the towns of Barrow-in-Furness, Blackburn, Nelson, Oldham, Southampton, Stoke-on-Trent, Swansea, Wolverhampton, Rotherham, and West Ham. Where local resistance persisted, the local Committees were simply suppressed by the Central Government and commissioners appointed in their stead. Others followed the policy of West Ham where the locals announced: 'We were threatened with supercession, and in face of that threat we prefer to keep our poor under our own care and do what we can for them rather than hand them over to an arbitrary commissioner from whom they could expect little humanity.'

This intrusion of the Central Government at grass roots level did much to make the oppositional grass grow greener. The Government had placed much reliance on the mixture of passive indifference and vehement hostility towards the N.U.W.M. displayed by the majority controlling the leadership of the principal trade unions. Some of these leaders saw in the N.U.W.M. a dangerous and potentially disastrous challenge to their whole structure of theory and practice developed since the defeat of 1926. For others the fact that the N.U.W.M. was under Communist leadership was in itself an almost totally sufficient ground for putting its isolation or elimination at the top of the agenda. It was said that Ernest Bevin's suspicious hostility towards the Soviet Union was due to the fact that he considered the Bolsheviks as essentially a splinter party which had formed a break-away union. That description was more literally true of the feelings so many leading trade union officials had about the N.U.W.M. There were also those among them who sincerely believed that the immediate sectional interests of the better paid workers could only be damaged by any association with the interests of the unemployed. The effort of the T.U.C. to isolate the National Unemployed Workers' Movement was only partially successful. It certainly prevented the development of a united action by the industrial workers against the policies of the City which might have been overwhelming and could even perhaps have been revolutionary. But in the lower echelons and at local levels, numerous trade union officials disregarded or openly defied the T.U.C. by working closely and in the most practical fashion with the organizers of the N.U.W.M.; raising money, arranging accommodation for marchers, agitating and speaking from platforms on their behalf, the situation provided a breeding ground for left-wing militancy in the trade unions. 'Unity in action' involved also local Labour parties, trades councils and co-operative guilds. At the beginning of 1934 the United Front Congress in support of the Hunger March, assembling more than 1,400 elected delegates from all sections of the trade union and political working class movement throughout the country, had Bermondsey Town Hall put at its disposal and received an official welcome from the Labour Mayor of the borough. In the context of those days it was a spectacular event. The alignments and cogitations within the trade union movement occurring at that time had consequences which long outlived the N.U.W.M. itself. They were in part responsible for the slow but powerful growth of organized left-wing influence in the T.U.C. and the leadership of major unions which became a notable feature of industrial and political life in the seventies.

New allies
Many voices which had been faint, out-shouted, gagged or suffocated during the years of gloom, panic and defeatism were now heard. People began to listen more carefully than before to what medical officers of health and

Overleaf: All over the British Isles men marched. Unemployed in Trafalgar Square; Scottish hunger marchers in London (left above); Irish hunger marchers (below)

other doctors were saying about near-starvation and the dangerous diseases caused by poverty in huge tracts of Great Britain. Doctors who previously had thought that in the prevailing climate nothing was to be done took heart and contributed to the agitation. A similar process was set in motion in the Churches. The peculiarly English institution of Parsons' Freehold, making numerous parsons invulnerable to economic, political, or ecclesiastical-disciplinary pressures, put them among the few totally independent individuals in the country, and safeguarded and nurtured eloquent clergymen of the Church of England in their protests against government policy. The 'Nonconformist conscience', never quite asleep, expressed itself, particularly in South Wales, in overt and practical support for the demands of the unemployed. In March 1934 Neville Chamberlain, Chancellor of the Exchequer, speaking at a Conservative Party dinner in Birmingham, stated that he was being overwhelmed with letters from all kinds of organizations and individuals urging him to restore the unemployment benefit cuts. He had even been stabbed in the back by the Archbishop of Canterbury. The prelate had written to *The Times* urging 'all Christians' to demand that the cuts be restored. Chamberlain said: 'I thought it was a pity that the Archbishop should suggest, as it seemed to me he did by implication, that Members of Parliament require to be reminded of humanitarian feelings.'

The fears and the determination to resist which had come newly to life among professional people of the middle class were summarized and expressed in the recreation of the National Council of Civil Liberties in February 1934. It was originally formed, at a meeting in the crypt of St Martin's in the Fields, for the purpose of protecting, by vigilant observation and bearing of witness, the hunger marchers of 1934 against police violence. It had wider implications and consequences. Harold Laski, Henry Nevinson, C. R. Attlee, Vera Brittain, A. P. Herbert, and H. G. Wells were among the signatories to the significant letter which announced the foundation of the Council:

'The present hunger march has been preceded by public statements by the Home Secretary and the Attorney General (who has already hinted at the possibility of bloodshed) which we feel justify apprehension. Furthermore, certain features of the police preparations for the present march—for example, instructions to shopkeepers to barricade their windows—cannot but create an atmosphere of misgiving, not only dangerous but unjustified by the facts.

'All reports bear witness to the excellent discipline of the marchers. From their own leaders they have received repeated instructions of the strictest character, warning them against any breach of the peace, even under extreme provocation.

'In view of the general and alarming tendency to encroachment on the liberty of the citizen, there has recently been formed a Council of Civil Liberties. One of the special duties of the Council will be to maintain a vigilant observation of the proceedings of the next few days. Relevant and well-authenticated reports by responsible persons will be welcomed and investigated by the Council.'

The retreat begins
In face of the broad counter-attack spearheaded by the N.U.W.M. the government retreat began.

That a major retreat was coming was evident to all who could read the signs of the times as early as the afternoon of 25 February, when the marchers gathered in Hyde Park.

The hard Birkenhead line had been abandoned. The new orders issued to the police, particularly the verbal instructions given to their officers, directed them to observe restraint and avoid taking the offensive.

To prevent provocation the main body of the mounted police was stationed at a considerable distance from the rallying points of the crowd, only just visible in the misty drizzle.

Thus between 100,000 and 150,000 Londoners were able to attend the proceedings undisturbed and disperse in peace. Similar orders to the police ensured that the mass lobbying of M.P.s which went on during the next couple of days took place without violent incident. Then, as now, as many reporters have found, the behaviour of the police on major political occasions is a nearly infallible pointer to government policies.

On 17 April it was announced that standard rates of benefit to the unemployed would be restored in July to their old level.

It was a retreat.

Super-Board—1935

But it was almost immediately evident that the retreat was designed to cover a redeployment and a shift of strategy. Hannington and the leadership of the N.U.W.M., together with trade union militants everywhere, continued their agitation. They were of course aware that the Government must attack again. The matter at issue was too fundamental, the objectives outlined in long-ago 1931 too valuable, for the main thrust to be abandoned. The militants were confident in the strength of support they had gained in the country since the beginning of 1932. But they expected the other side to move vigorously. They were right.

Less than half the three million now unemployed and their dependents were directly affected at all by the restoration of the cuts in the standard benefit rates. (Even at the new or restored level payments at those standard rates were officially admitted to be 'not a living wage'.) Those not affected had exhausted their benefit rights and were subsisting on the dole payable only after the administration of the Means Test. But the Means Test was administered by the local Public Assistance Committees. The Government already had experience of how gravely such local committees could be affected by local opinion, local pressures, local evidence of hunger and disease. Temporarily these undesirable pressures had been removed by the appointment of commissioners from the Central Government or threats to appoint them. Measures to transfer the whole administration and control of these payments from the localities to the Central Government were already on the Statute Book.

They were now put into action.

The elimination of popular pressures near the grass roots was much, but it was not enough. There was still the danger that popular pressure might be exerted through Parliament. The supreme Unemployment Assistance Board, set up in late 1934, was therefore declared an independent body. It would, that is to say, be independent of any direct parliamentary control. Criticism and interference by persons elected either at local or national level could thus simply be cut out. As in the summer of 1931 those in power rightly judged that ordinary processes of democracy could seriously damage or impede their enterprise.

The amounts decreed as payable under the new U.A.B. from 7 January 1935 were then announced. There were to be bold reductions right across the board. Possibly even more important than the reduction in cash payments were regulations putting new and sharper teeth into the Means Test. They could bite into the money of the unemployed at many points. It was seen as essential, for instance, to increase the extent to which unemployed parents could be mulcted in respect of money earned by their children if these were in work. From now on only one-third of the earnings of son or daughter up to twenty shillings, and only one-quarter of the excess over twenty shillings, would be regarded as the earner's own, the rest would be registered as available to the unemployed parents, and thus under the Means Test be used to reduce the amount payable to them. (Some government sociologists worked out that this was a way of maintaining or instilling a wholesome sense of family. As things were, the unemployed and their children were clever enough to note that if the children disappeared from home with their earnings the parents would be better off. Many families were forced to show their family feeling by disrupting themselves.)

Resistance was immediate and sustained in every sector. The anthracite miners called a twenty-four hour protest strike. The South Wales Miners' Federation called an All-Wales conference and set up a council of action. In that area 300,000 people demonstrated. In Scotland and on Tyneside, as in South Wales, protesting women smashed the windows and sometimes stoned the doorways of the U.A.B. offices. Protests came not only from innumerable individual borough councillors and county councillors but from whole county councils and local authorities speaking as elected bodies. Groups of doctors protested, religious organizations of all denominations protested. And many local Labour parties joined with the Communists in protest. It was only with difficulty and some internal apprehension that the T.U.C. remained inactive except in issuing warnings of disciplinary action against trade union organizations participating in any action in which the N.U.W.M. was involved. The depth both of feeling and of division in the Labour and Trade Union Movement was important at the time and significant for the future.

The rout
W. H. Mainwaring, Labour M.P. for East Rhondda, expressed the feeling of the Opposition elements inside and outside the House when he closed his speech with the words:

'I hope the working classes of this country will pay heed to what is said and done here today and that from now onwards the agitation which is at such a height in South Wales will spread like a flame throughout the country and that the English and Scottish working classes will join with the Welshmen and make the demand that come what may these damnable regulations must be withdrawn.'

80

The public gallery cheered.

For five more days menacing reports poured in upon the Government.

Then on 5 February 1935 the retreat was sounded for the second time in less than a year. Oliver Stanley, Minister of Labour, rose to announce a standstill order. Applicants for relief were to get either what they would have got under the previous Public Assistance Committee's assessments or an allowance in accordance with new regulations, whichever was the higher. Past reductions would be refunded.

Even so, even then, the Government supposed itself strong enough to postpone the standstill for a fortnight. The resistance movement would not allow it. A fortnight is a long time for a family on the starvation line. The final blow came from Sheffield. On 6 February, 40,000 unemployed from the great iron and steelworks of the city and from the mines of Yorkshire marched to Sheffield's City Hall demanding that the City Council receive a deputation. The deputation would demand immediate restoration of the cuts to the unemployed. Overpowering large forces of police, the demonstrators reached the City Hall. The deputation entered but the Council refused to receive them. They refused to leave. Police were called to throw them out. A mass of demonstrators trying to force their way into the Hall were charged by mounted and foot police. Fighting continued for some two hours. In the course of the battle the shopping centre of the city was partially wrecked. Police and demonstrators suffered heavy casualties.

Some members of the City Council simply took fright. Others reasoned that the events involving so many thousands of citizens in prolonged and violent action had sufficiently demonstrated the sincerity of the demands they were making upon their local councillors. The Mayor headed a deputation which hurried to London. The Mayor and Councillors saw the Minister. They told the story of those hours of battle during which the seizure of the Hall had seemed imminent. And some of them made it clear that if they had to return to Sheffield with 'no' for an answer they could not be responsible for the consequences. The Minister made the final capitulation. He authorized the Councillors to put the standstill into immediate operation and immediately pay back the amount of the cuts already made.

From the headquarters of the N.U.W.M. messages were immediately sent to all District Committees of the Movement calling upon them to demand the same treatment in their areas. Within twenty-four hours enormous demonstrations of unemployed were marching in all the principal cities and towns, demanding that what had been done for Sheffield should be done for them. There was no need for the Government to make any formal concession. Under pressure of the events in Sheffield and the subsequent demonstrations the attempt to delay the standstill broke down in chaos. The standstill and the repayment of reductions already made came into operation immediately almost everywhere.

Thus in the middle of the decade a brief period of equilibrium was reached. Certainly the impetus of the attack had been halted. Neither side had been finally defeated. But the shape and directions of the battle were shifting.

5 The New Consumer

1935 *And the kindly light of Woolworths*

Every eighteen days a new branch of Woolworths was opened in some city or town of Britain. The Woolworth people in New York had £5 million earmarked for use as a grant in aid for the British company. Given the stormy winds that certainly did blow in England it was reckoned that a million here and a million there might have to be shipped across in the financial lifeboats. The lifeboats never had to be called for. In New York it was a widely held opinion among the prudent that anyone launching any enterprise in England at that time was going to sea in a sieve. 'And everyone said who saw them go/Won't they be soon upset you know/ For the sky is dark and the voyage is long/And happen what may it's extremely wrong/In a sieve to sail so fast.' The Woolworth advisers on the other hand said that they knew by years of experience that British conditions were about right for the kind of craft they operated and that looked at in the right way a carefully constructed sieve could be a lot less sinkable than any heavy-built galleon. William L. Stephenson of Birmingham, formerly an English buyer for the New York store of Wanamakers, was the mastermind of the Woolworth operation in England. Soon after Guy Fawkes's Day in 1909, when the first British Woolworth store opened in Liverpool, Frank Woolworth, luring the young Stephenson away from Wanamakers, told him: 'If we go bust you're bust. If we make a go of it we'll look after you.' Going bust seemed the most likely alternative. But Frank Woolworth, and subsequently Stephenson, prospered largely by taking the view that almost everything most people said about the character of the English people, their deep-rooted traditions, their snobbery and their unconquerable individualism, was—when you came down to the harsh facts of life— boloney. They were told that English people with more than a penny or so to spend liked their shops to be little or at least small enough to have a personal individual air. Also the English would be shy of wandering about the store in the American manner before making up their minds what to buy. But the shy, traditionally-minded English liked the American-type store well, so well that a second Woolworths was at once opened in Liverpool. The English liked that even better. The place was enthusiastically mobbed, the counters were overthrown, the salesgirls knocked down, and the goods looted. In Stephenson's view it was an auspicious beginning. Its memory inspired him to what seemed in the early thirties impudent audacities. The appearance of impudence and audacity was deceptive. Studying the charts, he and the people in New York could see that the English weather was not wholly unfavourable.

Brooding on the reports from London, students in the Woolworth Building could see plenty of negative factors. As a source of new consumer demand three million unemployed could be written off for a start. Very poor at the beginning of 1931, they were going to be much poorer still at the end of it. May-ism was already in the air. The capacity in that sector to buy cheap consumer goods was certainly not going to rise and probably was going to fall. But the unemployed had never figured largely in the Woolworth operation. More important were figures showing the buying power—or lack of it— of the employed. Charts prepared by the experts showed that a little under 50 per cent of adult male employed workers were earning less than 55 shillings

Previous pages: An early Woolworth's branch; left: W. L. Stephenson, Woolworth's British boss; and mass-produced luxury radiogram plus cocktail cabinet

a week. A little over 20 per cent were earning less than 45 shillings. Taking the value of money as it then was it was reckoned that between 50 and 53 shillings a week was the minimum needed to keep a man, wife and three children above the absolute poverty line. Be the books cooked never so tastily, the figures totted up to the statement that approximately three million men were living below a standard 'below which', the social experts said, 'no worker should be forced to live'. One and three-quarter million women were on the same level. They were not likely to be renewing their lipsticks very often, or buying many pairs of the new rayon stockings. For them to burn out a saucepan or break a jug was a small disaster not to be automatically remedied by popping round to Woolworths.

There were other less calculable factors, all supposedly negative. People were suffering from mental depression and hopelessness. Even among those relatively well placed there was a spiritual pulling in of horns. Nobody was in a mood to try anything new: not even a new Woolworths store in their town.

Assurances of better goods and cheaper would not suffice to change their buying habits. The surrounding gloom was so deep that even the kindly light of Woolworths would, it was feared, fail to lead them on.

But Stephenson was looking at people who still did earn a little money. And here the effects of the slump could prove actually favourable. The slump had, though with less abrupt violence than in the United States, jolted British attitudes, knocked some old bits of thinking about a bit, sharpened people's economic eyesight. Millions who had any money left at all were not going to let habits or traditions impede them when it came to getting value for money. If the new Woolworths in an old town could provide better value for money, then the available money would come to Woolworths. Stephenson's personal experience of more than twenty years had developed in him a particular fingertip feeling for the characteristics, some steady, some quick shifting, of that large segment of the population which, so far as Woolworths was concerned, mattered. It was a segment which included everyone between a shadowy line drawn somewhere through the middle of the middle class and another drawn through somewhere near the top of the working class.

From that day to the present no one in Britain has ever been able to agree about the middle class. To deny that there is a middle class with an upper middle class, a middle middle class and a lower middle class would be pointless. But as to where the upper middle shades into the middle middle, and the middle middle into the lower middle, every observer and statistician can write his own ticket. It is said that the way a family furnishes its front parlour, living room, or lounge, shows it to be of the lower middle class. But suppose the place is burgled, and the family uses the insurance money to refurnish in a quite different style? Has it thereby changed class or not, or what?

In the analyses spread out in the Woolworth Building what was called the Factor of the Three Differentials was very visible. There was the Geographical plus Job-base Differential. It would have taken a very clumsy analyst not to notice that in Britain, although everyone and everything felt the effects of the slump, the old industries such as coal mining, cotton, and shipbuilding felt it a lot worse than, for instance, engineering, particularly electrical engineering and allied works. The new industries centred in the Midlands, the London area and the south-east. The population drift was that way from the north and from South Wales. Indices of consumer demand which were true of the Fife coalfields or Lancashire were untrue of almost everywhere from Luton to Maidstone and Dagenham to Reading.

Differential Number 2 was represented by the Function Factor. More important, at least in this context, than the above-mentioned shift within industrial production was the shift of earning capacity, and hence of consumer demand, out of productive industry into service industries and the distributive trades. It was in fact going on so fast that, although this could not have been precisely foreseen in the Woolworth analyses, by the end of the decade nearly a third of the gainfully employed personnel of Great Britain was engaged not in producing goods, but in servicing people or things, in selling, or in the bureaucracy necessary for the administration of the organizational apparatus of government and industry. The unit of personnel concerned could be a garage mechanic, a stockbroker's clerk, or an ex-officer trying to exist by selling the novelty of vacuum cleaners or the bound wisdom of the *Encyclopaedia Britannica* from door to door. What was true of the factory workers in both the old and the new industries could not accurately be stated of people in this sector.

The third Differential was provided by the factor comprehensively known as the Factor of Comparison and Expectation. This was a product of one or both of the first two Differentials. Even when apparently stagnant to the naked eye, every society is seen under the microscope to be in a state of flux. Particularly to the purveyor of consumer goods the important areas are not those near the centre of each social area. There, immobility, sometimes productive and sometimes stagnant, can persist over long years. The action is at the edges where displaced persons move from one area to another. A young man moves from a cotton mill in the north-west to an electrical engineering works in the south-east. He may be simply trying to insure himself against imminent unemployment. Or he moves because even a man reasonably assured of steady employment in a moribund industry can foresee no upward movement for himself and family. His real wage in the new job may be, possibly, probably is, a little better than in the old one. Even assuming it to be the same his outlook is changed and his spending habits with it.

In the thirties he looked back at what now seemed to him the petrified patterns of personal and family life in the mill town and compared them with patterns still newly forming themselves on the edges of London. He looked forward because, on the evidence of the expanding activity around him, there was something to look forward to.

The comparison and the expectation were both jolting.

The comparison helped him to consider what might be really value for his money rather than what the old folks had said was value, and the only value at that. The expectation also stimulated effective consumer demand. If you really wanted new crockery, lipstick, and a screwdriver, and it was possible to get good ones cheap at Woolworths, you were not afraid to lay your money out for the purpose lest at some future date you might not have enough left for a carpet. Paradoxically, even uncertainty about the future could, in relatively fluid circumstances, have the same effect. The very rich bought diamonds, and latterly have bought pictures and antiques, as a hedge against inflation and, if the worst came to the worst, revolution. The working class was not thinking in terms of a hedge. In the centres of the old industries common talk of the impending collapse of everything could produce symptoms of caution such as are usually associated with the peasantry. One of them was a drying up of consumer buying. The defensive reflex could consist in taking money out of the commercial bank and putting it in the supposedly safer Post Office Savings Bank, or even sewing it into the mattress. But in the slightly headier air of the new industrial communities the reaction could be in the direction of stocking up with what you needed now and could afford to pay cash for now. To this marginal extent even panic as well as hope could work for Woolworths.

This general assessment of the British scene was shared by experts very different from William Stephenson and his New York backers. When the big decision was taken to float Woolworths as a British public company with Stephenson as Chairman in 1931, Rothschilds handled the flotation.

And with a fingertip feeling for the way things were going in England which, by the hindsight of the seventies looks like genius, Stephenson started to put the shareholders' money into buying freeholds for the new stores instead of leases. In Stephenson's unwritten Social and Economic History of England, the important dates occurred every eighteen days with the opening of a new store. While the customers rattled in their sixpences for the necessities and the gadgets, the value of the floor, walls and ceiling enclosing them was on its slow unsteady rise towards heights then unimaginable.

Growth of this kind of consumer demand is a product of hope. In Greek mythology Elpis, goddess of Hope, was apt to be a wrecker. People were doing all right and 'then Elpis appeared to them and they were doomed'. The answer to the question whether people in one state of life or another take a Greek view of hope, looking at it askance, or welcome its presence as beneficent, can offer a quick little clue to the nature of the society they live in. Within the society the welcomers and the askance-lookers co-exist.

In societies like that of England in the thirties there were those who neither eyed Elpis with suspicion nor listened eagerly for her coming. They no longer believed in her existence. It was the salient fact noted by all social investigators of the long-term unemployed. And the mere presence of that mass of hopelessness deeply tinged the thinking of many not themselves so much afflicted. The colour of hopelessness, the sense that the only turnings out of Queer Street were blind alleys, could be discerned in much of the period's literature and more of its table talk, pub talk, club talk, talk in the works canteen, talk after the boardroom meeting was over, fireside talk, bed talk, and people in the street just talking madly to themselves. Seen back to front, the same basic hopelessness was equally visible in those books people read, those plays and films people saw, those radio entertainments they listened to, which at least purported to distract attention from reality. They did so because they considered reality too hopeless. It was a period when the organizers of mass entertainment in England automatically mis-understood or limited the meaning of the word. They conceived that entertainment must mean distraction. This belief was more English than American. The nihilistic political satire of 'Of Thee I Sing' could not have been acceptably translated into English terms. Yet in New York its success was enormous. The French Foreign Office took the corrosive satire so seriously that the French Ambassador was instructed to demand the excision of the song where the girl sang that she was 'an illegitimate daughter of an illegitimate son of an illegitimate nephew of Napoleon'. It was thought that at a delicate moment in international relations the song could lower the dignity of France in the eyes of the powerful American public.

Revealingly, English distractors when they turned thumbs down on social satire either invoked the libel laws or simply declared that they considered it would not entertain people. Here and there on the stage or the cabaret floor could be heard from inside the pretty waxwork the voice of a satirist screaming to be let out. At the time of Mussolini's invasion of Abyssinia Ronald Frankau had a song with the line 'I'd rather be an Ethiopian savage than an ordinary civilized man'. That got by. But there was another line in the same song which ended 'Let's find Hitler and kick him in the pants'. When he tried to transfer the song from cabaret to the B.B.C. he was in-structed to substitute the name of Carnera, the mammoth boxer, for Hitler. Privately he complained that satire in Britain was emasculated to the point where the authorities considered it more naughty for a person to be rude to a foreign dictator than to perpetrate a line which didn't even scan.

The small hopes sprouting towards the middle of the decade among workers in the expanding trades and industries were frowned upon by the Higher Orthodoxy in the City, and regularly deplored and censured by its spokesmen in pulpits and editorial chairs. The censures followed with some refinements the line of that *Times* message to the nation on New Year's Day 1930. The obsession with getting money to buy material goods was a weak-ness in the national character. It would have been frowned on by the Founder of the Christian religion. It was both immoral and, in the worst possible sense of the word, American. And if it was not absolutely immoral it was certainly inflationary. And that, in its effects on prices, on the value of money and on the value of fixed interest bearing bonds, was nearly criminal. In that kind of denunciation and in the attempts to create that kind of moral atmosphere, the determinedly hopeful spenders of the thirties, the people insistent on getting as good a time as they could for themselves and their families, experienced criticisms and warnings which became very familiar later to their successors in the sixties and seventies. Young people were particularly criticized. The orthodox view was that in the first place they had, ultimately because of the trade unions' hold on the wage scales, got themselves too much wage money. Not content with that, when it came to deciding what to do with it, they got their priorities wrong. They did save, certainly, and they did pay a lot to the insurance companies. But if they had spent less on con-sumer goods there would have been still more money saved and available for investment by the banks and the mighty funds of the insurance com-panies would have become mightier yet.

Mass entertainments: titillating tableaux proved popular

"Moonlight Madonna."

"Dawn."

TABLEAUX

Just a few examples of the beautiful tableaux which are a feature of each Revudeville.

Boom!

There was one road along which new consumer demand could be directed with socially beneficial results. People could use the money they saved to buy a house. For years the housing situation had been recognized even by the most conservative as a national scandal. The homeless, the slum dwellers and the suffocatingly overcrowded numbered many millions. The biting of the pullulating bed-bugs was thought unmentionable. But the ability or inability to live safe from the attacks of these little bloodsuckers silently marked differences in living standards as sharply as the presence and quality of window curtains.

The stench and disease-potential of the meagre communal lavatories was at least mentionable. Like fire hazards they were a danger to the community. Much higher up the earning-scale the housing shortage still eroded family life; it was seen by pundits as making for fecklessness and inefficiency, and

LUXURY HOUSES
To be Erected by HARWOOD NASH
The Architectural Builders

Weekly Repayment 15/4   £595   Total Deposit 3/5

Hugh   NO   Road Legal or Mortgage Costs

46.CHASE SIDE
SOUTHGATE "S".   Davies
Phone Palmers Green 5844/5

having undesirable political effects. Viewed objectively the housing situation was a national scandal because it at the worst created dangerous disease and dangerous discontent and at the best was a socially unstabilizing influence. In a leading article headed 'Building Societies: Their Record of Social Service' the *Daily Telegraph* noted:

'Before the war it was unusual for the middle-class man to be the owner of his home. Today the number of householders whose good fortune it is to be in so enviable a position grows consistently and rapidly. It will be difficult to exaggerate the influence of this silent revolution on the habits and outlook of the population. Viscount Cecil says truly that the ownership of property cultivates prudence. Clearly it encourages thrift, fosters the sense of security and self dependence, and sensibly deepens citizens' consciousness of having a stake in the country, and the influence is surely one which, spreading from the individual to the community and linking up all classes, must contribute appreciably to national stability.'

Dream homes—new luxury houses for £595

In logical pursuance of its general line of policy the Government had, at the end of 1932, cut off all building subsidies to local councils except where these were limited to the clearance of officially designated slums. This had been done at the insistence of and in close consultation with, the National Federation of Housebuilders. 'They say,' reported the Minister of Health, 'that on the withdrawal of subsidies houses will in their opinion be built in very large numbers to supply the whole of the demand shown by the waiting lists of the local authorities, and this building will continue until there is a margin of vacant houses comparable to that which existed before the war. I submit that it is impossible to neglect the weight of testimony of that sort, coming, as it were, from the fountain of knowledge on the subject.'

With the competition of subsidized council building out of the way, and the demand for houses ranging from the urgent to the desperate, splendid vistas opened for private enterprise. Money channelled into the real estate business and building could hardly, except as a result of extreme incompetence or half-crazy euphoria, fail to make more money.

It was not merely a bonanza: it was a boom. And it went booming on right through the thirties: the only boom there was, until rearmament got effectively under way in 1937.

By 1934-5, the annual rate of house-building had soared to 293,000. It remained at around that figure almost until the outbreak of war.

At the outset the beneficiaries, apart from the builders and the building societies, were almost exclusively of the middle class. The new houses were priced at around £600. The societies at the time customarily advanced 75 per cent of the purchase price at $5\frac{1}{2}$ per cent, repayable over 20 years. But the nearer the boom got to satisfying middle-class demand, the more evident it became that it was most profitable to widen the market by reducing prices. For this was a market which was not going to be saturated in foreseeable time. It was also a calculable market. It was simple to calculate by how much a reduction in price would attract new buyers on a scale which would maintain the overall profit, despite the lower price of the houses.

The average price was lowered to between £550 and £500. But the 75 per cent advance on that £500 left a down payment of £125 to be produced by the purchaser. That still kept half the white collar workers, and all but the most highly paid of industrial workers, out of the bidding. The building societies dared not increase their mortgage risks, even for the sake of vastly extended profits. The builders on the other hand were prepared to take a new risk to win new prices.

Arrangements were made by which the builders themselves guaranteed a percentage of the purchase price, and paid part of the guaranteed money in cash into a 'builders' pool' from which the societies could draw in the case of loss. The result was beneficial to all concerned. The building societies, with their new guarantees from the builders, could now offer up to 95 per cent of the purchase price, at the reduced rate of $4\frac{1}{2}$ per cent. The builders, in this expanding market, could produce houses selling at £480 instead of £500 or over. And that meant, in terms of cash from the buyer's salary envelope or pay-packet, a down payment of £24 and a weekly repayment of 13s 6d weekly over twenty years.

In social terms, it meant that a majority of the lower middle class could buy, or at least seriously consider buying a house. Such payments were also just within the reach, certainly within less than mere day-dreaming distance, of the most highly paid industrial workers earning £4 weekly or over. Since there were more than five and a half million skilled manual workers in the country at the time, it is probable that at least half a million of them were potential house buyers.

The great housing boom much alleviated the distresses and discomforts of the hundreds of thousands of families who could afford its benefits.

Since it was only made possible, given the general structure of the economic system, by letting private enterprise run very free, it produced a rich crop of financial swindles, bankruptcies and festering scandals. For many people the term 'speculative builder' was synonymous with 'financial shark'. With so much at stake—in profits for the builders and homes at last for the buyers—nobody except those who got mauled by frauds and racketeers was inclined to do much in the way of complaint or exposure. When it became desirable to bribe civil servants or elected officials, the money was available and corruption became so normal that it ceased to be thought reprehensible. Not that such corruption was at all new in kind: it was new only in extent. It established new standards of financial probity, particularly in municipal life.

Characteristically, it was common among people unwilling to recognize this development as a native product to point to such practices as instances of creeping 'Americanization'.

The Portia from West Wickham

To these and other criticisms, the most general answer was a loud So what? So those hundreds of thousands of people, millions of men, women and children, were getting houses to live in, most of them more or less watertight, most of them free from vermin. The standards of the British house-hungry could not be high. That a house be 'fit for human habitation' was the humble criterion of acceptability.

From time to time some furious neo-householder rebelled, and the rebellion would suddenly disclose, by protest meetings and letters to the newspapers and Members of Parliament, that many thousands of others had been resignedly suffering similar disillusionments. The names of Morell (Builders) and the Bradford Third Equitable Building Society became literally household words. The legal battles conducted against them by Mrs Elsie Borders, wife of a taxi-driver of West Wickham, Kent, held the headlines as it dragged its way from the Chancery Court through the Court of Appeal to the House of Lords, where it came to rest at about the time of the German invasion of Greece and Crete.

Mrs Borders had paid £693 for her house. She had done so on the assurance by the building society that it conformed to the local authority's by-laws, being built in efficient manner, of good materials. But the walls of the house oozed damp and big cracks appeared in them. Water dripped on Mrs Borders through the roof. The windows were for looking through only; they could not be opened. Out of the new woodwork beetles came swarming. The front door, at the moment of purchase a smartly up-to-date affair with glass panels, was now boarded up; the glass had fallen out. So had the plaster round it. The floor boards, seen at once to be warped, also shrank month by month. And whenever Mrs Borders ventured to touch the shrinking wood with her hand, electric shocks ran up her arm from the ill-placed wiring.

For three months she withheld her mortgage payments. The Bradford Third Equitable, designing to get possession of the wretched house and sell it a second time, sued her for repossession. She counter-claimed for re-payment of the instalments she had already made, plus £500 for repairs. She also demanded repayment of £500 she had been forced to spend on repairs. She said the Society had 'wilfully and fraudulently misled' her. She also, to the great alarm of the building societies and the builders, charged that the Bradford Third Equitable had broken its own rules by lending money on insufficient security. Morell (Builders) had gone into liquidation.

Described, inevitably, as 'the modern Portia' Mrs Borders conducted her own case. She spoke for eight hours in the Court of Chancery, which threw the case out. She went to the Court of Appeal which held that 'in this matter the Society's business was conducted fraudulently'. The Bradford Equitable, determined to exhaust the financial resources of the taxi-driver and his wife, went to the House of Lords, which exonerated it in May 1941.

Meantime, inspired by Mrs Borders, three thousand owner-occupiers went, as the saying was, 'on mortgage strike'. Thousands of others engaged in various forms of guerrilla combat with their landlords. The whole free-wheeling apparatus of the boom, the ramshackle financial machine which powered the productivity and profit of it, appeared to be in danger.

The Government made haste to meet the danger. In 1938 it brought in a Bill retrospectively legalizing the suspect and often reckless financial arrangements made possible by the 'builders' pool'.

The Bill was a very reasonable spelling out to the home-buyers that with-out the fullest freedom for free enterprise there would have been no houses at all, jerry-built or otherwise.

Posterity be damned

The public need being so great, and the flood of free money in the building business so desirable, there was no huge audience for those who viewed some of the long term consequences of the boom with alarm. They spoke of 'posterity' and how it would curse the day when the speculative builders ruined huge tracts of the countryside, created the enormous, unsightly and strangulating Sargasso Sea of the urban sprawl, and tied the road and rail transport systems of the great cities into knots likely still to be inextricable forty years on.

The house-hungry understandably replied with the well known question: What has posterity ever done for us?

It was certainly no time for egg-heads and premature anti-pollutionists to complain that the architects generally employed were the lowest of hacks, that the houses built were, for the most part, ugly beyond reason, and that these amorphous conurbations were being created in a manner ultimately disastrous to health and good living.

They could accurately predict that the working efficiency, in particular of London and the whole south-eastern region, was going to be lowered for long years to come. The railway system was not geared to the new conditions. The lines ran to the wrong places, or not at all to places where thousands were newly living. The suburban coach services were embryonic. And as they sprouted to meet the demand, they created the traffic jams which bedevilled transport thenceforth. (As an economy measure, the Government of 1931 had halved expenditure on road-building.)

More and more working hours were wasted, more and more leisure hours lost, as factory workers and office workers had to travel longer and longer distances between their homes and their places of work. The man in the cheap 'workmen's train' and the commuter became outstanding features of the social landscape.

As Toffler has emphasized in his book *Future Shock* (published in 1970), the pace of change is often more important in its social effects—particularly psychological and emotional effects—than the direction which the change takes.

The housing boom came to Britain fast, and went on moving fast. It gave the British social scene the biggest jolt it had had since the panic of 1931 and before the outbreak of war in 1939. The change directly affected only about one-third of the families in the country—the ones that could afford to buy the houses. Certainly for those who previously never had been house-owners, the change, even had it come gradually, would have been deep in its effects upon their outlook on the world. In any western society, the shift from being the temporary tenant of a flat, or even of a house, to becoming owner—and it is to be hoped permanent owner—of your house, is more convulsive, has greater impact over a wide intimate, emotional and psychological area, than the shift from one rented flat or house to another. The effects are intimately felt, particularly since they concern families rather than individuals.

The abruptness of the change redoubled its effect. Such changes have the effect of getting from here to there by jet plane after expecting, at best, to travel by bus.

And the existence of this third, or thereabouts, of the population, so suddenly experiencing changes in its way of economic life, of family thinking, had repercussions outside the groups directly concerned.

The families least affected, other than in the simplest material sense, by the boom were those of the middle middle class who, whether they actually had owned houses or not at some earlier period, had, so to say, the general habits of householders. They thought of themselves as being the kind of people who live in their own houses.

Much more affected were the new householders belonging to the lower middle and the most highly paid working class. Although none of them, and very few of their parents had owned homes, the idea of doing so was lively in British tradition; it was not just an idea, it was a sort of ideal.

To say that by circumstance of their all suddenly becoming householders, the distinctions between these classes had been obliterated, was a persistent pipe-dream of the upper sort. They believed, with the *Daily Telegraph*'s leader writer, that 'the influence is surely one which, spreading from the individual to the community and linking up all classes, must contribute appreciably to national stability'.

So firm was this belief in the boom as an eliminator of class distinctions, tending most helpfully to the *embourgeoisement* of the upper sections of the working class, that the promoters of building societies, such people as the directors of the Bradford Third Equitable, were seen as being in the nature of socially-minded philanthropists and enlightened saviours of society from social unrest. So highly were they rated that when an international congress of building societies was organized in London in 1933, the Prince of Wales was called in to address the delegates. He spoke, and other notables spoke, of the importance of the building societies as new elements in the construction of a new England.

Speakers and editorial writers of the day made it clear that their hopes for the stability of the system were anchored in the lower middle class. They believed, and they made no bones about it, that the lower middle class was, and always would be, the least class-conscious and most docile of the power orders; the *grands bourgeois* and the mandarins hoped and expected that the 'linking' of classes by house-purchase would result in decreasing class consciousness and increasing docility among the manual workers concerned.

They were sometimes right but equally often the supposedly cowed clerks, shopkeepers, and minor bureaucrats learned more about methods of organization, organized action and forward thrust from the working class home-owners than these latter learned of humility and resignation from them. It was not universally so. It could often happen that after the hard struggle required to get together that £24 down payment—likely to be the equivalent of two months' wages—and the unending further struggle always to have 13s 6d left in the pay-packet for paying off the building society, the fear of losing that arduously bought house became as obsessive and debilitating as the fear of unemployment in the cotton towns, the mines, or the shipyards. A man and his wife could feel that to risk loss of the house by, for example, joining in strike action at the works or 'standing up to the boss', and thus losing so and so many days', or weeks', pay, was to put at risk the most important thing in life.

Yet the proliferation of house-owners' defence committees, and the vigour of their demands, sometimes even reaching the news pages as 'mortgage strikes', showed that the fact of possessing a house, and the quality of being proud of it, frequently produced not fearful docility, but a new kind of militancy. In the ruling classes it was traditional to suppose—encouraged by traditional history books—that rootless men without possessions are more dangerous to the established system than men with something tangible to lose. The thesis seems to be not usually well documented. In many people the sense of having 'a stake in the country' serves to arouse sharply critical awareness of what is happening to the country, and them and their stake with it. And these new motivations were at work among the new householders of the lower middle class as well as among the skilled factory workers, the mechanics, and the taxi-drivers such as Mr Borders, husband of the house-owning but most notably militant 'modern Portia'.

96

The new suburbia

Contemplating the mass of this new proletariat of house-owners encamped in the new national suburbia, readers of the *Daily Telegraph* found matter for reassurance. These people had, as the saying went, taken on new responsibilities and above all new, inward-looking preoccupations. Their sense of themselves as 'family' men and women had been increased with the increased reality of the sense of 'home'. They were busy getting and finding the instalment payments for their furniture. They bought more and more radio sets, both for use and as status symbols.

In the view of sociological reporters, the radio set had by this date taken the place of the piano as a symbol of cosy lower-middle-classiness in the worker's home.

And these people did so love their little gardens. Horticulture was viewed by observers as the outdoors counterpart of the piano and, now, the radio set. The house-owning proletariat was evidently taking the advice of the disillusioned Candide to 'cultivate our gardens'. It surely meant that the garden would now soothingly distract the flower-lover's attention from politics, and all that they implied.

These assessments, though containing some important truths, were often flawed by the same kind of preconditioned misunderstandings which vitiated assessments made from outside and above of the supposed attitudes of the unemployed. Sociologists would go down to, for example, South Wales and come back with the news that things were not so bad after all. They particularly noted figures showing attendance at the local cinemas. They were as high as the cinema managers could wish. The unemployed were going to the pictures as often as twice a week. This was held to prove that they were a lot better off than the agitators pretended. It also showed that they were more interested in the Astaires and Jean Harlow and Edward G. Robinson than in Wal Hannington and the N.U.W.M. Otherwise they would have spent the picture money on a couple of eggs and a piece of cheese.

The observers did not usually ask themselves the question whether they, huddled in a slum house, grievously undernourished, and with nothing much visible ahead but hundreds and hundreds more days of the same, would not find a couple of hours at the pictures more satisfying than an egg, however cogently the nutrition experts might explain its high protein value. For the unemployed the cinema had taken over some of the functions of religion as described by Marx. 'Religion,' Marx wrote, 'is the sigh of the oppressed creature, the heart of a heartless world, the soul of soul-less conditions: it is the opium of the people.' It is generally known that the exhausted Chinese coolie sometimes preferred a drag on the opium pipe to an extra handful of nourishing rice.

Similar misjudgements were made about the new house-owners. The fact that they enjoyed cultivating their gardens, choosing the curtains, shopping for the new furniture and prowling Woolworths for utensils, was no proof that they had lost political consciousness. Even when, as some trend-spotters noted, some manual workers took to playing golf instead of football, it did not necessarily indicate the hoped-for change in their political outlook.

But it could be said, as it was often said by roving correspondents of

Continental and American newspapers, that there existed among these millions of, so to speak, replaced persons, a type of political apathy not found to the same degree in the older communities, based on the older industries.

And it was true, too, that the inward-looking preoccupations could and frequently did occupy attentions which in the older industrial areas had little to focus upon other than politics and religion.

But the observable apathy was not, in general, quite what many of the correspondents thought it was. It could not be equated with 'indifference'. How could people with a stake in the country, with a house and family and garden, be indifferent? Their apathy arose from the general conviction that, so far as the higher direction of affairs was to be concerned there was 'nothing much you can do about it'. You could vote in a general election. You voted, in 1931, to give the Government a 'Doctor's Mandate' to cure unemployment and in general put things right. There were still two million unemployed. You voted in 1935 for prosperity and peace by collective security. Average annual real wages fell by one per cent between 1935 and 1936, and the League of Nations had been thrown on the junk-heap.

And, increasingly, all questions relating to domestic economic policies or to international politics were answered from on high with the explanation that these matters were too complex to be understood by anyone except trained experts and persons having at their disposal stores of esoteric and necessarily confidential information. To ask to have the situation set out plainly enough to be understood by the plain man was silly, unhelpful, and could even lead to a rocking of the national boat.

To this extent, the new proletariat was not precisely de-politicized, but politically alienated.

Them v. Us

It was at this period that the image of Them and Us first became widely recognized in Britain. It was to become one of the most important elements in the national psychology. It extensively replaced the conception of the Two Nations. And in this new light some class divisions were obliterated: in the sense that manual workers and white collar workers, together with large sectors of the middle middle class accepted the existence of the distinction, and the antagonism between Us and Them.

By their very nature, They were never precisely identified. Indeed their identity shifted according to where you were looking at them from. They included bosses and bank managers and government inspectors and the directors of insurance companies, and undertakers, who took advantage of the grieved confusions of the bereaved to make them pay through the nose for a decent funeral.

But to the boss of the small factory, They were the heads of the great combine which ultimately controlled him; to the manager of the little local bank branch, and the salesmen and collectors for the insurance company, the front-line Men from the Pru, They were ignorant, faceless tycoons in London boardrooms; the undertaker told how They, by monopolistic practices, had raised the cost of coffin-handles.

All that was universally known among Us about Them was that They were

Idols: Jean Harlow (top), Clark Gable and Claudette Colbert (bottom), and film poster

out to bilk, mislead, confuse and thwart Us at every turn. In their speeches and writings They used a lingo of mystification especially designed to baffle Us. Official forms, their questionnaires, their manifestos, were framed so as to distort facts, and entrap all but the most wary among Us.

It was easy to confuse deep scepticism and suspicion with apathy, and even with indifference.

The owners and directors of mass circulation newspapers for the most part welcomed what they supposed was apathy regarding political issues and did what they could to encourage it. They thus produced a vicious circle. The political news—particularly the international political news—they published was so relatively meagre, so bowdlerized, so lacking in depth and intelligibility, that it repelled the reader, or threatened to suffocate him with tedium. In reply to questionnaires, he then truthfully answered that he took little interest in anything the papers printed except the sports news and the pictures. Pressed to speak frankly, he said that he also enjoyed accounts of murder and other crime, and sexual scandals. He 'didn't bother much' with the political items.

Armed with this information, the circulation managers and the advertising managers told the editorial staff that nobody really wanted to know all that much about the Japanese invasion of Manchuria, or what the Nazis were up to in Austria—unless and until they bloodily murdered the Chancellor—or who voted for what in the Spanish elections. People would, said circulation and advertising men, down-to-earth fellows who understood the man in the Saloon Bar, be at the best bored, at the worst uncomfortably disturbed, by a dispatch disclosing, as was afterwards revealed by Krupp von Bohlen himself, that 'the most important of the guns used in 1939-40 were being completed in 1933'. Only poorly paid Reds, with no money to buy advertised goods anyway, were in the least anxious to hear about efforts in France and elsewhere to organize some broad democratic front against advancing Fascism.

The vote of the circulation and advertising people, and of many editors too, was always in favour of what, with a ghastly self-revelation, they called 'human interest stories'. Their estimate of humanity and its interests was low indeed. No important series of political events, seriously treated, could be expected to hold for long the interest of a human being. Human beings were interested in food and drink and sex. They led, in fact, a dog's life.

There is certainly no way of calculating whether, in the existing financial and technological set-up of the big press, a cheap, 'non-quality' newspaper could have gained and kept a circulation of, say, somewhere between half a million and one million, by supplying the requirements of readers by no means indifferent to serious issues. The advertisers would, for sound reasons, have boycotted it. The circulation in the working class and lower middle class would be too small to justify paying for advertisement space in papers with much larger circulation. And in terms of available purchasing power, the 'quality' papers were obviously better media for advertisers.

Significantly, the B.B.C., not dependent upon advertising and yet seeking to suit an audience larger than the readership of any single newspaper, did, as a general rule, assume the existence of a more intelligent political interest

100

among its vast public than the mass circulation newspapers did.

These newspaper policies created a vacuum, an unfilled space between what they purveyed and what increasing numbers of people, particularly young people, wanted to know about what went on in the world.

Filling the vacuum

Stephenson of Woolworths had recognized the emergence of a new type of consumer demand in the Britain of the thirties—particularly the demand created by the shift of population out of the old into the new industries, and the sideways shift out of industry into distribution and services.

His fingertip feeling for the new was paralleled in another field by two men whose fingertip sensitivity equalled his. Both understood the eager interests underlying the supposed apathy or indifference of the new proletariat. Both had the compelling enthusiasm, organizing drive, and financial sense, to turn what other people had often dreamed about into effective reality.

Allen Lane's Penguin Books revolutionized the British literary and educational scene. Despite what all the sages and pundits told him, Lane believed in the lively existence of people who wanted serious information, scientific, sociological, historical and political, of the kind the mass circulation newspapers either could not, or would not provide, and was not to be easily found in weekly or monthly publications either.

A character in E. M. Forster's *Howards End* remarks that there is one thing worse than the confidence trick—it is the no-confidence trick.

The printed media of the period were all in greater or lesser degree guilty of the no-confidence trick. None of them were prepared seriously to bet that in the England of that day there were hundreds of thousands of people— particularly in the twenty-five to thirty-five age groups—who could confidently be trusted to provide a consumer market for the type of book which until then had been supposed to appeal only to the mandarins. The shelves and the rest of the furniture and the house were still being paid for by instalments. Books were not to be got on the instalment system. Yet to possess a book rather than simply borrow it was an important need. Lane, creator of Penguin Books, supplied it.

Victor Gollancz, founder and organizer of the Left Book Club, also displayed a talent amounting to genius in the understanding and supply of the new market: in his case, of the most politically alert sectors of the market.

Newspaper reluctance to give adequate play to serious political, particularly international political news, the bowdlerization and emasculation of such news, all created an imbalance between the demand for intelligible, serious news and the supply of it. Gollancz used the imbalance and the weight of the newspapers' own inhibitions, to ensure success for the Left Book Club. Membership of the club and the hugely greater readership of its books were found in the same strata as the readership of Penguin Books. The members and readers could be said to be people of specialized interests. The books were political and topical.

But in fact a large section of the area they covered was ground which could have been covered daily and weekly by an intelligent press, ground

101

which very numerous political diplomatic and foreign correspondents were covering in reports which never saw the printed page or appeared only in truncated travesties. (The extent to which important international news was stifled, slanted, or repainted in the British national press was thrown into high relief by the contrasting breadth and depth of foreign correspondents.)

It was correctly pointed out, sometimes with indignation, that publications of the Left Book Club were propagandist.

It was also correct to say that they were often, though not always, nor even as a general rule, Communist in approach, direction and conclusions. From the standpoint of anyone looking at the thirties, the point of interest and significance is simply that books of this character should have found so ready a market and should have been, as was generally agreed by observers from all quarters, so eagerly read and so immediately influential. There was after all no material or theoretical obstacle to publishers or organizations of other opinions entering the same market. The conclusion had to be that so far as this mass of the people was concerned the evidences of apathy and insularity told only half the story.

The course of events in the middle and late thirties demonstrates sufficiently that the influence of all those newly nourished faculties of criticism and knowledgeable scepticism was not by any means decisive. Its existence may even be said to have created dangerous illusions. For many observers of that scene hoped and expected from year to year that now, or next week or next year the informed masses, stimulated by the knowledge newly made available to them, would raise their voices loudly enough and even act effectively enough, to abate the pride, assuage the malice and confound the devices of their government.

This did not come to pass.

Instead a series of omissions, of negative events, of non-happenings, were the most notable features of the middle and latter years of the decade. The inward-looking tendencies, the insularity of the family, the couple and the individual prevailed.

The Yanks come
Among all the warnings as to the deterioration of the national character, the enfeeblement of traditional institutions and barbaric, nearly brutish, irresponsibility of the young, the claim was made that the country was becoming Americanized. It was usually put in the form of an accusation or charge, amounting to a charge of moral and intellectual delinquency. As a charge it was preferred from very different quarters and from very various motives. But it had a basis in truth. This was discerned in, for example, Woolworths.

It was an American outfit. When the English company was floated the American company retained fifty-two per cent of the shares. Its methods, first imported in 1909, were then, and continued to be, adaptations of American methods based on American experience and observation of what made western society tick, and could make it keep on ticking. These American methods, in so far as they differed from the British and the European, were products of the discovery by operators in the American part of the System of

102

new facts and developments in what was loosely called the consumer society. Cramming their discoveries into an inadequate nutshell one could say that they had either discovered, or at least taken a new look at, the working masses of the wage and salary earners as not only producers but consumers. Like all such discoveries it seemed, once made, to have been simply a discovery of the obvious. But the traditional structures of British and European industrial systems and the thinking of financiers and industrialists in Britain and Europe delayed full acceptance of this as a valid discovery and of its recognition and exploitation as essential for survival. This American social know-how was backed and propelled by vast natural resources, the existence of a comparatively open domestic market and the concentrated financial power of the great American combines. Americanization at, so to speak, the top, the penetration of British and European financial and industrial institutions by American capital, was already far advanced in the thirties, though trivial in comparison with the positions occupied after the Second World War and the Marshall Plan.

But the know-how and the methods of operation in relation to the consuming masses could not have been successfully imported into societies rigidly and immutably petrified in an un-American mould. Partly in independence, partly in an interaction with the society of the United States, British and European societies had been Americanizing themselves. Since Americanizations, whether native or imported, implied a new recognition of the function of the mass of the consumers in the economic process, it could be represented as a kind of democratization of economic life. American politicians and pundits had long adopted and propagated the notion that this kind of 'democratization' could be more or less generally equated with political democratization.

The doctrine was preached despite extensive, often calamitous, often violent, real life demonstrations in the U.S.A. that although the two uses of the word democratization might sometimes somehow come to mean the same thing they did not do so in existing reality. But it was this supposed characteristic of Americanization or Americanism which caused British statesmen, thinkers, and leaders of the upper sort in general to observe it with alarm and utter their warnings against it. It seemed to them to involve openly or obscurely some tendency towards equalization. It seemed to be giving the masses a new status, a new right to certain demands and satisfactions. It was this apprehension and suspicion which lurked just under the surface of much chit-chat and head shaking about Americanization. Many of the chatters and shakers were themselves involved at high directorial level, or as shareholders, in businesses which had in fact been penetrated by American capital with profit, immediate or envisaged, to both sides. But there was a sense in which the apprehensions and warnings were justified. The fact was exemplified in the newspaper field, for instance in the case of the J. Walter Thompson advertising agency and the *Daily Mirror*.

The agency, American owned and ostentatiously American styled, was at that time the leading advertising agency in Britain, and in consequence one of the most powerful factors operating to affect the conduct and content of British newspapers. Naturally nobody would ever agree as to the exact

103

extent of the influence exercised by advertisers on editorial policy: very few would deny that it was great. And a large volume of that influence was channelled by the J. Walter Thompson agency.

In 1934 the *Daily Mirror*, then owned by Lord Rothermere, was scruffy in appearance, and its wing Right. Its circulation and finances ailed. A new management turned the problem over to the J. Walter Thompson agency. As its formula for success the agency recommended transformation of the paper into the semblance of an American tabloid. The advice was acceptable on its own merit. The formula was the more readily adopted because of the implication that if that were done J. Walter Thompson would be in the position to swing large advertising appropriations in the direction of the *Daily Mirror* and if not, not. In the limited sense of the word there was no political significance in the change. Indeed some saw in the British version of the tabloid formula—the extended picture and headlines space, the large area occupied by the strip cartoons, the chopping up and chopping down of news stories—a kind of de-politicization. What space or niche was left for serious political information?

The same sort of critics who forty years before had derided and deplored Northcliffe's new *Daily Mail* as 'written by office boys for office boys' said the *Mirror* was written for morons for morons. Things turned out quite otherwise. The success of the new tabloid depended by definition on its appeal to the masses. And so the logic of the situation compelled it to the position of increasingly identifying with Us against Them. And significantly its most popular and influential commentator became William Connor, an abrasive radical. Enthusiastically and deliberately he constructed his column, signed 'Cassandra', as a loudly brash megaphone voicing in the demotic vernacular the enthusiasms and grievances of Us. While the quality press was still mincing words about Nazis and Fascism being 'helpful' to the British Foreign Office, crying, or at least mumbling, 'peace' when there was no peace, Cassandra stamped up and down the street shouting and vulgarly pointing and asking who was that so-called Emperor who not only had no clothes but was grossly pot-bellied into the bargain?

The Cassandra column and all that it implied was the beginning of a process which culminated in that wartime showdown between the *Daily Mirror* and the Government.

In this entire sequence of events those who discerned political dangers in Americanization could see their apprehensions justified.

Among all the other things it had said the J. Walter Thompson Agency said that the tabloid form was the proper form for a mass circulation newspaper because it was the form best adapted to new patterns of transport. The housing boom uncontrollably throwing up houses all over the environs of the cities resulted in more and more people having to travel farther and farther between their homes and their places of work. On the long crowded journeys you needed something to read but it had better be something manageable in size. Reading in the bus was one way of salvaging something from the loss of leisure time involved by the new distances to be covered twice daily.

Suburban and short-haul bus services suddenly multiplied and extended

The Daily Mirror's *famous columnist saw through Hitler earlier than most*

CASSANDRA

AS I write these words, the infuriated little man is screaming his head off on the radio.

My German is almost non-existent, but one or two phrases that I can understand are charged with the usual venom of revenge and limitless hate.

Personally, I don't give a hoot what he says. It doesn't make any difference now.

Apologists for this fellow say that he really does believe what he says—at the actual moment he says it.

I've no time for liars intoxicated with the glamour of their own mendacity.

Switch the dog off!

A fully motorized Britain—traffic jams (left), a traffic-free street, and a demand for a 30-m.p.h. speed limit

themselves. But in 1931 just as it war being repetitiously announced that Britain was entering the motor age, the long-term policies of the Higher Management had required that expenditure on road building be halved. By later standards the roads of the mid-thirties would seem open roads and a pleasure to travel on. But the traffic jams had begun and they'd come to stay.

Car-crash

The social shifts brought about by the shifts of trade and industry, had created the housing boom and nourished the flagging motor industry. Problems and attitudes resulting from the frictional mixing of old and new were succinctly distilled in the words of the coroner at an inquest upon a woman of eighty-six killed by a motor car. He said, 'Old ladies who go about this way cause any amount of danger to other people. In trying to avoid them, motorists and cyclists may find themselves in difficulties.'

In 1927 the Society of Motor Manufacturers and Traders had calculated that numbers of the British working class would not, at any reasonably foreseeable time, have enough money to buy motor cars. Not all members of the middle class would get them either. Potential car buyers, they reckoned, would be found among about one-third of the income-tax-paying population. An output of approximately one million cars would bring the market to saturation point. But the world prices of everything, including the materials of motor car construction, fell. Falling prices widened the potential market and the scope for mass production thus increased enabled further lowering of selling prices.

The average price of a car in 1920 was £684. In 1930 it had gone down to £279 and by 1938 stood at £210. The price of petrol fell from 3s 9d in 1920 to 1s 5d in 1930, and had risen only by a penny a gallon in 1938. By the mid-thirties the supposed saturation point had been reached and passed: there were more than one and a quarter million cars on the roads. Five years later there were more than two million. And more of them were small cars. At the beginning of the decade cars of 10 h.p. and under accounted for approximately 30 per cent of cars sold. By its end the figure was 60 per cent.

Even so the motor car remained an acknowledged, visible and nearly ubiquitous badge of class.

> Oh heaven defend the poor working girl
> She has such an awfully hard time
> The Rich man's daughter drives haughtily by
> My God, can you wonder at the crime!

Crushed in the suburban buses, peering over the tops of the tabloids, office workers and factory workers were not necessarily or directly incited to crime by the sight of the bank manager's daughter or the vicar's niece driving past them through the urban sprawl in their 10 h.p. car. But the private motor car did remain a symbol of classed vision, one of the world's goods inevitably belonging to Them rather than Us. The British motor car had no social kinship with the American flivver and its great-grandchildren. The situation was illuminated on each election day. Labour candidates and their supporters declared that the number of cars available to their Tory opponents for bringing voters to the poll had scandalously rigged the chances in favour of the Tories. Richard Ackland claimed that in the election of 1935 he had only forty cars at his disposal for canvassing and transport of voters, while his Tory rival had two hundred. It was declared that dozens of seats were lost to Labour in this way: that the motor car was determining the composition of Parliament. There is no way of proving the degree of that influence, particularly as most Labour voters in need of a lift to the polls were intelligent enough to look like Tories for the duration of the ride. But looking at the picture of the thirties it is important to recall that there really was some substance in the Labour complaints.

The economic and social status of motorists turned up the heat and sharpened the edge of controversies which revealingly arose on matters less directly political. William Plowden, in his excellent book *The Motor Car and Politics 1896-1970* (Bodley Head, 1971), devotes a chapter to the subject of what he calls 'middle class killers'. The title aptly evokes the atmosphere of the period.

Because of the class character of the motorists the problems of 'death on the roads' and 'the toll of the road' almost always evoked class animosity. They were at it again—killing people this time.

In 1930 the motorist had got rid of the twenty-mile speed limit. Observe the results. In 1933 the Pedestrians' Association complained that 'The Ministry of Transport has permitted to be unleashed on the roads the forces of destruction which it is beyond the powers of the police to control.'

In the Commons Moore-Brabazon spoke up for the motorist. People who tried to curb them were relics of a past age. 'I have,' he said, 'been motoring long enough to have been slashed in the face by people with whips. I am surprised that such people still survive.' And when you came right down to it, why was there such a rumpus when the deaths on the road amounted to only seven thousand? 'Over six thousand people,' Moore-Brabazon noted, 'commit suicide every year, and nobody makes a fuss about that.'

Continual controversy about the penalties properly to be imposed for killing or wounding living creatures with motor cars threw useful light on the British attitude to animals. A Bill was passed making it an offence not to stop after killing certain creatures. The Act of 1903 had made this an offence only if the dead one was a human being or horse. In 1930 the list was enormously elongated. It now named not only human beings and horses, but dogs, cattle, donkeys, mules, sheep, pigs and goats. There was understandable indignation at the omission of the cat. In England a Member pointed out, 'the cat is one of the most loved and prized of animals'. Lord Cranborne, who had remained silent on other clauses of the Bill, spoke to say that he would 'like to put in a plea for the goose and the ducks'. To this the Minister harshly replied that the highways 'were not meant for the perambulation of these animals'. Hartington reminded Members that when *Kismet* was playing at the Haymarket a camel had had to walk along Jermyn Street twice daily and four times on matinée days. Was it to be callously run down and slain while the motorist drove on without stopping?

6 Spectre
at the Jubilee
1935 *An old king and a new dictator*

Before there was any recorded historical form to go by, people celebrated the Spring Solstice with acclaim because something had
happened which might not have happened. The fact that over a
number of years spring had followed winter was no proof that it
would always do so. The gods might decide to alter the entire schedule,
probably to the detriment of the human race. Later it seemed that the re-
current repetition of the seasons could probably be taken for granted. Like
the striking of clocks, the festivals marked the expected and anticipated
passage of time. For all labouring mankind they were a brief moment of
sanction and guiltless leisure, permissive also of jubilation and spree. The
Venerable Bede notes that 'the ancient peoples of the Angli began the year
on the 25th December when we now celebrate the birth of the Lord; the
very night which is now so holy to us, they called in their tongue Nodra Niht,
that is, the Mother's Night, by reason we suspect of the ceremonies which in
that night-long vigils they performed.'

Irregular celebrations, wakes for the dead, days of jubilee, mark more
than the passage of planetary time. They draw attention to a unique event
underlining the special significance of a happening, or a character and a
lifetime. They invite people to stop and think about the meaning of that
thing or series of things that occurred and is now being celebrated. They, too,
are permissive periods.

The tribal chiefs, the people in power in the community, seek to persuade
all to accept their version of the significance to be attached to the event.
They wish the maximum possible number of people to interpret the event in
the desired sense. Where a consensus on the true interpretation exists, the
political colouring and content of the affair can be heavily and uncom-
promisingly emphasized. In other cases, the consensus can only be reached
at the level of vague emotional generalizations.

Some celebrations are imposed by the event they celebrate: if by the
blowing of God's wind or the accurate gunnery of our sailors the enemy
fleet is sunk without trace, public rejoicings must follow. Others are invented, so to speak, backwards. That is to say, those in charge think first
of a desirable political interpretation and emphasis, and then set up an
event to provide the occasion for that interpretation. Evidently these
artificially created occasions have more meaning as signs of the times than
those which are imposed. Thus if the United States Government were
suddenly to proclaim the anniversary of the Boston Tea Party a national
holiday accompanied by symbolic destruction of goods imported from
Britain, that would be taken as a sign of deteriorating Anglo-American
relations. When the British National Government announced in 1935 that
from 6 May the quarter-century of the reign of George V would be joyfully
commemorated on a national scale, it was widely understood that the
Government felt in need of a tonic and, from its analysis of the national
mood, judged that from the existing ingredients a festival injection could
produce just the tonic needed. There had never been such a thing as a Silver
Jubilee before. To decide that one should be held now was audacious. Many
expert government supporters advised against it. People would ask, they
said, just what precisely they were supposed to be celebrating. Was it, for

112
Previous pages: The King and Queen drive to St Paul's; inset: the new spectre

instance, simply the fact that the King had remained on the throne for twenty-five years during which his cousin the Tsar of Russia had been murdered, his cousin the German Kaiser forced into exile, and his relative Alfonso XIII of Spain also compelled to abdicate and flee his country? As a theme for national rejoicing it seemed reminiscent of the first Austro-Hungarian communiqué of the First World War: 'Lemberg is still in our possession.'

The same trepid advisers forecast, and they were not entirely wrong, that oppositional elements would find it easy to remark that it must be assumed to be a matter for celebration merely to have survived twenty-five years of predominantly Tory or National Government.

A flop, counter-productive in effect, was pretty generally predicted.

Political considerations apart, people claiming to understand the well-known British character said and wrote at length that organized, elaborate, and flamboyant expressions of feeling such as were envisaged must be alien and repugnant to the phlegmatically reserved temper of the British people. In the event, these calculators proved to be as wrong as those who so many years before had warned Frank Woolworth that the British character would not accept Woolworths. The spree was enormous, universal and highly permissive. In a land where, especially in the north and midlands, the village bands and town bands were still the pride and joy of their localities, the brass bands and the silver bands played as they had not played since the announcement of the Armistice in November 1918. Flags there had been no occasion to unfurl since the German Grand Fleet surrendered at Scapa Flow flowed from windows and streamed from flagpoles, giant or dwarf. In the squalor of the narrow back streets the decorations were so lavish that people walked as though under tossing roofs of bunting by day and fairy lights by night. They ate together at long trestle tables in the street and drank from Jubilee mugs. They had bonfires in the streets, they danced and kissed in the streets. The park attendants had to call for extra trolleys to cart away the huge litter of discarded condoms. It was a genuine jamboree.

Peep-show of Britain

International telescopes were trained on Britain. Experienced observers from the Continent and the United States came to observe and report upon the phenomenon: also to assess its significance in terms of Britain as a decisive, perhaps at the moment the decisive factor in the political situation of the western world.

Most reporters see what they are conditioned to see. It is in general what the editor and the folks back home expect them to see. In reporting it they are sincere. In enumerating the number of flags flown, recording the volume of decibels in the cheers for the King as his carriage passes, they believe they are reporting 'the facts'. These nuggets of fact had their importance. First, they proved that if the Silver Jubilee was a gimmick of the National Government, it was a successful one. Secondly, the huge outburst of jubilation and jollification, sometimes rising to hysteria, also very un-English, demonstrably surpassed the calculations of the government calculators. No public relations man could have foreseen this enthusiasm.

But enthusiasm for what?

Here 'the facts' stopped short of an answer.

Demonstrably there was a consensus about something. Anyone who supposed it was about the excellence of the National Government would have been proved wrong by the results of the General Election of November 1935. (The National Government was by this time led by Stanley Baldwin, the Conservative leader. MacDonald had resigned as Prime Minister in June, taking Baldwin's Mace as Lord President of the Council.) At that election, 11.8 million voted for the National Government. 8.3 million voted against it (they sent back to Parliament 432 supporters of the National Government, 154 Labour members, and 20 Liberals); or it could be said, and it was said hundreds of times, that this proved something or other about the native British reverence for the king and monarchy.

But that deduction had to be at least seriously amended when, in just over a year, the Government was able, with a minimum of trouble, to force the then reigning King to abdicate.

Much nearer the mark were certainly those who saw in the cheering crowds an expression of personal affection for the ageing King. Very different types of people who went about among those crowds at the time were convinced of that fact. The old boy, it was felt, certainly had had his worries. And, unlike some one could mention, he certainly had not made anything out of it. It was a matter of common belief that the King was always being messed about and pestered by the bloody politicians. What they were expressing was not reverence because he was powerful, but fellow-feeling because he was harrassed and supposed to be almost powerless. He had become, paradoxically, virtually one of Us—endlessly harried, deceived, and generally done down by Them. Indeed, some of the older people still vaguely thought of the King much as the man thought of Providence when he said, 'That there providence had been agin me from the beginning, but there's one above as'll see he don't go too far.'

The consensus of exuberance had been achieved by draining the occasion of almost all political content. As to just why they were merry-making, cheering and waving flags, every group and individual could write their own ticket. To be asked their reasons would have seemed an impertinence. Everyone longs for some distruption of the dreary and often ugly routine, particularly of industrial life. Many of them have to make do month after month with a street accident or a fire on the way to work. Even heavy drinking can become a routine. In so far as there is any truth whatever in the view of the English character as phlegmatic, it may possibly be that the English require more than some other peoples a sudden powerful impetus or else some kind of official sanction and blessing for public outbursts of glee. The Silver Jubilee provided such sanction and blessing from on high.

Seeing it Red

Reporters who looked a little below the surface concluded that emotions were so various and particoloured that it was impossible to make any worthwhile judgement about 'the mood' of Britain at that time. Typical was the case of an American reporter who, not content with counting the bunting,

114

decided to take soundings in the offices of the *Daily Worker*. Alone among political groups, the Communists had denounced the Jubilee as a confidence trick, an attempt to obtain respect under false pretences. The *Daily Worker* so denounced it daily. Hundreds of thousands of leaflets, hundreds of speeches were devoted to the theme. On the night before the Grand Royal Procession to St Paul's, the Communists strung across the Strand an enormous banner, ornate with loyal sentiments. The police stopped the buses while they got it into place. As the royal cavalcade proceeded slowly between the dense and cheering masses on the pavements, an unseen hand twitched a string and a few yards ahead of the King's car the banner unfolded. The enormous piece of bunting now hanging down almost to windscreen level displayed the words '25 years of hunger and war'.

The American reporter's conversation with the people at the *Daily Worker* office was interrupted by a telephone call from the secretary of a Communist Party sub-district in Bethnal Green. He wanted advice. Three Street Jubilee Committees of the local people had combined to buy the materials to construct a big and elaborate bonfire at the intersection of the streets. Now the police had intervened and forbidden the bonfire as being certainly an illegal obstruction and probably a grave fire hazard too. The Committees had reasoned with the police, but got nowhere. In frustration and despair they had appealed to the local Communist Party. What, asked the local secretary on the telephone, in view of the strong anti-Jubilee line of the Party, was he supposed to do? He had telephoned the Party headquarters for advice, but they were closed for the evening. The reporter listened with some amazement to the brief discussion which followed and its outcome. The inquiring secretary was told to stand by and in the meantime assure the people from the Street Committees that help was on its way.

From the office a dozen telephone calls were urgently made.

Within an hour there converged upon Bethnal Green Police Station two high-powered solicitors, one of them representing the Council for Civil Liberties, two barristers, one of them a King's Counsel, and three M P s, one a Communist, the other two from the left of the Labour party.

The police had no idea what had hit them.

Under the legal and political barrage they surrendered unconditionally. The ban on the bonfire was lifted. Within half an hour it was burning gloriously.

To the reporter's interested questions the busy man in the *Daily Worker* office seemed to have little time to give extensive answers. They said simply, 'Why shouldn't the lads have their bloody bonfire? Why should the police muck them about? The people have given a lot of time and money to make that bonfire a success.' The reporter said afterwards that on that night he had learned a great deal about the situation in Britain, but just what he had learned he could not be entirely sure.

The view from Berlin
The task of the German reporters at the Silver Jubilee was crude, simple and of grievous international importance. They were rigorously instructed as to what they should see and report. They, too, were for the most part sincere.

115

They too truly believed what Hitler saw fit for the German public to believe. The image of England as presented by the Silver Jubilee played a major role in German thinking, including thinking in the top ranks of the Nazi party, at a period when momentous issues were in the balance.

Viewed from Berlin the appearance of a united Britain, even of a united Commonwealth, which the Silver Jubilee was designed to present, was patently fraudulent. Then, as in succeeding years, Hitler's information about Britain—other than the military and industrial information obtained by espionage—came from three sources. There was the staff of the regular embassy. Its reports were as suspect as were its political sympathies. They were increasingly disregarded. The second were the reports of the Ribbentrop Bureau in Berlin which Ribbentrop, long before he became Ambassador to London, had established as a kind of parallel Foreign Office in the Wilhelmstrasse. Information from this source, like Ribbentrop's own dispatches from London later, were phenomena of a strangely paradoxical character. To a reasonably informed Englishman they could appear to have been composed by moronic and maligned children who had never visited England or got beyond the third form in their study of English history. They showed a misunderstanding of every British institution from the constitution onwards. Where demonstrable facts seemed likely to nullify deductions made, the facts were distorted or suppressed. The character and behaviour of leading personalities as represented in these reports and dispatches would have been unrecognizable to intimates of the persons concerned. Trivialities were magnified into significant events, isolated happenings into trends. The whole Bureau could be described as a rich mine of misinformation. And yet, as though some ignoble but powerful imp had determined to make humiliating game of the truly expert, the well informed, and the laboriously truthful, it happened with hideous regularity that the obsessed fanatics and crooks of the Ribbentrop Bureau mysteriously got their sums right when people who knew better were getting them wrong. It has often been a matter for wondering remark that Hitler, who knew nothing whatever of England so far as personal experience was conerned, for the greater part of the thirties and especially at crucial moments, displayed a bizarre and seemingly miraculous 'fingertip feeling' for what the British Government was likely to do in any given situation.

The possessed
It would be convenient to explain this, in the lingo of an earlier age, by saying that he was possessed of a devil. In exchange for his soul he had been granted power to enter at will the minds of potential enemies and above all potential friends. Reluctantly discarding such a convenience one may suppose that for him and for his agent Ribbentrop, and for Ribbentrop's sub-agents, ignorance at one level of reality was a positive asset. A toad's-eye view of the world, and in particular of England, was unimpeded by the paraphernalia of expert knowledge.

Too ignorant, arrogant, and impatient to bother to know the difference between an elm and a beech, they clearly and simply saw the wood. Another factor of life facilitated them. Being themselves base, greedy, corrupt,
116

cowardly, arrogant and vain, a criminal sixth sense, the common 'larceny in the blood', intuitively signalled to them the liveliness, however carefully concealed, of these qualities in other men and groups of men. Those people in Berlin understood the people they had to deal with in Paris and London the way a heroin dealer can smell out and understand a corrupt policeman. The analogy is close. It was still possible to present England as the beautiful garden of law and order, the champion of civilization.

Hitler's third source of information about England was provided by those numerous influential individuals and groups who, for the most various and in some cases more or less subconscious reasons, were prepared at any moment of decision to aid or obliquely abet his policies. These became identified later exclusively as 'the Cliveden Set'. This shifting congeries, including Lords Lothian and Londonderry, Lady Astor, and Dawson, editor of *The Times*, repeatedly denied its own existence. Observers were thereby reminded of the defensive remarks made by Thomas W. Lamont, partner of J. P. Morgan, when the House of Morgan was accused of organizing a 'power trust' in the United States. 'Some of you,' he told reporters, 'have painted a frightening picture of a sinister group at work plotting vast designs, exerting unseen influences upon the Government itself. It would be better, it would be more accurate, not to write in that strain. There is no such group, there are no such plottings. What you can say, what I would very much prefer you should say, is simply that we at the House of Morgan, and others interested in the development of electric power, are standing around in a co-operative frame of mind.'

Member of 'Cliveden set': Lord Londonderry and friends

But in reality those who, in England, as the bands tuned up for the Jubilee, brought aid and comfort to Hitler, were a great deal more widely spread. They included the purely pacifist wing of the Labour Party, led by the still revered and influential George Lansbury. In their ranks were men who sincerely believed that absolutely anything, including the extermination of the Jews, was better than international war. There were many others who found pacifism a usefully opportunistic slogan with a calculable appeal to people preoccupied with paying off the mortgages on their newly bought houses. Objectively speaking they were allied, not at all paradoxically, with the chiefs of the War Office, Air Force and Admiralty, who claimed rightly that the armed forces were prepared for nothing but long years of peace. And at the centre and on the right there were all those who, without being members of the self-denied Cliveden Set, yet believed in a general way that Hitler was a barrier against Bolshevism, a salutary threat to the Soviet Union, and the kind of man who knew the right medicine to give the trade unions. England was half full of the kind of democrats who saw in any advance in the power of the working class a threat to democracy. They were the people who a decade before had applauded Mussolini on the grounds that he had made the Italian trains run to time. Given a free hand Hitler would ensure that central and eastern Europe, possibly all the way to the Urals, would be regulated as punctually as the 8.15 to Milan.

As it 'should' be

The position has been succinctly stated, perhaps even a little understated, by Alan Bullock, Vice Chancellor of Oxford, in his valuable book *Hitler: A Study in Tyranny* (1952).

'Although,' Bullock writes, 'Hitler's attitude towards Britain was modified later by a growing contempt for the weakness of her policy and the credulity of her government, the idea of an alliance with her attracted him throughout his life. It was an alliance which could only, in Hitler's view, be made on condition that Britain abandoned her old balance of power policy in Europe, accepted the prospect of a German hegemony on the Continent and left Germany a free hand in attaining it. Even during the war Hitler persisted in believing that an alliance with Germany on these terms was in Britain's own interests, continually expressed his regret that the British had been so stupid as not to see this, and never quite gave up the hope that he would be able to overcome their obstinacy and persuade them to accept his view. No British government, even before the war, was prepared to go as far as an alliance on these terms, yet there was a section of British opinion which was sufficiently impressed by Hitler's arguments to be attracted to the idea of a settlement which would have left him virtually a free hand in Central and Eastern Europe, and Hitler, if he never succeeded in his main objective, was remarkably successful for a time in weakening the opposition of Great Britain to the realization of his aim. The policy of appeasement is not to be understood unless it is realized that it represented the acceptance by the British government, at least in part, of Hitler's view of what British policy should be.'

It was in this sense and in this context that the spring of the Silver Jubilee marked the opening phase of a period which lasted with many zigs and zags, and such spectacular diversions as the formal declaration of war in 1939, right through Hitler's victorious attack on France up to the moment when his manoeuvre at Dunkirk had failed to produce a peace offer from Britain.

118

His orders to his generals to halt or delay the final encircling attack on Dunkirk were issued in the belief that the return of all those many thousands of soldiers to Britain, their equipment lost, spreading up and down the country their stories of rout, of the incompetence of their own High Command, the treachery of the French, coming at a moment of Britain's total isolation, would enable his old acquaintances in high places to speak out once again. Success had calloused his fingertips at last.

All right so far

The themes and mood of the Silver Jubilee were regarded as auguring well for the prosecution of Nazi policy. In the welter of emotions aroused it could be seen that one among them was a profound sense of quiet self-congratulation on mere survival: not by any means in the cynical sense referred to above in meaning miraculous survival through so many years of gross misrule. By casting the eye back over those twenty-five years the Jubilee was intended to focus, and did focus, attention on the fact that after the biggest war in history, and the biggest slump in living memory, here we all are still alive, alive-oh, the vast majority of us not even maimed, a majority at work and earning money, a new Woolworths opening somewhere every eighteen days, and blessed old George and grand old girl surviving too and:

> All the King's horses and all the King's men,
> They march up the street and they march back again.
> Do they go to fight the foe?
> You might think so, but oh dear no.
> They go because they have to go
> To put a little pepper in the Lord Mayor's Show.

It was an occasion very apt to reproduce the gentle optimism of the man hurtling groundwards from the roof of the skyscraper who shouted as he passed the window of the sixteenth floor, 'All right so far!' Even if it caused people to dwell somewhat on the past the joyous atmosphere caused them to do so principally with the thought, 'Goodbye to all that'.

In other words the fact of survival so heavily emphasized suggested that provided nobody rocked the boat survival could quietly be continued indefinitely. It seemed harsh and unreasonable to suppose that Providence intended this Jubilee to be regarded merely as a euphoric moment between crisis and catastrophe. Even pessimists could allow themselves to hope that it was not so. Elpis, that dangerous goddess, was dancing in the streets.

Even had this state of mind produced by the Jubilee been entirely ephemeral, which it was not, the impression of the British attitude it conveyed to Berlin was an event of serious political importance. There was a parallel here with the resolution passed by a very large majority in the Oxford Union in 1933 that 'This house will in no circumstances fight for King and Country'. His agents reported to Hitler, who had only just achieved power, that this was an ultimate signal of Britain's decadence and inertia.

Informed people in Britain tried to point out to them the exaggerations and distortions in this interpretation. They sapiently explained the nature and eccentricities of the Oxford Union. They said that, rightly considered, the Union vote was not a proof of decadence or even of pacifism but simply a

119

means of expressing in as pungently shocking a form as possible the disgust of the younger generation at the way affairs had been conducted in the past and were being conducted at the moment. The well informed people were correct in what they said. But even then the malign imp was at work. For practical purposes the ignorantly ham-handed arithmeticians in Berlin had got the sum right. Never mind about the details, the Union resolution really was a signal that the mood of Britain was one propitious for the Nazi designs.

Fair enough

Tapped in Berlin in May 1935, the barometer could be seen as moving a tick or two towards Fair. During the previous nine months there had been some hitches and set-backs. Dollfuss, Chancellor of Austria, had been viewed by the Nazis as an impediment to their plans. They had assassinated him. But the results were unsatisfactory. It had produced a hostile, even threatening, response from Mussolini who still regarded himself as the guardian of the states beyond the Brenner Pass. It had improved relations between Mussolini and the French and British governments. In France, Barthou, Foreign Minister, had presented a similar impediment. Earlier in 1934 the Stavisky scandal and the general reek of corruption in high places had been successfully exploited by the French Fascists. It had looked briefly as though these imitators and allies of Hitler against the Jews, the Bolsheviks and democrats, might actually seize power and bring about the fall of Paris without a German division having to move.

Led by the Communists, the French democrats were able to rally and defeat them in the streets.

Despite their corrupt and Fascist chief Chiappe, the police in the main remained loyal to the Republic and at a critical moment fired on the Fascists. Barthou was the outstanding figure in the Government which resulted from the crisis. He denounced and sought to thwart Nazi aims with a vigorous and uncompromising frankness found quite shocking in London. He toured eastern Europe constructing a line of political and military defence pacts against Hitler. Using Croatian nationalist thugs as gunmen, and with the active connivance of their friends in the French Ministry of the Interior and the High Command of the police who withdrew protection, the Nazis organized the assassination of Barthou and his ally the King of Yugoslavia on the quay at Marseilles in October 1934. But in its results this assassination, too, was a flop. The French Government pursued and extended its policies in the East. In the first week of May 1935 one event occurred which was ominous for Hitler and astounded most of Europe. The Soviet Union signed a Treaty of Mutual Assistance with France. It was a move to compensate the dangerous and alluring weakness of Russia. Many Communists were shocked, regarding it as a betrayal of the principles of Marx and Lenin.

In March 1935 Hitler banged the international barometer. He formally repudiated the essential clauses of the Treaty of Versailles by announcing German rearmament and the reintroduction of conscription. The needle could have jumped to Storm. Britain and France might not only have recognized this as a fateful moment but drawn from it practical conclusions of a kind inimical to Hitler. Other considerations apart Hitler had been forced

Assassination: King Alexander with Barthou (top); after the shooting (bottom)

60 68-CA6

to take the risk by two major factors in the situation. The fact, as distinct from the admission, of German rearmament was already too obvious to be at all disguised. To slow it down to the point where passionate denials that it was in progress could be at all credible would in the first place have produced friction with the industrialists whose schedules and production lines would have been disorganized. The profitable war contracts they had been promised in those 'forest glades' would have been delayed. Similar frictions with the Army High Command would have been inevitable. The support of the High Command both before and immediately after Hitler's assumption of power had been secured by irrevocable promises of immediate rearmament and huge expansion of the army. The army, too, was part of the second factor compelling Hitler to take the risk he did in the spring of 1935.

The urgent purge

In the summer of 1934 the always latent possibility of a 'second revolution' conducted by the beef-steak Nazis, brown outside and red within, was deemed by Hitler and the army to be emerging from a possibility into a probability. Röhm, Chief of Staff of the S.A., was demanding that the S.A. should take over as the new army of the new Germany. As he said, the radical revolution of the new Germany was incomplete. The High Command of the old army, the industrialists, and the Junkers who had combined to assist Hitler to power, were now procuring the miscarriage of the revolution or aborting it. The hundreds of thousands of organized and armed men who would have followed Röhm were not Communists—certainly not in any doctrinal sense of the word. But they were certainly in part infiltrated by Communists and might in the whirligig of time actually have allied themselves with the Communists. In 1934 they were simply and savagely aware that Hitler's coming to power had not produced for them the results they had expected. Röhm knew and many of the others were beginning to suspect the extent to which Hitler had sold out the supposed revolution before it took place. They were becoming as the saying went 'radicalized'. On 30 June 1934 Hitler murdered the leaders and defeated the incipient revolt. But he had not remedied the grievances or satisfied the aspirations which had seemed to bring ruin and his mixed horde of gangsters, adventurers and genuine beef-steak men within reach of power. It was a matter of urgency to assuage the grievances with the prospect of employment in the new armament industries, and canalize the aspirations in the direction of an aggressive, glorious, and victorious nationalism. Since man does not live by bread alone, and the spiritual impulse is as powerful as the material, the repudiation of the Treaty of Versailles was a real substitute for more tangible good things.

Everything depended upon the British reaction to the challenging announcement. The British Government had already ventured, despite pacifist opinion in the country, to disclose its intentions to take some steps towards the rearming of Britain on account of 'the general feeling of insecurity which has already been incontestably generated' by news of secret German rearmament. Sir John Simon, British Foreign Secretary, was about to visit Berlin. Hitler tapped the barometer again by ostentatiously declaring that he had a bad chill and could not receive Sir John.

Dancing-time

The British Government immediately humiliated itself by announcing that the Foreign Secretary would go to Berlin as soon as Hitler felt better. At that, Hitler, on 16 March, took the decisive step of announcing to the Reichstag the news that the German Government was tearing up the Treaty of Versailles by reintroducing conscription and building up an army of thirty-six divisions. John Simon and Anthony Eden then confirmed the accuracy of his intuition by going to Berlin as though nothing had happened.

The gesture emphasized divergence between British and French policy. It was a move in a dangerous little dance which became repetitiously familiar in the following months and years. The pattern of the dance was simple. Move 1: The followers of the anti-Germany policies initiated by Barthou acted in Moscow and the capitals of eastern Europe to construct a defensive link around Germany. Move 2: They were denounced as fanatical Germanophobes, warmongers and friends of Bolshevism. Their policy, it was charged, was not only futile but disastrous; because, and this was the vital essence, if France were to take a hard line towards Germany, Britain would certainly let her down. Move 3: The British Government made gestures of friendship, sometimes almost fawning, towards Hitler's Germany. To their critics at home they declared that, other weighty considerations apart, it was not possible for Britain to take a hard line in the West because, owing to the strength of pacifist, Germanophile, and anti-Russian feeling in France, the French would let the side down. Move 4: The pacifists, Germanophiles, and anti-Russians in France adduced the latest British actions as proof of their contentions that Britain was not to be relied upon. Their influence was thereby increased to the point where it could reasonably be adduced by the British Germanophiles as proof that the French were not to be relied on as allies in an anti-Hitler front.

Several considerations made it impossible for the Western Powers to register unprotesting acceptance of Hitler's actions. Sir Robert Vansittart, Permanent Secretary at the Foreign Office, was strenuously anti-German. With some, though insufficient reason, it seemed to him that Italy could be cajoled, bribed, and pressurized into joining France and Britain in an anti-German policy. He had the support of the majority of permanent officials at the Foreign Office.

The weakness of the whole design was that for Italy to join an anti-Hitler policy in Paris and London, the existence of such a policy was a precondition. If the Foreign Office had some ham, it could have some ham and eggs, if it had some eggs. In France, where Laval had succeeded Barthou, the followers of Barthou were still strong and saw the British Foreign Office as their ally. Above all, Mussolini could not afford to swallow silently and humbly the contemptuous insult represented by the Nazi murder of his protégé Dollfuss in Vienna only a few months before and the continuance of Nazi preparations for the subversion of Austria. Immediately after the murder he had moved Italian troops up to the Brenner Pass. In April he agreed to a meeting with the British and French at Stresa. It was a way, or at least it seemed to be a way, of keeping his options, if he still had any, open.

By suggesting to opinion in Britain and France that Italy might still be drawn into a serious alignment against Germany, he expected to paralyse any effective or threatening British or French action against the Italian attack upon Abyssinia for which preparations were already far advanced. And on the reasonable assumption that in the end he would have to ally himself against the West, he could suppose that this ostentatious flirtation with the Western Powers would raise the price he could ask from Hitler for such an alliance.

Farce at Stresa

In the circumstances, the Stresa Conference could not be otherwise than

Diplomatic farce at Stresa: MacDonald (second left), Flandin (centre), and Laval (second from right)

farcical. The champions of international law and order who came together there to display to Hitler their unity and determination consisted of Ramsay MacDonald, still British Prime Minister, whose mind was partially unhinged, his degree of influence in his own government standing at zero; Sir John Simon, Foreign Secretary, who had already shown his approval of Hitler's general line and detested Sir Robert Vansittart; Laval, French Foreign Secretary, who was financially subsidized by Mussolini; and Mussolini himself who contended with MacDonald, bribed Laval, and announced in advance of the Conference that he did not expect very much to come of it.

He was right.

All that came of it was a declaration that 'The three powers, the object of whose policy is the collective maintenance of peace within the framework of the League of Nations, find themselves in complete agreement in opposing, by all practicable means, any unilateral repudiation of treaties which may endanger the peace of Europe and will act in close and cordial collaboration to this purpose.'

The declaration was one of those documents of which it was rightly said that there was even less in them than met the eye.

The Stresa Conference was in fact another of those non-events which yet by the negativeness of their nullity can shed light on the way things are really going. Those, who, in an ecstasy of wish-fulfilment, read into its final communiqué indications favourable to the policy of Vansittart, or alternatively to the hopes of those millions who still believed in the League of Nations as a peace-keeping force, spoke and wrote joyously of 'the Stresa Front'.

The references to the League were particularly welcome in Britain. By hindsight, it is difficult to realize that what was often called 'the League Idea' was among the most powerful of imponderable political forces in Britain during the thirties.

It was as intangible, as pervasive, and as uplifting as laughing gas; except that it was not to be laughed at. For it emanated from the most tragic memories and anguished hopes of one generation, and the quietly respectable aspirations of another. To be seen supporting it also provided those who had neither memories, hopes nor aspirations and wanted only what they called a quiet life, with a sort of certificate of good conduct.

To the elder generation the formation and existence of the League had been an official proclamation that the horrors and barbarism of the world war would never occur again; that civilized western man had come to his senses; that the nations were now going to behave with the level-headed common sense of a British county council, settling by argument acrimonious, perhaps, but non-violent disputes and conflicts of interests arising between the various boroughs, townships and rural districts. The Idea acquired an immense moral force. It had affinities with the so-called Non-Conformist Conscience. It suggested a cleansing of international life, an end to the corrupt and secret dealings of principalities and powers which were supposedly responsible for the Great War.

Since in Britain—particularly at the political centre and among the social democrats just left of centre—'excessive nationalism' was on record as one of the causes of the war, the supra-nationalist flavour of the League was attractive, while not spoiled by any suggestion that genuine national sovereignty would be infringed or eroded. The younger generation of League supporters shared these general conceptions but with sharp sceptism as to the degree to which the original Idea was being allowed to manifest itself in practice.

With every month and year that passed they saw mounting evidence that the League Idea was being betrayed. But this in no way reduced their enthusiasm for the League. On the contrary, in a somewhat paradoxical fashion, it increased such enthusiasm. What was seen as a sabotage of the

126

League roused an indignation which fused naturally with indignation against the Government's domestic policies. If the Tories of the National Government were betraying the League just as they were acting rapaciously and repressively against the working class at home, that was a reason for political opposition. For huge numbers of people the League, too, had become an ally and instrument of Us against Them. Celebrants of the Silver Jubilee could feel that it was just the kind of good thing that George V and Queen Mary were surely in favour of.

Slippery Sam

Just two months after the Stresa declaration Ribbentrop came to London as Hitler's special envoy. He negotiated with Sir Samuel Hoare, Foreign Secretary, known, by a correct public intuition, as 'Slippery Sam'. Ribbentrop was brutally rude, insulting and dictatorial. He was said to have 'intimidated' Sir Samuel. So Alexander Cadogan, later one of his principal subordinates at the Foreign Office, has testified that Hoare was of a cowardly and treacherous nature. It is possible, though on the evidence unlikely, that some other member of the National Government might have been found to possess a self-respect which made it impossible to stomach Ribbentrop. But in the present case questions of personal qualities do not arise. Hoare's

'Slippery Sam' Hoare, Foreign Secretary, on skates with champion Sonja Henie 127

thinking on the subject of relations with Hitler was fully in line with that of the rest of the Government. Almost anything that could bring Britain and Germany closer together was to be welcomed, not to say grabbed at, however contemptibly feeble the action might appear in the eyes of Hitler, however treacherous in the eyes of the French.

Within a fortnight, in June 1935, Hoare had signed with Ribbentrop an Anglo-German Naval Agreement which regulated the relative sizes of the British and German fleets. Strategically the agreement had little importance. The relative percentage strengths permitted to the two fleets took no account of the fact that the British tonnage allowed was made up of elderly ships scheduled for world-wide tasks, whereas the German tonnage was in ships newly built or building, whose activity in war would be concentrated in the North Sea, Baltic and the Western Atlantic. The agreement regarding submarine strength was equally deceptive. Under the pact Germany was permitted to build up to forty-five per cent of British submarine strength or a hundred per cent 'in exceptional circumstances'. In case of war Britain would be dependent upon her merchant fleets for supplies. Against these the submarine would be Germany's only weapon. Since Germany's merchant fleet would automatically be blockaded at the outbreak of war, the value of the submarine to Britain was very small in comparison with its value to Germany.

As this fact must be apparent to the most myopic, the pact contained a clause by which Germany guaranteed never to use the submarines against merchant vessels.

In the longer term the pact had no strategic importance at all since Hitler had emphasized that his attitude to treaties was a traditional one common to most governments: he would repudiate any treaty which had become inimicable to his interests as soon as he felt it safe to do so.

The practical effects of the Anglo-German Naval Agreement were of another kind. It had been negotiated secretly without the British Government informing, let alone consulting, the Governments of either France or Italy. In the few years remaining before the catastrophe, the agreement became the unanswerable argument of the French Germanophiles; the blatant symbol and proof of British perfidy. It afforded a quite reasonable excuse for every perfidy committed in Paris. It made nonsense of the Stresa front. It demonstrated to Mussolini that his allies at the British Foreign Office under Vansittart were, when it came to the crunch, powerless. Since it was negotiated bilaterally and without the least reference to the League of Nations, the Agreement enfeebled what was left of the League as an instrument of collective security and endorsed Hitler's policy of referring bilateral agreements to multi-lateral treaties of security.

Angry British critics of the Treaty wrote furiously that the Government must have taken leave of its senses; its members must be stupid, ignorant or both. With the exception of the Prime Minister, often not quite in his right mind, the members of the National Government were neither very stupid nor very ignorant. They were perfectly aware of the strategic and political consequences of the Agreement. They considered that these were a worthwhile price to pay for close and friendly relations with Hitler.

The Agreement was not an aberration, it was a development in a long-term policy which could be justified on many grounds. Fundamental to the role of that policy was the understanding, not officially proclaimed but strong and clear, that there existed a genuine basis for the fullest co-operation between Britain and Germany. Some supporters, and many critics, of that co-operation crudely paraphrased the policy as being one of turning Hitler's war drive from West to East.

But this was to assume that it was a matter of indifference to Hitler whether he attacked westward or eastward.

It was not.

On the contrary, his deepest and most sincere desire, expressed many years before in *Mein Kampf*, was precisely to avoid the mistakes of the Kaiser's war; to establish not only cordial relations but an actual alliance with Britain and the British Empire; to extend the power of domination of the German master race over eastern Europe and to the Ukraine and the Urals; and by so doing both to complete the historic mission of the Teutonic Knights, and lead a more up-to-date crusade which would destroy Communism and save the capitalist system not only of Germany but of the world.

In such a policy the British Government, the City of London and the British Higher Management could honestly and sensibly concur. The British Government's policies of 1935 and 1936 became stupid only by hindsight, after failure to reach the desired objective. Even as late as 1941 when Hitler invaded Russia, he and some of his advisers assumed that after a dangerous hitch the policies could still be resumed. And even then, even in London, there were still influential people who hoped for, and even expected, the same thing.

The euphoria of the Silver Jubilee reported by his agents had helped to convince Ribbentrop that that was a time when any act of supposed reconciliation between the protagonists of the First World War would be welcomed or at least not too widely criticized in Britain. The same mood which assisted him was helpful also in enabling the Government to drop the encumbrance of Ramsay MacDonald as Prime Minister. It was now possible to dismantle the façade of a Labour, a 'socialist', Prime Minister as front man of a Tory Government.

The Devil's Diplomacy

1936 *Abyssinia and the Rhineland*

For the German Government, the estimated behaviour of Great Britain was the crucial element in all calculations. Three clues to what might really be going to happen as distinct from what might appear to be happening were immediately available.

In June 1935 a clue appeared when the organizers of the national Peace Ballot, a unique referendum, published their results. Since before Christmas, volunteer canvassers had been collecting answers to five questions. First, should Britain remain a member of the League of Nations? Eleven million answered 'Yes'. Secondly, are you in favour of all-round reduction of armaments by international agreement? Ten million favoured that. It was like being asked whether they were opposed to sin. The fact that around ten rather than around eleven million voted 'Yes', was explained by the scepticism many felt as to whether, given the character of the various governments, any such international agreement was sufficiently practical a proposition to be worth voting about. The same applied to the third question. It was whether a person was in favour of abolition of national naval and military aircraft by international agreement. Ten million or so were in favour: they were sincerely opposed to the destruction of their own and other peoples' cities by aerial bombardment—including, it was generally and officially assumed throughout the thirties, bombardment by poison-gas bombs. Ten million, answering question four, favoured prohibition by international agreement of the private manufacture and sale of arms. It was a period when books such as *Merchants of Death*, all with huge circulations, factually exposing the lucrative machinations of the armament industrialists in all countries, had been misunderstood to signify that private manufacture of arms actually caused war. It was hoped, and even supposed, that by nationalizing Vickers, Krupp, and Schneider-Creusot, the causes of war would be nearly abolished. Question five was qualitatively different. It required the voter to face a situation which anyone could see might really arise at any moment, and to state whether or not he would support positive action in the matter.

It asked: 'Do you consider that, if a nation insists on attacking another, the other nations should combine to compel it to stop by (a) Economic and non-military methods; (b) If necessary, military methods?'

As was to be expected, the millions split on 5(b). 6,700,000 voted 'Yes'. But twenty per cent, 2,300,000, who had almost all voted 'Yes' to everything else, voted 'No' to this one. To make up this last figure, the pure pacifists who in principle must oppose military measures, were joined by an incalculable number who hoped and supposed that economic sanctions would always prove effective. Their miscalculation, though catastrophic, was intelligible.

The writers of historical text books for schools, reacting over-violently to the practice of their predecessors, who had devoted so much space to battles and treaties and so little to mineral resources, steel output and banking, had produced a fashion of thinking according to which the politics of power could be fully assessed by the methods of chartered accountants.

The fact is important in any examination of the thirties. For this sort of thinking affected not only the millions who voted in the Peace Ballot but also very many people of political power, particularly in Britain and the

Previous pages: Crisis—German troops march into the Rhineland

United States. They were prone to share the weakness of William Pitt during the war against France, as described by Macaulay: 'It was pitiable to hear him, year after year, proving to an admiring audience that the wicked Republic was exhausted, that she could not hold out, that her credit was gone, that her *assignats* were not worth more than the paper of which they were made—as if credit was necessary to a government of which the principle was rapine, as if Alboin could not turn Italy into a desert till he had negotiated a loan at 5%, as if the exchequer bills of Attila had been at par.'

These primitive economists could, certainly, argue that if and when economic sanctions were fully and generally applied they might bring about the downfall of the transgressor. They never were so applied. And the flaw in the argument was that the very nature of the System they were supposed to safeguard ruled out the possibility of such application. People forgot even such small but vivid instances of the supra-national workings of finance as the fact that after the fateful torpedoeing by the Germans of the *Lusitania*, a large part of the insurance losses were borne by firms in Hamburg.

As a clue, the Peace Ballot was important. It was as apparent to the German Government as to everyone else that in its dealings with British public opinion the British Government would have to employ considerable artifice and guile: would even, from time to time, have to bend its policy for fear of having it broken.

The other two available clues were of a different character. One was a sharp rise that summer in the export from Britain of every sort of manufactured goods useful as war materials, and the re-export of raw materials essential for the same purpose. No informed businessman could doubt that Mussolini was very soon going to attack Abyssinia. No alert exporters would overlook the opportunity thus offered for the sale of war material. Since businessmen everywhere were pushing into that Italian area, there might have developed a buyers' market in which the Italian purchasers could have used the sharp competition to force down prices. But this tendency was contradicted by another. Here the results of the Peace Ballot and all that they implied played a certain role. No informed person could study them without realizing that it could be dangerous to bet everything on the assumption that the British Government would not feel bound to initiate and participate in economic action by the League of Nations against the aggressor.

There could be economic sanctions.

It was therefore essential for Mussolini to stock-pile war material before such a development could take place. This had to be carried out in a hurry, and the Italian Government's urgent need created a sellers' market.

The third clue was provided directly by the British Government. During that same summer, at the request of Mussolini, it banned the export of war material to Abyssinia.

Mussolini had at his disposal well-placed observers of the London scene; notable among them Vladimir Poliakoff, formerly Diplomatic Correspondent of *The Times*, the principal commentator on European affairs of the *New York Times*, and unofficially close to Vansittart. The likely course of the British Government during the summer and autumn did not require much expertise to map out.

The eleven million Peace Balloters were its bug-bear.

On 11 September, Samuel Hoare, in a speech at Geneva described by *The Spectator* as 'Britain's Lead to the World' declared: 'The League stands, and my country stands with it, for the collective maintenance of the Covenant in its entirety, and particularly for steady and collective resistance to all acts of unprovoked aggression. The attitude of the British nation in the last few weeks has clearly demonstrated the fact that this is no variable and unreliable sentiment but a principle of international conduct to which they and their Government hold with firm, enduring and universal persistence.'

On 3 October the Italian Army entered Abyssinia. On 7 October the League formally declared this to be an act of war in disregard of the Covenant.

On 19 October, as the Italian troops advanced, the League voted to lift the embargo on arms to Abyssinia, which could now no longer have been delivered. Under the guidance of the British delegation, the League sharply reduced the range of the economic sanctions which, under the Covenant, should have come automatically into effect. Under the Covenant, oil exports to Italy would have been stopped. The Italian Government privately admitted that if the Covenant were really enforced in this particular the effect might be disastrous for the Italian attackers. The League—Foreign Secretary Eden guiding the knife—castrated the Covenant and excluded not only oil but a long list of other useful goods from the operation of sanctions. The list of embargoed goods was long, but its effect had been nullified in advance by the stock-piling. Imports of Italian goods to League member countries were banned.

On 25 October Prime Minister Baldwin announced a General Election for 14 November. Support for the League of Nations was one of the Government's principal campaign points. The League, the Peace Balloters were assured, 'remains, as heretofore, the keystone of British foreign policy'.

The embattled Haile Selassie appeals to the League . . .

RESTORATION OF CONFIDENCE.

In relation to the Abyssinian war 'there will be no wavering in the policy we have hitherto pursued'. The Government was returned with a majority of 247 in the House of Commons. (As usual, the British electoral system grossly falsified the state of Parties in the country, and quite distorted the wishes expressed at the polling booths. Rather less than ten and a half million voted Conservative. The Conservatives got 432 seats. Eight million three hundred thousand voted Labour. Labour got 154 seats.)

On 9 December it was announced that Samuel Hoare had made a Pact with Laval under which nearly two-thirds of Abyssinia's territory was to be ceded to Italy, or turned into an area reserved for Italian economic use. This enormous reward would, however, only be offered to Mussolini if he stopped the war. Had he done so, he would have achieved a huge advance without fighting: his troops were still not within sight of most of the territory he was to be given. Abyssinia as an independent state would have been extinguished.

The pact

Though predictable by those familiar with the style and real aims of the National Government, the announcement produced a degree of shock and fury rarely paralleled in British politics. To those who were shocked by the betrayal and final ruin of the League were added numerous others who, without being enthusiasts for the League, were indignant at having been so brazenly lied to and swindled, their votes obtained under the most gross of false pretensions.

Hoare had to be temporarily jettisoned. He excused himself in a long resignation speech to the House of Commons and sat down, crying.

The Abyssinians conducted a ferocious but almost certainly foredoomed defence. The Italians found the going a great deal rougher than they expected. Although the Abyssinians had been starved of arms by the summer's

. . . but the League could do nothing for the Emperor

Abyssinians in action (above) and parading before Emperor (below) British news headlines

Mussolini, checking his sights

embargo, the morale of the Italian infantry and mechanized units was low. The war to establish, as Mussolini proclaimed, 'the glory of a Fascist Empire' was not popular with them or their families. It became necessary to risk— if it can be called a risk—incurring international horror and repugnance by resorting to the use of poison gas. In the absence of an Abyssinian air force, the operation was easy. The gas was either dropped in canisters or sprayed direct from the air. The eyes of the defenders were particularly affected, being burned by the gas. Years afterwards foreign observers were still struck by the number of blind men, former fighters against the Italians, still to be seen in the streets of Addis Ababa.

On 1 May the Emperor of Abyssinia fled from the capital. A week later Mussolini proclaimed the annexation of Abyssinia.

The prospect pleases

Viewed from Berlin, the policies of the British Government during 1935, and their results, could be deemed satisfactory.

As has been disclosed by the captured German archives, Hitler in the mid-thirties had high hopes that diplomatic conflict between Britain and France, and possibly open war between France and Italy, would reduce to zero the risk of serious action by the West, when the moment came for his attack upon Czechoslovakia, itself designed as the first crucial move in the 'Crusade to the East'. The acute frictions of the Abyssinian war period had been happy auguries. At the same time, the British Government had on the whole maintained itself only slightly shaken by the Peace Balloters and the revolt of the supporters of collective security. Indeed the flamboyance of the Government's mendacity and cynicism had worked better to Hitler's advantage than would a more subtle deception and tergiversation.

For it was immediately apparent that the Government's successful display of contempt for the British public had created a new spirit of defeatism, of helpless apathy and of cynicism. It deepened the suspicion, and further disseminated the belief, that They were bent on getting away with murder, had got away with murder, and would do so again at the first opportunity to the further discomfiture of Us.

This same cynicism with regard to the Government was the only honest motivation of Labour Party policy on disarmament. It was pointed out at the time, and has been pointed out over again *ad nauseam* ever since, that the realization of collective security, specifically the organization of a successful defence barrier against Hitler, was not consonant with a state of relative disarmament. To restrain Germany you must be prepared to fight Germany: it followed that you must support the rearmament of Britain.

That was the Government's public case and the case of many who opposed the Government, but could not find it reasonable to oppose rearmament.

On this issue the Labour Party consisted of a coalition of notions, only made to cohere by the necessity of keeping the Party, as such, intact and assembling the largest possible aggregate of votes. The pure pacifists had no ideological or other problems. Despite defeat at the Brighton Conference of 1935 and the substitution in October of Attlee for Lansbury as Leader, they remained influential. Their support could be engaged by any non-pacifist group, such as the Communists, which opposed government policy on rearmament.

It was thus necessary for the Labour leadership to seek to detach them from the extreme Left.

Pacifism, uncluttered by moral principles, appealed also to the amorphous and nearly inert mass of opinion which, influenced by the factors of comparison and hope, took good note of the fact that things were better in 1936 than in 1932, appreciated the housing boom with all that that implied, and concluded that things were relatively a bit better and might get a little better still, provided there were not international rows and upsets and interruptions of the tenor. Among wide sections of the English people at that time the atmosphere resembled that of a prison where, after riot, some improvements in diet and general conditions have been made. It is the consensus of the majority among the inmates that although direct action against warders and 'trusties' may have promoted the change, the thing to do now is to do nothing liable to disturb the new conditions.

Such opinions were held by the Tory Working Man. But they were held, too, by very numerous citizens who, by tradition or observation, were most apt either to vote anti-Conservative or to abstain.

After its disembowelment of the League in 1935, the Conservative Government in its propaganda found it useful to appeal to all seekers after the quiet life by suggesting that the Labour Party, by continuing to support the League and the notion of collective security, was in reality a party of warmongers. They had, for example, official Italian statements to prove that had oil sanctions been imposed during the Abyssinian War, the Italian air force would have dive-bombed the British Mediterranean Fleet. (The Italians did, in fact, make a practice of sending air squadrons to any major outdoor celebration attended by the British Ambassador, Lord Perth, and having them dive spectacularly and with terrifying uproar just above the box where he and fellow-diplomats were installed. His reports stressing the awful power of the Italian air force were much used in London by the opponents of the League and the friends and agents of Mussolini.)

The Labour Party, forced to lean over backwards in demonstration of its opposition to war, could hope to keep the supporters of the League, the near-pacifist and the quiet-lifers together only by a programme of which the appeal was that it appeared to approve of armaments only for the purpose of enforcing, by collective action, collective decisions of the League.

Its general programme at the period has often been described as both dishonest and meaningless. It was certainly very soon shown to be dishonest. For when, in 1936, the outbreak of the Spanish War offered an opportunity for the member states of the League, in particular Britain and France, to take action, the Labour Party supported the Government in laying a lethal embargo on arms for the Republic, changing its position only after months of pressure from its own members.

Meaningless it was not. It served to present the Labour Party as the natural rallying point for all those who quite simply felt that to pay for and produce arms for the use of the National Government on the understanding that the weapons would be employed solely in the defence of the League and against aggression by the Fascist dictators, was a contradiction in terms, the sickest of sick jokes. (In this connection one may recall that the slogan 'Whose finger on the trigger?' played a notable part in Labour's electoral successes after the Second World War.)

The scepticism plus cynicism plus sullen apathy with which a huge minority, perhaps even a majority, of the British electorate viewed re-armament under the National Government has been often construed by historians and commentators as explaining and excusing the Government's policies of complaisance and complicity with regard to Hitler and his aims. The Government, according to this reading, had to embrace Hitler for fear of being eviscerated by him.

The reading is mistaken. At no time did Hitler desire to attack Great Britain. In this matter there was no divergence between his public utter-ances, spoken or written, so many of which were more or less crudely constructed lies, and what he said and wrote in a secrecy only broken by his defeat and the capture of his archives. He would, as the archives show, fight Britain only if Britain, improbably, interfered with his planned attack on Czechoslovakia. He wanted, at the best, British friendship and British support for his Teutonic expansion and crusade eastwards. At the worst, he wanted to be assured of British non-interference with that obsessive enterprise.

The British Government was aware of Hitler's obsessions and long-term designs. It was not seeking to rearm as a defence against German attack. What it hoped for—and in the thick of a big deal the hope was reasonable— was that a rearmed Britain would be able to secure in return for its support a better price, and a stronger position for Britain in the loose Anglo-German partnership envisaged in the West. As a particular, limited example, it could get better terms for Britain in its dealings with the international steel cartel, in which the German steel industrialists were now the dominant force.

Years before, at a naval disarmament conference, Ramsay MacDonald had been asked by an American reporter: 'Since Great Britain is not arming against America, against whom is she arming?' In a reply which is a classic in the repertory of evasion, MacDonald replied ('in ringing tones' according to the reporter's account): 'Great Britain is not arming against anyone. The size of the British Fleet will be determined solely by the factors in the situation.'

The tones of Baldwin and Neville Chamberlain now rang out to the same effect. They could not let the bells proclaim that the practical purpose of rearmament was to facilitate a bargain with Hitler.

The attitude of the Labour Party in this respect did not excuse the ob-eisances of London towards Berlin. To oppose rearmament under the National Government was not to weaken the defences of Britain against Fascism and Nazism.

An anti-Government day-dreamer could dream thus: 'If we one day, some-day, somehow, anyhow, can brew up enough assorted votes to put the Government out; if we can produce from our own ranks a genuinely anti-Nazi, anti-Fascist Government [a dauntingly big "if"]; if that Government can then go ahead with a crash programme of rearmament, involving the control, if not the formal nationalization of all the armament industries— why, then, friends, democrats and Red revolutionaries, we can, on equal terms, join the French, the Czechs and the Russians in a cast-iron, foolproof encirclement of Germany which will successfully confront and confound all Hitler's devices.' It was a dream many Labour Party supporters pure-heartedly dreamed. It did not correspond with the facts of the days it was dreamed in.

Paris-Moscow

These, to the German Government, were heartening developments. But all was marred, the vision of the future jarred and blurred, by another develop-ment; expected, but not less menacing for that.

The signature in May 1935 of a Treaty of Mutual Assistance between France and Russia was rightly seen in Berlin as an event superficially menacing enough, and—examined in depth—having many points of even more sinister significance.

One: for years, the policy not of Germany only, not of the West only, but also of Japan, had been largely determined by the relative economic and military weakness of the new Soviet state as a central fact of life in the world of the Great Powers.

At the same time, political and social hostility to the socialist state had secured its almost complete diplomatic isolation.

Now both these aspects of the situation were radically changed. The weakness of the Soviet Union was to be seriously compensated by alliance with France, still a major military power. It could be inferred, too, that the French Intelligence Services considered that even the original weakness had been eliminated to a serious extent: the French General Staff would not otherwise have agreed to accept the obligations of the Treaty, including the heightened tension between France and Germany which its signature must produce.

Equally, it was shown for the first time that the supposedly reliable and overriding social, class antagonisms in the capitalist West could, under such pressures as Germany was exerting, be subordinated to the interests of national survival.

Two: the decision of the Kremlin Government to ally itself with a western capitalist power, despite the risks involved, indicated an ominous shift of policy, perhaps of political power, in Moscow. The military risks were self-evident: a German attack might well be accelerated. Politically it implied a major reorientation of Soviet policy and, by extension, of the political lines of the Comintern.

It represented a defeat, most unwelcome in Berlin, for what the Germans described as the Russian isolationists. They were not so called in Russia, and were not a defined group; or rather, they could only be defined, as it were, backwards by the line they followed. The isolationist trend involved construing the principle of 'building socialism in one country' as implying maximum aloofness in relations between the Soviet state and other states. The capitalist world was seen as composed of states which, despite their

savage internecine conflicts and contradictions, were not basically differ-
entiated. Only the most limited, *ad hoc* arrangements between Soviet and
capitalist institutions could be valuable to the Soviets: for example, the
ending, in the late twenties, of the long and often violent fed between the
Soviet oil producers and the Standard Oil. (The Rapallo Treaty of recognition and commerce between Russia and Germany in 1922 was concluded
in circumstances too peculiar to be in any way exemplary.)

Ideologically, this isolationism could be shown as expressing a kind of
Simon-purity of Marxist doctrine. It was most notably so expressed in the
Comintern, where there had already been long and bitter contentions
between those who adhered to the doctrine that all bourgeois governments
were essentially indistinguishable, and those who insisted on differentiating
in accordance with the shifting of situations, stresses, and balances of power.

The Franco-Soviet Pact marked a sharp, perhaps irreparable, break with
isolationism. One fact alone sufficed to show that it was not to be considered
a mere gesture, another brief *ad hoc* arrangement: being essentially of
military nature it required co-ordinations in the military field which could
be of value only if they were treated on a long-term basis.

Three: the treaty purported to be defensive in character. But in Berlin,
reports from Moscow and indirectly through Paris, where German agents
had wide access to secret information, it was calculated that the defeat of
isolationism might be a milestone in a longer journey. It was thought that the
Pact signified such Russian confidence that soon the Soviet Union might be
preparing to face the dangers of taking the lead in the organization of a
more forward-looking anti-German policy in Europe; a policy in which
preventive action might well be seen as the best means of effecting a successful defence. Admiral Comans presented to Hitler a document he saw had
been processed for the German Intelligence by a sympathizer at the Quai
d'Orsay. It disclosed secret military clauses of the Pact, involving plans for
joint Franco-Russian action with Czechoslovakia.

French and Russian entente: Laval (left) with Litvinov (centre)

Four: however the tremendous speculations under Point Three were to be evaluated, it was clear that the absolute avoidance of war, which for so long had been almost the whole objective of Soviet policy, was no longer to be relied upon as still axiomatic in Moscow. Peace at almost any price was now an obsolete aim.

Five: at that particular moment, under the influence of the followers of Barthou and the surge of anti-Fascist feeling produced by the premature attacks of the French Fascists in Paris and other cities, it had been possible, as already noted, for a Pact with the Bolsheviks to be signed—though not yet ratified by the Chamber.

It could already be foreseen in Berlin that the Comintern would now extend and intensify its efforts to develop not merely the United Front of Communists and Socialists, but the new conception of a genuine Popular Front to rally not only the Communists and Socialists but also anti-Fascist radicals of the bourgeois parties and the parties themselves.

Such a development would certainly be extended to England. But there all the evidence pointed to its being negated by the rigidly and even ferociously anti-Communist policies of the Labour and trade union leadership.

In France, on the other hand, the signature of the Pact must call for a major effort to strengthen the Germanophiles and the Fascists, and to re-create and sharpen an overriding fear of Bolshevism in the propertied classes.

How the money rolled in

The effort was made. German subsidies poured into Paris. Payments to Fascist leaders already in good standing were increased. Other payments procured new leaders and new recruits. The flood of German money was so great that it caused greedy and damaging dissensions among the payees. Men and women of some distinction in their particular spheres, eager to take German pay, complained that they had been rated at an insultingly low scale, or that unworthy rivals had made off with the funds. Some of them in their indignation disclosed the facts to anti-German officials in the Home Office or to the anti-Fascist press. Some threatened to have recourse to the courts to recover bribes allegedly due to them and improperly pocketed by others.

Newspapers were launched, bought up, or bribed, either directly or by the pressure of advertisement agencies controlled by the Germans. Politicians on all levels were ruthlessly blackmailed. They were encouraged to engage themselves in financial swindles and then threatened with exposure unless they denounced, as required, the menace of international Communism. The sex lives not only of homosexuals but of heterosexuals too became arduous to themselves and costly to the State. If articulate and influential, they must endlessly proclaim the advantages of Franco-German friendship and the evil character of the Bolsheviks. If lacking gifts of persuasion, they must exert themselves in the thefts of state secrets. Otherwise their irregular sex lives would be exposed either to the public, to their wives, or one or other mistress. Whores of every degree and both sexes were gainfully employed to keep the stew simmering.

The money, taking the long view, was not wasted. But the campaign failed to achieve its immediate objective. On 11 February the Chamber of Deputies ratified the alliance with Moscow by 353 votes to 164.

Hitler drew the necessary conclusions. Since secret subversion had failed, momentarily, to bring home the bacon, a spectacular blow must be dealt in the West such as would expose to all, and particularly to the Russians, the corruption and disarray of the Western Powers.

A new Röhm

There was another motive for speedy action, and action of a particular kind. This motive force was inside Germany, at work all over Germany.

The 'blood purge' of June 1934, the victory of Hitler, the industrialists and the Army High Command over Röhm and the other leaders of the 'beef-steak Nazis' had not solved the problems or lessened the tensions which had brought Röhm's second, radical revolution to a point where its success was credible to many, and certainly to Hitler.

Nobody had expected them to do so. Certainly nobody in power supposed that the threat of the 'second revolution' could ever be otherwise than blunted or diverted: it could not be eliminated. Even to attempt to eliminate it would have meant the dismantling of the entire German economic system as established and operated under Hitler.

The threat came in part from disappointed adventurers, the unrewarded banditti of the Nazi Party's struggle to power. But in so far as they were radicals, they were opposed by the High Command. And without the High Command there was no possibility of a successful *putsch*, conducted without reference to the mass of the working people.

The normal weapons of working-class action had been removed. The trade unions had been suppressed. Collective bargaining was illegal. To strike was illegal. The only organization available for workers was the Labour Front, which was not a Labour organization at all. It was sometimes compared by American observers to a company union. It was not even that. For the employers were themselves members of the Labour Front. Even officially there was no pretence that it existed to protect the rights, let alone advance the interests of the working class. Its stated aim was 'to create a true social and productive community of all Germans. Its task is to see that every single individual should be able to perform the maximum of work.'

The gradual drainage of the 'pool of unemployment' by the rearmament, at first secret, then avowed, could, even after the destruction of the trade unions, have created an upward pressure on wage rates. The danger was appreciated by the Nazi state. Measures were taken to nullify the natural effect of a situation where jobs were demanding workers. In 1935 came the 'work book'. It gave full particulars of every worker, his particular trade, employment record. Without it, he could not legally be employed. If he tried to leave a job for better pay elsewhere, his employer could seize the work book and so imprison him in the job. (Three years later, labour was fully conscripted: no one could change his job without state permission.)

At the depth of the depression, when Hitler came to power, wages in Germany were at a record low. He forced them lower yet. Between 1933 and

1936, the wages of skilled men fell, according to official German figures, by a little under 5 per cent. The wages of the unskilled fell by more than 6 per cent.

Compulsory contributions to the Nazi Party and organizations under its control increased the size of the cut.

The value of moral values

Watching all this, reading the official statistics, doing sums, many Westerners, particularly in the British Labour Party, concluded that a spirit of anti-Nazism must be growing in Germany. They made, in fact, the same mistake they had made about economic sanctions, and for many of the same reasons.

They imagined that surges of opposition, spirits of revolt, etc., occur, automatically, like the striking of a clock, when its hands reach, statistically speaking, a certain position.

Many such economical thinkers were prepared to admit that in the Soviet Union the political attitude of vital sections of the working class and poor peasants was not determined exclusively by rise or fall in their material benefits and standard of living. Even the most sceptical of the economically-minded realized that the sense of participation in the building of the first socialist state was a factor as powerful as it was statistically incalculable.

And certainly it could be seen as easier to rouse workers' enthusiasm for the creation of a workers' state, than to stir it on behalf of what Hitler had to offer. But this very fact enhanced the importance of the immaterial factors, the spiritual shot in the arm. Though correctly described by steel tycoon Thyssen as 'that stammering drunkard', Dr Ley, head of the Labour Front, spoke truth when he said: 'We had to divert the attention of the masses from material to moral values. It is more important to feed the souls of men than their stomachs.'

The notion of diverting attention from domestic misery by staging triumphs in the foreign field is often over-simplified: as discontent brews at home, the dictator starts a war, or forces a neighbouring state into some humiliating concession. The psychology of diversion is more complex. The exact nature of the diversion is of critical importance.

As a diversion, Mussolini's war against Abyssinia was meagre in results. Recreation of the glories of Imperial Rome was not adequately alluring to the Italian worker. He could not identify with Caesar. He was not diverted from his oppositional attitude, which consisted not in revolt but in sloppy work, bad time-keeping, absenteeism, and the swindling of state and employer by all possible means, traditional and novel.

In Germany the glorification of 'the Thousand Year Reich' was certainly the overall diversionary impulse. But the German masses did not by any means desire glorification at the price of war—unless Hitler could guarantee a small walkover-type war, with few casualities and no rise in the price of foodstuffs. As Haji Baba of Ispahan so truly said: 'If only there were no dying in the case, how the Persians would fight.' Glorification, as justification of long hours for low pay, must be peaceful.

It must, in the first instance, take the form of defying and annulling the Treaty of Versailles. For reasons, some of them factual, some invented or, so to speak, refocused first by the right-wing nationalists and then by the

145

Overleaf: Germany's industrial might—the Krupp works, the Krupp family, and financial genius, Schacht

Nazis, Versailles had become the cause of all Germany's ills, above all the symbol of the humiliation of the German spirit. It had sought to destroy the Good in Germany and elevate the Evil, personified by the Jews and the Bolsheviks. Opposition to Versailles was therefore religious and ethical in character.

With the leaders of that religious revival, millions could identify on the spiritual plane. The rearmament of Germany, which was an integral part of the revival, facilitated this identification by bringing it rewardingly on to the material plane. It ended the long nightmare of unemployment.

The English steel-worker who had been unemployed for years and then, in 1936, got a job, had a job. Period. No spiritual uplift was built in. The formerly unemployed German had a job and plus the job he was making steel to make Germany great and good again. He asked no more than everlasting rearmament with no war.

And in this he concurred with Krupp and Thyssen. For it is a mistake to suppose that the tycoons of the armament industry positively want a major war anywhere. Such wars are profitable while they last but history saith an ending to such good things must be, and also there are risks: the war, as it did in Russia in 1917, may knock the whole lucrative system to bits. In this sense the armament makers are pacifists: their dream is of an unending peace, with war endlessly just around the corner.

In the winter of 1935-6, reports of 'rising discontent' in Germany poured out of the country. In British Labour circles they were received with uncomprehending satisfaction: uncomprehending in the sense that the discontent which really existed was equated wishfully with anti-Nazism. The murmurers were no more anti-Nazi than Röhm had been. They had supported Nazism from the outset. They had rejoiced in its victory. They demanded only that it now proceed to new victories over financiers, bloated capitalists, Jews, and the Old Guard of the Junkers and the Army, seen as stunting the fresh growth of the New Germany.

Nobody can possibly know whether the situation was as dangerous in January and February 1936 as it had been in May and June 1934. But it is certain that Hitler believed it to be so, and the High Command believed it, and Dr Schacht, head of the Reichsbank, believed it, and through him his opposite number at the Bank of England, Montagu Norman (with whom he was intimate), and the heirarchy of the City of London believed it.

Every person who has risen to power is conditioned to believe that others, seeking power, are going to operate in the same fashion as he did. Gangsters, speaking generally, are more afraid of being toppled by other gangsters than by the police. They understand the nature of the gangster's operation.

Hitler and his colleagues were all conditioned to the politics of demagogy combined with the threat, or the reality, of the terrorist *putsch*. Among them and around them were many whom they rightly suspected of plotting to exploit existing mass discontents to support a *putsch*. Memory of their own successes in this line inclined them to exaggerate existing dangers.

The High Command, always fearing that the notion of a new, revolutionary Nazi Army could be revived, shared some of the suspicions, and helped to foment them in order to get Hitler's agreement to an extensive counter-action, a new purge.

The London bankers were sufficiently alarmed to request from Schacht, early in the year, assurances that such counter-action against beef-steak tendencies would be taken vigorously and in good time. Otherwise the credibility of Hitler as the bulwark against Bolshevism would be destroyed, and with it a principle *raison d'être* of the City's policy towards Germany.

Right up to the first week in March 1936 it was believed in the City that the desired and, supposedly, most urgently necessary action against 'the second revolution' was about to be taken. Schacht confirmed that this was so. He may, in fact, have believed it. As late as the afternoon of 6 March, when it was known in Berlin that the Reichstag was to be convened in emergency session next day, it was generally surmised that it was to hear the announcement of the new purge.

But another option was open. A diversion of precisely the kind indicated by the situation was available.

There was one area of potential operation in which a single act, the movement of a couple of divisions, could effect the most spectacular repudiation of Versailles imaginable: a symbolic defecation upon the pages of the Treaty of a nature intelligible to the coarsest and least instructed of onlookers.

A military occupation of the demilitarized Rhineland was not only prohibited by the Treaty: under Article 44 it constituted a Hostile Act, one calling for immediate counter-action. The demilitarization of the Rhineland was also guaranteed by the Locarno Pact of 1925, of which Britain, France and Germany were the principal signatories.

The point of no return

The invasion of the Rhineland had been prepared, as a contingency plan, in secret conferences between Hitler and the highest of the High Command for at least nine months. The occupation had been planned under the code name *Schulung*. The generals supposed that the contingency would arise only at some distant point when the balance of forces, particularly the expected embroilment of France with Italy, would be such that either the West would be incapable of military counter-action, or else German strength would be sufficient to face resultant war.

But the pressure of political developments, specifically the signature of the Franco-Soviet Pact and the creeping menace of the 'second revolution', combined to whisk the invasion of the Rhineland out of the contingency basket on to the immediate agenda.

Up to the last fortnight before the decision—momentous and unprecedented even in the list of Hitler's audacities—the High Command and the Reichsbank still stressed the risks of the invasion and their preference for internal action against the aspirant successors of Röhm. Hitler, rightly, told them that they were mistaken in their assessments.

With his profound understanding of the German masses, and his sufficient grasp of the real character and motives of the people in power in Britain and

149

France, he insisted that to decodify *Schulung* into plain language would be to kill two birds with one stone.

To reduce the Treaty of Versailles to so much lavatory paper and publicly flush it down the international drain would provide in Germany just that 'food for the souls of men' which the Head of the Labour Front was crying out for. Nothing could better divert the attention of the potential followers of conspiring *putschists* from 'material to moral values'. At the same time, nothing could more rudely unveil the true preoccupations of the British Government, and the mutually internecine treacheries of London and Paris.

The reports of the naval and military attachés, the warnings of the non-Nazi Ambassador, might say otherwise: Hitler's instinct told him that the British Government, and his own well-wishers in positions of power at Westminster, in the City and at Printing House Square, would immediately see his action for what it was: the last turning point, the moment of truth, the moment when the last bets were to be placed before the croupier called 'Rien ne va plus'.

Dusseldorf, 1936: Hitler's triumph—the Rhine is crossed

At dawn on 7 March, a force of between 30,000 and 40,000 German troops began the march westward across the Rhine bridges. At 10 a.m. the German Foreign Minister informed the British and French Ambassadors of the invasion, denounced the Treaty of Locarno and suggested new plans for peace.

At midday, Hitler addressed the Reichstag. His themes were the evils of Versailles and the menace of Bolshevism. The first evoked the deep response of Germans. The second was sympathetically received in London and Paris.

William Shirer, author of *The Rise and Fall of the Third Reich*, immediately wrote in his diary a description of the scene when Hitler announced that the troops were on the march:

'Now the six hundred deputies, personal appointees all of Hitler, little men with big bodies and bulging necks and cropped hair and pouched bellies . . . leap to their feet like automatons . . . All the militarism in their German blood surges to their heads. They spring, yelling and crying, to their feet . . . Their hands are raised in slavish salute, their faces now contorted with hysteria, their mouths wide open, shouting, shouting, their eyes, burning with fanaticism, glued on the new god, the Messiah. The Messiah plays his role superbly. His head lowered, as if in all humbleness, he waits patiently for silence. Then his voice, still low, but choking with emotion, utters the two vows.

'"First, we swear to yield to no force whatever in restoration of the honour of our people . . . Secondly, we pledge that now, more than ever, we shall strive for an

understanding between the European peoples, especially for one with our Western neighbour nations . . . We have no territorial demands to make in Europe!"

'It was a long time before the cheering stopped. A few generals made their way out. Behind their smiles, however, you could not help detecting their nervousness . . . I ran into General von Blomberg, [Minister of Defence] . . . His face was white, his cheeks twitching.'

They will do nothing

Von Blomberg had never more than half believed that the French would not counter-attack. He and General Beck, Chief of General Staff, had agreed that any French military counter-move must be followed by instant German withdrawal. Even Hitler was not absolutely certain that the tremendous coup had succeeded. He said afterwards, 'If the French had then marched into the Rhineland, we would have had to withdraw with our tails between our legs, for the military means at our disposal would have been wholly inadequate for even a moderate resistance.'

But he told the generals that he did have absolutely certain information to the effect that the French would not march. Whether that information was in the form of personal assurances such as he might easily obtain from his supporters in Paris and London, or was based on his general assessment of all that he knew by report and by instinct, it was correct.

And it was correct because it was based on an appraisal in depth of political attitudes and long-term political objectives rather than of day-to-day detailed news.

The German naval and military attachés, necessarily reporting immediate naval and military indications, were in the main alarmist in their messages to Berlin. But Leopold von Hoesch, German Ambassador in London, had some political understanding. He was intimate with the Royal Family, and in particular with Edward VIII, who had repeatedly voiced, to the Ambassador and to his English friends, his sympathetic attitude to Hitler and his aims.

Von Hoesch had always assured the Berlin Government that Britain would not forcibly oppose German occupation of the Rhineland. And it was accepted by almost everyone that if Britain refused to act, France would do nothing either. There were minority groups in the French Foreign Office and at the French War Office who favoured independent French action. They believed—rightly according to the German archives and the testimony of the generals at post-war Nuremberg—that the French Army alone could force an ignominious German withdrawal, probably without a shot fired.

General Jodl testified at Nuremberg: 'Considering the situation we were in, the French covering army could have blown us to pieces.'

Speaking in 1942, Hitler said, 'A retreat on our part would have spelled collapse.'

Even von Hoesch at one moment was half convinced by his attachés and other informants who told him there was at least a likelihood that the British would take forcible action, even if this were believed certain to lead to war.

He immediately motored to Fort Belvedere to see the King. According to his own account, he persuaded Edward VIII to 'intercede for peace' with Prime Minister Baldwin. At midnight the King telephoned. Fritz Hesse,

Wehrmacht chief Blomberg arrives in England

correspondent of the official Nazi News Agency, and virtually a member of the Embassy staff, was present when the King rang to say, 'I've just seen the Prime Minister. There won't be war.'

Von Hoesch was under the ludicrous misapprehension that his trip to Fort Belvedere and the King's intervention with Baldwin had 'saved the peace'. Very few journeys have been less necessary. Baldwin and his Cabinet certainly did not need Edward VIII to 'persuade' them not to act effectively against Hitler. They never had any intention of so doing.

Some contemporary, and many more subsequent commentators have written as though the Government's behaviour were the result of excessive caution and, in some cases, of cowardice. It is suggested that had the Government been aware of the facts as known to Blomberg, Jodl and Hitler himself, it would have taken, or supported the French in taking, necessary action to repel the German invasion. Their error is fundamental. The Government, and the City of London, were well-enough informed of the German situation. It was not one which required extended or expert espionage to assess. The channels of information between London and Berlin at the highest levels were numerous and wide.

Unacceptable consequence

It could be assumed that joint Anglo-French military action, even an unmistakable threat of such action, would have had immediate results. But what results? Immediately, the failure of Hitler's diversion. Consequently, the failure of those food supplies required for the soul. The recreation, therefore, in a very much intensified form of the dangerous internal situation existing before the Rhineland coup. For the humiliating failure of the coup could be seen as not merely a setback for Hitler, but a probable disaster.

And the end result would have been the emergence in Germany of just that state of affairs which was most unwelcome to the British Government: a state, at the best, of uncertainty, at the worst of a radicalization of the Nazi movement. In fact, the Anglo-French action would have produced the very situation which a few over-optimistic Communist crystal-gazers had hopefully foreseen before Hitler became Chancellor. Following the delusive notion of what Marxists denounced as 'worsism', they imagined that the worsening condition of the masses under the Nazi regime, the disillusionment which certainly occurred, and the elimination of the bourgeois political parties and their allies, would automatically lead to the collapse or overthrow of Nazism, with Communism as the automatic replacement.

Some Communist calculators, who understood British attitudes less well than Hitler, certainly supposed that somewhere along the line—somewhere within a few years of Hitler's taking power—the Western Powers would stand up, as the saying went, to Hitler. They would administer a smart external blow to his entire contraption. He would thus be forced into a premature and, for him, disastrous war, or else to a 'retreat from glory' which would destroy his domestic prestige and power.

These prognosticators were wrong. Yet they, in foreseeing no automatic collapse, but collapse as a result of external action, were not alone in their general judgement of the position. The view was shared in British governmental and City circles.

The difference was that while the Communists would have welcomed such action, and supposed it would be taken, the British Government, foreseeing just the same consequences, were determined not to take it. Why, they understandably asked, should they contribute to the creation of possibly uncontrollable unrest in Germany? Conditions of uncertainty disadvantageous to international finance and commerce? Conditions which could deteriorate to anarchy? Could even deteriorate, even more disastrously, as they saw it, towards Communism?

Hitler estimated that 'a retreat on our part would have spelled collapse'. And the dominating notion of British policy in that first fortnight of March 1936 was not that action against Germany might mean war, but that it might mean German collapse.

Charade

In this sense the spectacular and seemingly crucial political and diplomatic activity of the days following the invasion were a black charade.

Flandin, French Foreign Minister, flew to London that spring to go through the motions of asking for British support for effective action. It is true that in France, particularly at the Foreign Office, and within the Cabinet itself, the advocates of such action were more numerous and powerful than they were in London. Flandin's trip was not entirely farcical. Had he received any sign of British encouragement, the advocates of action might possibly have had things their way. There was that much truth in the over-simplified picture of a France, eager to act against Hitler, but held back, impeded, and threatened with betrayal by Britain.

During the critical days, the War Offices of the Three Powers engaged in a grotesque parody of a tribal war dance. They advanced, they weaved, shook weapons, retreated, ululated in a frenzy of professional nervousness. They were frightened, as well they might be, of their native politicians; frightened of hidden tricks up the enemy's sleeve; frightened above all of making some blunder with disastrous consequences for which they would be made to carry the blame.

The Defence Ministry in Berlin, as the archives show, was gnawed by fear of getting the sack, or worse, if it seemed to vacillate in carrying out Hitler's directives, and the gamble succeeded by equal fear of any serious confrontation by the French.

In Paris, the War Office, heavily permeated by Germanophiles and Fascists, nevertheless maintained in important posts energetic opponents of Germany, who foresaw that while resistance to Hitler might be a turning point in the history of western Europe, surrender now could endanger the whole credibility of France in the eyes of the Kremlin. Two years earlier de Gaulle had published his *L'armée du Métier*, which was ignored by the French War Office and eagerly studied by the German Defence Ministry.

But both these groups were outnumbered by men notoriously as lazy as they were incompetent. Indeed the entire set-up at the French War Office offered an instructive preview of the situation as it was at the moment of the collapse of the French war effort in 1940. The balance of forces within that crucial department was similar on both occasions. The difference was that in 1940 it was probably too late for the results of treachery and inertia to be counteracted. In 1936, the military force required to put the German High Command into reverse was relatively so small, and the nervousness of the German generals so great, that the unready condition of the French military machine as a whole need not have inhibited the limited local action required.

However, the opponents of action were able to point to the consequences of incompetence as proof that the French Army could not possibly counter-invade the Rhineland.

In London, an able high official of the British War Office, seeking to describe its condition, quoted the remark of one of William Gerhardi's characters describing Tsarist Russia: 'There are clever men here, and there are honest men, but there are no honest clever men, and if there are they are certainly heavy drinkers.' As in Paris, there was a number of men in high positions who favoured an immediate riposte to the German move. There was probably a larger number of officers who, for political and social reasons, were profoundly hostile to any show of hostility to Germany. But even if these latter had been fewer than they were, they would have had the overwhelming professional support of those who argued, convincingly, that the army was in no shape to be engaged in major war, and assumed, less cogently, that counter-action in the Rhineland would lead to major war.

For these reasons, pacifism found its strongest support in the War Office.

The situation at the Admiralty was similar. The Sea Lords took up an impregnable position on the line that the British Navy was able and willing to undertake any task except such as might involve risk of armed conflict.

Press and profile

The British press at this juncture was powerful in its immediate impact on opinion in all three countries most immediately concerned, and equally significant in its disclosure of the real attitudes of the newspaper proprietors.

Considering that its editor, Dawson, had for long been deeply engaged in the intrigues of the advocates of friendship with Hitler, the behaviour of *The Times* was predictable. It headed its leading article of 9 March 'A Chance to Rebuild'. Yet, however predictable, this open acclaim for Hitler's lethal coup, coming from the most powerful organ of the British press, and the one most nearly expressing majority opinion in the Government, was a heavy blow to the *morale* of the anti-German activists in France, and to the still embryonic anti-Hitler faction in the German High Command. Conversely, it provided Hitler with breath to utter a hearty 'I told you so', and the Germanophiles in France with great store of ammunition for a campaign to demonstrate that, however anyone might regret surrender to Hitler's demands, the perfidy of England had made it inevitable.

The defection to support Hitler's policy by the mass-circulation papers, the *News Chronicle* and the *Daily Herald*, was domestically more important. The *News Chronicle* was, so to speak, the guide, philosopher and friend of several million readers who included the most sincere enthusiasts for the League of Nations, and collective security.

156

Overnight, the *Chronicle*, after the ritual sighs of regret that Hitler had seen fit to act with such rude crudity, welcomed the new situation created, and urged acceptance of new Hitlerian peace proposals.

Vehemently furious members of the *Chronicle*'s staff, their judgement enflamed by a just sense of betrayal, explained the whole sordid turnabout with details of recent reorganization of personnel, and above all by the fact that Sir Walter Layton, Chairman of the company, had suddenly assumed close editorial control of the paper. Sir Walter was an associate of Lord Lothian. Lothian, formerly Philip Kerr, and a private secretary to Lloyd George, was hand-in-glove with Dawson of *The Times* and among the most active organizers of support for Hitler in British high places. The fact, together with Layton's affiliations in the City, was certainly important. But equally so was the simpler fact that business consultants took the view that high-principled support of the League and collective security was not a circulation-getter: pacifism, apathy and hope were better money-spinners.

The support of the *Daily Herald* for Hitler's policy was less jolting in effect. It was jointly owned by Odhams Press and the T.U.C. Its business affairs were in the hands of Odhams. Its political line was directed by the T.U.C. In the battles for mass circulation, the paper had been drained of serious political content. Its political influence was meagre. In the Rhineland crisis the businessmen and the circulation-minders were of the same opinion as those at the *News Chronicle*: an activist, anti-Hitler line would not pay off. The political directors from the T.U.C. were aware that the T.U.C. and the Labour Party were at least divided and uncertain. Without belief in the principles of pacifism they calculated that a pacific line would be better, in terms of circulation and votes, than a call for resistance to Hitler. In their unending struggle to document themselves as quietly reasonable persons, fit to govern again, they were in great horror of being smeared as war-mongers. They were deeply influenced, then and later, by the fear of being supposed so passionately anti-Fascist or anti-Nazi that these class sentiments could affect their cool assessment of the situation.

History is regularly seen in the act of post-determining itself. It is supposed that because one of two things did happen, the other could not have happened. On this supposition to speak of any climactic event such as Hitler's march across the Rhine as a turning point is thought not to make sense. The supposition is a mechanistic and defeatist distortion of reality, denying—and when accepted, actually eroding—human intelligence and will-power. In a particular matter, such as the invasion of the Rhineland, the deleterious effects of this kind of pseudo-philosophizing are immediately visible. The parties responsible for the outcome publicly wash their hands, claiming they could not have done anything else. Acceptance of the *fait accompli* is held to be a virtue. Thus, so far from attempts being made to nullify it, the accomplished thing is taken as a new starting point. Hitler and his supporters call for a new deal: Hitler starts the new round with better cards.

Russia in Europe
Many of the multifarious and proliferating results of the Rhineland coup of

7 March 1936 were listed with most admirable terseness by A. J. P. Taylor in his *English History 1914-1945*:

'Germany, it was hoped, would settle down now that her unequal conditions had been ended. Arthur Greenwood, deputy leader of the Labour Party, for example, found the situation "pregnant with new and great possibilities for the future of the world". The hope was not fulfilled. The Council of the League met in London. Only Litvinov, the Soviet representative, proposed sanctions against Germany. His advocacy was enough to damn the proposal. The Council resolved, though not unanimously, that the Treaties of Versailles and Locarno had been broken. Hitler was invited to negotiate a new arrangement for European security, to replace that which he had destroyed. He responded to the invitation: he had "no territorial claims in Europe", wanted peace, proposed a twenty-five year pact of non-aggression with the Western Powers. The British government sought further definition, with a list of precise questions. To this Hitler did not reply. Silence followed.'

In two sentences, Taylor drew attention to the 'new and great possibilities' with which the situation was really 'pregnant'—with a child not at all resembling the infant of Greenwood's imagining.

Litvinov, alóne, proposed sanctions. And 'his advocacy was enough to damn the proposal'.

This Soviet intervention was a new public advertisement of the profound development in Soviet foreign policy of which Russia's entry into the League of Nations and the signature of the Franco-Soviet Pact had been the first sign. The whole development was described without exaggeration as marking 'Russia's return to Europe'. The latest move confirmed the apprehensions of the Nazi Government regarding the formations of the shift of direction in Moscow. The shift was made in a confident calculation that self-isolation, seen as necessitated by Russian weakness and need for peace at almost any price, was no longer the enforced principle of policy.

Like isolationists in the United States, though for most obviously different reasons, the political directors of the Soviet Union had held 'avoidance of foreign entanglements' to be axiomatic. Every treaty of mutual assistance, and membership of the League of Nations, was an entanglement evidently involving a risk of war. Until recently, advocates of such entanglements being accepted. such risks taken, could have been denounced within Russia as traitors to the Soviet state and its objectives.

The rise of Litvinov expressed and symbolized the change of balance and direction in Moscow. Coining the slogan 'peace is indivisible' he was by no means issuing a ration of pacifist bromide. It was a slogan of collective security. But it was also a declaration of intent to participate in military sanctions against an aggressor. And the German Government was aware that the line between 'aggression' and 'potential or threatened aggression' was a fine one. The way things seemed to them to be going just behind the scenes in Moscow, it was desirable for them to start wondering where, in the long run, that line might be drawn.

To state, truthfully, that Litvinov's advocacy of sanctions was sufficient to damn sanctions, is a brief statement of the sum total of several different factors, among them, these:

First, to join the Soviet Union in action against Hitler would have been to abandon the entire basis of Britain's policy towards Germany. Ever since

Hitler came to power, British policy had accepted the general thesis that peace in the West without major and painful concessions by the Western Powers, could only be achieved by agreeing, in effect, to a disinterest in eastern Europe.

It was perfectly consonant with the policy of those very powerful elements which considered that British policy should strike a more positive note: Germany, they held, should not merely be unimpeded in eastern Europe, but actively encouraged in the Teutonic Crusade to the East. Among the supporters of these differing, though barely divergent policies, it was common ground that Germany was to be seen as a 'bulwark against Bolshevism'. The phrase emphasized the domestic role of Nazism in the heart of Europe. And again, there were those who preferred that the bulwark be transformed at a suitable time into a battering ram. But whether the policy preferred was the relatively passive or the relatively aggressive, it would not be squared with joint Anglo-Russian action against Germany.

Secondly: to accept the Russian proposal for joint sanctions would be to acknowledge and facilitate the 'return of Russia to Europe' in a quite unacceptable manner. It was less than seven years since Britain had resumed the diplomatic relations with the Soviet Union which had been broken off in 1927. It was only twelve years since Britain had officially recognized that the Soviet Government existed. But the recognition and the resumption of diplomatic relations had been politically possible only on the assumption of Russian weakness and isolation. That was a very different pair of shoes from recognition of Russia as a power in Europe, and a potential military and economic partner in collective action against Germany. To the British Government the notion was damnable, and Litvinov's proposal damned.

The third damnable quality of that proposal was less ponderable but equally potent. Its acceptance would have immediately brought to the surface and canalized all the subterranean waters of anti-Communism in Britain. The notion of collective, possibly military, action with the Bolsheviks would have horrified people right across the board from the Royal Family, whose cousins and cousins-once-removed had been shot by these same Communists at Ekaterinburg, to leaders of the Labour Party and T.U.C.

A Labour Government had resumed diplomatic relations with that weak and isolated Russia. It was still just possible then to represent the Soviet Union to the British Labour voter as an experiment, noble or otherwise, but one which had probably failed, and certainly had not produced a state powerful in international terms.

But if one admitted that the experiment had somehow or another, despite its gross deviations from Labourist principles, succeeded in putting together a machine that visibly worked, and a state with which close military and economic co-operation was desirable in the interests of peace, then it was going to be that much more difficult to denigrate and ridicule Communism wherever it was to be found: new prestige for the Soviet Union would rub off, dismayingly, on the tiny British Communist Party.

Another damnable result.

'Silence followed.'

It was raucously broken by the uproar of war in Spain.

8 The Battle for Spain

1936-9 *Triumph for the Right*

Throughout the spring of 1936, there took place in Spain a development that was convulsive, spontaneous, tumultuous and, supposing the word had any meaning, democratic. In the February elections, the parties of the Popular Front had won 278 seats in the Cortes. The parties of the Right, combined in the National Front, had 134 seats. Despite intimidation by the landowners in rural Spain, which was traditional, and on this occasion intensified, the vote for the Popular Front was 4,176,000. The vote for the National Front was 3,780,000.

In the Popular Front were included the Left Republicans and the Republican Union with 126 seats between them, the Socialists with 99, the Catalan Separatist Left with 36, and the Communists with 17.

Outside Spain, the event was noted with generally calm incomprehension. A general election had taken place, a shift to the Left had been registered.

Europe north of the Pyrenees was in the main ignorant of the state of mind of the Spanish working people; was indifferent to it; and would in any case have found it unintelligible.

Those whose business it was to observe the course of events found it impossible to convey their nature and significance to populations cocooned in their own political habits. Some tried to translate Spanish into French or English by seeking comparisons with the mood of revolutionary Europe in 1848, or of the Paris Commune of 1871. The translation was rough indeed, the analogy distant.

It was justified in one sense only: in Spain now, as in those great European explosions of the nineteenth century, hundreds of thousands of people—in Spain millions—were motivated and propelled by a good hope that the moment had come when man could remake his world; that he could master his circumstances; that liberty could cease to be an empty word, and work be no longer a dreary one. They did not accept that Utopia must be a sick delusion.

In the rest of western Europe such hopes, which had once been their own, had become objects of melancholy mockery among people numbed by seemingly endless failure and disillusion. Passing much of their lives in routines both tedious and corrosive, they were accustomed to the view of a future which to some looked black, to others grey, and bright to very few. Without theology, they had yet succumbed to a belief in the consequences and penalties of Original Sin. They were told, and told each other, that large hopes were wills-o'-the-wisp because you can't change human nature. They felt, like the people of Kansas City in the song, that they'd gone about as far as they could go.

When any news of what the Spaniards were up to did percolate to them, they concluded that the Spaniards must be mad. The French explained this collective insanity on the ground that the people were Spaniards; the English on the ground that they were Latins.

The advanced industrialization of the more northerly western countries had not produced any general or lasting sense of potential human mastery over material things. On the contrary, and for reasons which were evident in every factory, mine and office, the common phrase said that man was increasingly 'the slave of the machine'.

162

Previous pages: The guns of Spain—Republican forces in action

In Spain in those days it was as though the powerful aspirations of nineteenth-century Europe, the gigantic acts and projects of scientists, philosophers and technologists, had been disinterred from the rubble they had been buried in and found to be not dead but waiting only for a kiss of life to recover and expand their vivacity in a new context. Mad as March hares, those Spaniards supposed that now that what they thought was democracy had broken through to what they thought was power, it would very soon, very fast, proceed to the establishment of a state of affairs in which the resources of that rich land where most people were miserably poor would be at the disposal of the people for their use and benefit.

Their historians told them, and they were a people very much aware of history, that in the days of the Roman Empire Spain had been distinguished by the single epithet 'opulent'. When the Moors held southern Spain in the Middle Ages, travellers had described the journey from east to west of the country as a trip through a vast expertly and elaborately irrigated garden where a great population lived prosperously among its rich crops. Orators on hundreds of platforms proclaimed these facts in hundreds of villages. The villagers, working for only a few months of the year at starvation wages on millions of neglected acres, believed that the land would soon be theirs. And it would be a new land. The scientists and the engineers together could irrigate those acres, making them as productive as they had been under the Moors; much more productive, because modern technology, no longer strangled by the landowners, could make three blades of grass grow where one had grown before.

There would be schools everywhere, beginning with the travelling schools already starting to perambulate the country. Everyone would learn to read. Good books would be as cheap as wine. Everyone would know what could be done, and how to do it.

In the factories of Barcelona, Madrid and Bilbao, the working people, already highly literate and informed, knew that Spain, coming so late to the industrial revolution, had an industrial plant more generally up-to-date than any in Europe, uncluttered by the relics and paraphernalia of long and slow development. Now, in this new democracy, it would be possible to organize things rationally for the profit and pleasure of the factory people and of a whole country starving for industrial goods.

Viva Yo!

In that crazy country, when people looked around them and saw what should be done and were told that it couldn't be, they answered simply: Why not?

Explorers from the north came back with tall travellers' tales. They had not actually seen, like Othello, 'men whose heads do grow beneath their shoulders'. But they had seen millions of professing Christians who seemed to be treating the Sermon on the Mount as some kind of blueprint for the just society. They had seen priests hounded violently from their villages not because they were priests but because their conduct, as agents and accomplices of landowners and usurers, was then declared demeaning to the Christian religion. They had seen voters who believed that they, at the

163

ballot boxes, had voted to take the destiny of the country into their own hands. for their own good and the good of that same country. They had heard workers and peasants ceaselessly chanting a slogan which perfectly expressed their philosophy: Long live the Republic! Long live Democracy! Long live Me!

That final, exultant Viva Yo! particularly astounded the northern explorers. These cock-eyed Spanish people, suffering perhaps from a touch of Mediterranean sun, had evidently not heard that up north the best-established sociologists had proved that you cannot glorify the individual except at the expense of the collective, and vice versa. Hopeless to try.

The Spaniard of those days could have been described in words spoken thirty-five years later by de Gaulle, when he said: 'If what I have done had not carried hope within itself, how could I have done it? Action and hope are inseparable. It certainly seems that only human beings are capable of hope. And remember that in the individual the end of hope is the beginning of death.'

Such were the general motives and aspirations of the working people, expressed in a cloudburst of newspapers, leaflets, manifestos, big speeches from radio stations and rostra, smaller speeches at the street corners or the travelling platforms of lorries, still smaller ones shouted in the hubbub of cafes and bars.

The same passion which united them in agreement on the broad objectives of the forward march divided them on the question of the best route to take. The Anarchists, who made up the membership of the largest political and trade union organizations, had—at least officially—boycotted the elections. Officially and on principle they regarded parliamentary systems and the resulting governments as delusive impediments to the achievement of the good life in a good Republic.

It was said of them that they believed freedom could be achieved with no weapons other than an encyclopaedia and a pistol, or even, in a more traditional way of thinking, the works of Bakunin and some sticks of dynamite. As a rough caricature, the crude picture expressed elements of truth.

But the huge Anarchist Union, the C.N.T. was in the cities at least as authoritarian as the Socialist Union, the U.G.T., and as politically sophisticated as Tammany Hall at the height of its power. Nobody imagined the C.N.T. would have achieved its power had it been otherwise. Some Anarchist leaders explained some of the seeming theoretical contradictions by showing that in its methods and objectives the C.N.T., in the cities, was not in fact anarchist but syndicalist.

Membership of the F.A.I., the guardians of the Anarchist faith, the political wing and flying squad of the movement, was more fluid and in practice, thought not in theory, less controlled. Its practical and ideological impact was greatest in rural Spain, where real power was decentralized, and where the traditions of pure Bakuninism had been least disturbed by economic change.

The C.N.T. shook the new Government of the Popular Front by strikes. The gunmen of the F.A.I. fought pistol battles with right-wing Socialists.

The Socialists were passionately split between the so-called reformists led

164

by Indalecio Prieto and those led by Largo Caballero who, at that time, called for immediate revolution.

The leaders of the Left bourgeoisie saw the Popular Front as essentially an indispensable, if precarious, barrier to counter-revolution: to the destruction of the Republic that had succeeded Alfonso XIII, and the ruin and repression of the middle class, particularly the professional class, by the feudalistic landowners, the financial monopolists, and their allies in the ferociously reactionary hierarchy of the Spanish Roman Catholic Church.

The Communists, tiny in numbers, had possessed the energy and organizational know-how to bring about the creation of the Popular Front. The policy of seeking to establish Popular Fronts, to include working class and middle class elements in a broad, united opposition to Fascism, had been adopted at the 7th Congress of the Comintern in 1935. By some, it was seen as a purely defensive policy. To view it thus was mistaken, since in the Marxist dialectic there could be no, so to say, static separation of the defensive and the offensive. Still, it did recognize that the menace of Fascism to the whole working class and to broad other sectors of the population was not only real and immediate but was the most important factor in the entire situation. The strategy of the Popular Front was defensive in the sense that it demanded the subordination of ultimate and necessarily divisive aims to the necessities of the defence against Fascism.

Many observers and explorers from the north, observing and exploring the fierce, often physically violent, divisions between the parties of the Popular Front itself, and between those parties and the Anarchists, concluded that the visible divisions were more important than the visible unities. Their habits of mind inclined them to misunderstand the mood of the Spanish people at that time. It was, for them, a phenomenon so novel that they supposed it must be mythical.

It was a mistake disastrously shared by the Spanish enemies of the Popular Front. Well aware of the existing divisions, they supposed that under violent pressure the component parts of the Front would fly apart. It was soon proved that the unity of the people in terms of their essential aims was a greater force than were the problems that divided them. The growing unity of the different groupings of the people was a most notable political development of the Civil War.

Drugged euphoria

Nobody can be astounded by the incomprehension, or contemptuous of the judgement, of the observers from the outside. But it is astounding, and yet is certainly true, that in the enthusiasm, the euphoria, (which some saw as the delirium), of the spring and early summer of 1936, very large numbers of Spaniards did not believe that civil war was imminent; certainly did not believe it inevitable. The euphoria of hope had produced a truly mad confidence in the power of the democratic process. It was seriously imagined that the will of the people expressed at the polling stations would democratically prevail: the enemy would recognize it, and folding its tents steal away. This more or less mystical way of thinking was—oddly enough, considering their experience in industrial struggles—most pervasive and

165

debilitating among the Anarchists. Opposed in principle to the state, they saw the election results as presaging a rapid collapse of the state power. Their strategy and behaviour at that time ignored the probability that the state power would not collapse but would be seized by the common enemy.

This fatal underestimation of the opposing forces, within Spain and elsewhere in Europe, can be explained, so far as it affected the masses of the people, by that euphoria, that naïve confidence in democracy. Among many of the political leaders less simple-minded calculations played a role. By a paradoxical contradiction, it was seen by almost all the leaders concerned as politically advantageous to play down the menace of Fascism, to represent it as a bogey.

The leaders of the bourgeois parties reckoned that if the menace were to be treated as both real and really imminent, then it would follow that everything must be done as quickly as possible to develop the trade union and other working class militias as para-military forces capable of dealing with military revolt. But that meant arming the workers. It meant a major transfer of power to the working class. Such a step was naturally alarming.

To the Socialist Leftists, acknowledgement of the imminent reality of Fascist attack would have involved acknowledgement that the first priority must be mobilization of the widest possible forces for the counter-attack. It would have inhibited Caballero from such statements as his speech at Cadiz in May when he said: 'When the Popular Front breaks up, as break up it will, the triumph of the proletariat will be certain. We shall then implant the dictatorship of the proletariat, which does not mean the repression of the proletariat, but of the capitalist and bourgeois classes.' His assumption that the break up of the Popular Front must result in working-class victory paralleled Anarchist assumptions about what would happen at the break-up of the Republican state.

In the programme of the Communist Party, the defence of the Republic had priority. But the party was weak in numbers and tradition. Its position, particularly in relation to the youth organization in which the Socialist and Communist Youth Movements were now merged, required the maintenance of close relations with Caballero. And at the same time it remained, at many levels, on better terms with the Anarchists than existed between the Anarchists and any other non-Anarchist grouping.

All the conspirators
Despite the wishful ignorance which brought bliss to many, informed people were aware that the army chiefs, the bankers, the landowners and the hierarchy were planning the nullification by political intrigue and gang warfare if possible, otherwise by armed revolt, of the results of the February elections. (Bankers, landowners and members of the hierarchy were often the same individuals. The Church was one of the greatest landowners and also controlled the great Bank of Bilbao, among other financial institutions.)

Even before the final election results were in, General Franco had demanded that the provisional Prime Minister declare a State of War so as to prevent the formation of a Popular Front Government. Less generally

166

known were the visits of Spanish generals and other leaders of the Right \ Rome and Berlin, where they secured financial and general support. Even at that stage, the Right assumed that it could not win a civil war without aid and comfort to be supplied by Hitler and Mussolini. Their reports of just how much assistance other than financial they thought they had been promised varied.

Even with financial aid assured, and military aid confidently and (as it turned out) rightly expected from Italy and Germany; even though they would have at their disposal trained and well-armed troops against the working-class militias, the leaders of the Right understood that some kind of spiritual appeal must be produced to pull against the enthusiasms of the Republicans.

The problem was serious, and never completely resolved, in the sense that different and sometimes contradictory appeals had to be made to stir emotions other than the deep and natural fears of loss of money, land, and power which were sufficient motivation for the rich, the landed and the powerful, but not for these unprivileged in the system now seen as threatened by the democratic surge.

Since the whole *raison d'être* of the counter-revolution was to re-establish the power of the hitherto ruling classes, and to recreate a land safe for bankers, landowners and the hierarchy, the creation of an acceptable counter-revolutionary ideology involved, as in Italy and in Germany, myth-making, mystification, political fraudulence and chicanery of a grand kind. Hitler had created an ideology and a demonology powerful enough to defeat the Left and partially drug those who for so long, and sometimes so dangerously, expected the 'second Nazi revolution'. But Hitler's drugs were prescribed specifically for German subjects; liberation from the Treaty of Versailles was a major ingredient. Mussolini's patent medecines would not work quite satisfactorily either, in Spain; indeed some of them were definitely contra-indicated. In particular, talk of colonial glory and colonial conquest was repugnant to the people of a country so recently bled white and humiliated in its campaigns in Morocco. There was also the circumstance that the type of Spaniard the Right must seek to appeal to in general hated and despised the Italians, regarding them much as the same type of Englishman did.

Some of the early Italian Fascist slogans, programmatic announcements, and methods of organization were imported, repacked in a hurry, and ostentatiously labelled 'Made in Spain'.

Germany provided appeals at a different level. The racialist conception of the Master Race, in this case Spanish, not Nordic, was an important element in the propaganda of the Spanish Fascists, the Falange, whose task was to rouse enthusiasm in particular among the impoverished and frustrated youth of the country. The lurid mysticisms of Blood and Soil were transferred to Spanish blood, Spanish soil.

In Germany, the ideology of the Nazi philosophy-makers was essentially, and often overtly, non-Christian or anti-Christian. Distortions of Nietsche were prominent in their armoury of delusions. This was an area where the Falangist philosophizers had to walk warily in the alliance with the Spanish

Roman Catholic Church. They did not, in fact, always walk warily enough. The divisions between the Falange, which had to be able to claim that it represented the masses, and in particular the youth, and the hierarchy were obtrusive during the Civil War and became more so after it.

Viva la Muerte!

But at a certain level, it was actually easier to avoid conflict between Spanish Catholicism and the notions of the Falange than it had been to reconcile Nazi doctrine with the relatively sophisticated Catholicism of Germany.

Politically and doctrinally, the sees of Toledo and Seville were a long step from Vatican City. The teachings of the Spanish bishops were viewed by numerous Roman leaders and directors of opinion, including some influential Spanish Catholics, as dismayingly and, in the end, disastrously obscurantist. Politically, those teachings identified the Church inelectably with the interests of finance-capital. Doctrinally, they dragged it down to a level where it could be identified as the enemy of human reason and human intellect.

At that level, there need be no contradiction between the teachings of the Christian bishops and the grossest fantasies of the Nazi cultists. They could not only coexist: they could cohabit and spawn some brutish offspring. Our observers from the north, bemused by the enthusiasms of the Popular Front, were equally confounded to discover among the Rightists, and notably in the province of Navarre, beliefs and motivations which reminded them not of the European movements of the 1840s, but of the mass hysteria and mass sadism, justified and promoted by religious arguments, which afflicted Europe during the 'witch-craze' of the sixteenth and early seventeenth centuries. As Professor Trevor-Roper has pointed out, those who supposed that the witch-craze was merely a horrible aberration, its causes eliminated for ever by the advance of humane reason, were found, in the twentieth century, to be grievously mistaken. The grotesque forgeries of the Protocols of the Elders of Zion in the 1890s became the Bible and inspiration of Fascist and Nazi propaganda in northern Europe in the thirties, and were held to justify the torture and extermination of Jews, Communists, liberals and intellectuals.

The same deep wells of human barbarism were being tapped in Spain. They were found richly productive.

These black gushers helped to signal the fact that the conflict in Spain concerned the whole of Europe, not on the immediate material plane, but as a conflict between different estimates of the nature and potentialities and purpose of *homo sapiens*.

The conflict was tragically dramatized in Salamanca on 12 October 1936, almost three months after the outbreak of the Civil War, in the confrontation, which became famous, between the philosopher Miguel de Unamuno, Rector of the University of Salamanca, who at first had supported the rebellion, and the leaders of the Fascists, the military and the Church. The scene is described with succinct vividness by Professor Hugh Thomas in *The Spanish Civil War*:

168

'On that date the day of the Festival of the Race, a great ceremony was held in the ceremonial hall of the University of Salamanca. There was the Bishop of Salamanca. There was the Civil Governor. There was Señor Franco. There was General Millán Astray. And, in the chair, was Unamuno. After the opening formalities, Millán Astray made a violent attack on Catalonia and the Basque provinces, describing them as "cancers in the body of the nation. Fascism, which is Spain's health-giver will know how to exterminate both, cutting into the live healthy flesh like a resolute surgeon free from false sentimentality". A man at the back of the hall cried, Millán Astray's motto: "Viva la Muerte!" Long live Death! . . . Several Falangists, in their blue shirts, gave a Fascist salute to the inevitable sepia portrait of Franco which hung on the wall over the dais.

'All eyes were now turned to Unamuno, who slowly rose and said: "All of you are hanging on my words. You all know me, and are aware that I am unable to remain silent. At times to be silent is to lie. For silence can be interpreted as acquiescence. I want to comment on the speech—to give it that name—of General Millán Astray. Let us waive the personal affront implied in the sudden outburst of vituperation against the Basques and Catalans. I was myself, of course, born in Bilbao. The Bishop", here Unamuno indicated the quivering prelate sitting next to him, "whether he likes it or not is a Catalan from Barcelona."

'He paused. There was a fearful silence. No speech like this had been made in Nationalist Spain . . . "Just now", Unamuno went on, "I heard a necrophilous and senseless cry: 'Long live Death'. And I, who have spent my life shaping paradoxes which have aroused the uncomprehending anger of others, I must tell you, as an expert authority, that this outlandish paradox is repellent to me. General Millán Astray is a cripple. Let it be said without any slighting undertone. He is a war invalid. So was Cervantes. Unfortunately, there are all too many cripples in Spain just now. And soon there will be even more of them if God does not come to our aid. It pains me to think that General Millán Astray should dictate the pattern of mass psychology. A cripple who lacks the spiritual greatness of Cervantes is wont to seek ominous relief in causing mutilation around him."

'At this, Millán Astray was unable to restrain himself any longer. "Abajo la Inteligencia!" Down with intelligence! he shouted, "Viva la Muerte!" There was a clamour of support for this remark from the Falangists.

'But Unamuno went on: "This is the temple of the intellect. And I am its high priest. It is you who profane its sacred precincts. You will win because you have more than enough brute force. But you will not convince, because to convince you need to persuade.

'"And in order to persuade, you would need what you lack: Reason and Right in the struggle. I consider it futile to exhort you to think of Spain."'

It was Unamuno's last lecture. He was placed under house arrest and died at the end of the year.

Factors in the battle
The military attack began on 17 July. Decisive factors in the first weeks, during which the course of the two-and-a-half years of war were really shaped, were these:

First: the politically intelligible but fatal hesitation of the Popular Front Government in offensive, and still more in defensive preparations to resist the rebellion led by the generals. Enough information was available to the Government to show that a whole list of high-ranking officers ought, for security reasons, to be arrested. The argument used against taking such action was that it would have precipitated a military revolt which otherwise might not take place. By hindsight it can immediately be seen that the argument was hopelessly flawed: an attack by the Right was inevitable, and

169

would inevitably be timed to occur before the Government was consolidated.

But this was obvious not only in hindsight. The evidence was already plain enough to see in June 1936.

For instance, Alvarez del Vayo, a leading Socialist, later Foreign Minister, was in London at the end of June and told many who talked with him many facts about the conspiracy, both in Spain and between the intending rebels and the German and Italian Governments. Unwillingness to act against the generals and other conspirators was linked with the Government's nervous reluctance to take steps to enable the working-class organizations to arm and give some training to their members in para-military formations. This reluctance could be ascribed simply to fear of the working class and its demands. Less crudely, it was argued that to act in that way would be in some sort a 'betrayal of democracy'—since it would in effect alter the democratic balance of power produced by the ballot boxes in February.

No one can say what would have happened if the thing that did happen had not. But it was certainly the opinion of level-headed and militarily experienced assessors on the Republican side that militias, armed and organized for military action in time, could have crushed the military revolt in many other cities as they did most notably in Madrid and Barcelona.

Second: immediate aid by Italy and Germany in the form of transport planes certainly made possible the swift—to the Government unexpectedly swift—transport of the rebel forces from North Africa to Spain. This hugely increased the effects of the Government's lack of defensive preparation.

170

Academic martyr Unamuno; evil genius Ribbentrop (left); Franco's victory smile

It made possible the rapid consolidation of the separate risings, and the initial thrust up the Tagus valley to the suburbs of Madrid.

The German planes transported the first troops to Seville, the Italian planes gave fighter cover to the ships which transported the next detachments across the Straits.

Of considerable, though lesser, importance was the effect of bombing by Italian Capronis of the column, led by the Anarchists, which on the outbreak of the revolt had marched out of Barcelona to recapture Saragossa from the military rebels.

Third: the resistance of the Republicans, and their blocking of the rebel advance after the first thrusts of the attack, was astonishing to the leaders of the revolt, in particular to Generals Franco and Mola. (It was General Mola who, advancing upon Madrid from the north, coined the phrase which, together with the name of Major Quisling, O.B.E., became an international description of the Fascist traitor within the gates. Mola boasted he would take Madrid because he had four columns advancing upon the city from without, and a 'fifth column'—*una quinta columna*—within the city, ready to rise against the defenders at the crucial moment. The immediate result of the statement was the arrest and often the shooting of large numbers of suspects who might otherwise never have been suspected.)

The blocking of their advance forced a re-thinking of all the rebel plans, military and political. It convinced the rebel leaders themselves, and—more importantly—convinced Mussolini and Hitler that the rebels, lacking

171

adequate mass support within Spain, were at least unlikely to succeed without Italian and German aid in men and armaments on a greater scale than had ever been contemplated.

Britain's 'No'

Fourth: outweighing in importance all the above factors was the immediate intervention by the British Government to prevent the French Popular Front Government sending arms to the Republic. Within a week of the military attack upon the Republic, the British Government had first warned, and then threatened the French Government with dire consequences if it persisted in its first decision to carry out its contractual and international obligations by acceding to the Republic's instant request for arms. On 25 July, after Léon Blum, French Prime Minister, had returned from a disastrous visit to London, the French Government announced that it refused the Spanish Government's request.

By a shabby and ramshackle compromise, it agreed that it would not actually prevent the Mexican Government buying French arms to send to Spain, or prohibit arms transactions with private dealers. The result was disastrous for the Republic. The immediate and massive supply of arms which as the legal government it had a right to expect was cut at the most critical moment. The substitute arrangements ensured fatal delays and maximum confusion.

Many critics considered that the blame for the disaster lay as much with the Republican Government as with the British. It was argued that they should have been sufficiently informed about the motives and aims of the British Government to foresee that it would, and could, exert the necessary pressure on the French Government to cut the supply. The Madrid Government should have imported and stored in advance of the revolt arms to the value of twenty million francs which had been contracted for in a Franco-Spanish Treaty of 1935.

To this criticism the Government could again reply that such shipments would have 'precipitated' the enemy's action. There was another reason, more cogent though certainly bizarre. It was that leading members of the People's Front Government, unpardonably peninsular in their ignorance of Britain, and hallucinated by the notion that a 'democratic Britain' would not act in open hostility to the Republic, were genuinely astounded and dismayed by the behaviour of the British Government which, on recent form, was entirely predictable. As anyone who was at all intimate with the Republican leaders could testify, many of them maintained until more than half way through the war, and in the teeth of all the evidence, that soon, somehow, the British would change their attitude.

To visiting politicians from England and to British journalists, who warned them of their error, they kept insisting that 'the British people' might be slow to act, but yet would surely see that it was in their interest to support another democracy against Fascism. In thus confounding the interests of the British people with the interests of British Government, they displayed, as Lenin said in another connection, 'a naïveté which in a child would be touching, but is repulsive in a person of mature years.'

172

Manpower and material

The Republicans had all the mass support and all the manpower they could effectively use in battle. What they lacked in terms of human beings were disciplined men, trained men, and above all men with some experience as officers.

The Right, officially known as the Nationalists, had trained troops—notably the Army of Africa. This consisted of the Spanish Foreign Legion and the Moorish trained in the campaigns of colonial Spain against their own rebellious people. These were first-rate fighting forces. They had a majority of the officers of the Spanish regular Army. But these proved by the end of the first phase of the war to be insufficient to overcome the Republican defenders. The advance of these fully equipped forces against the Republic, whose arms supply had been blocked or disrupted by the British and French Governments, was blocked and defeated.

At that time, General vom Faupel, Hitler's representative at the Nationalist Headquarters, in agreement with the head of the Nazi Condor Legion, reported that if Franco could be supplied with one German and one Italian Division at full strength a decisive breakthrough could be made. The German Foreign Office advised that two Divisions would not suffice. In the event, the Foreign Office advisers proved right. The aid, in manpower and—by Germany—in aircraft in the end enormously exceeded the prognostications of late 1936.

The particular and temporary needs of the Republic in the matter of manpower were supplied at the most critical moment by the formation of the International Brigades. They were decisive in the battle of Madrid. Their recruitment, organization, transport and training were the powerful, and to the Fascists terribly disconcerting, weld of Communist know-how, discipline and military experience, with the dedicated and furious *élan* of anti-Fascists of all political creeds and nations of Europe and the Americas. In numbers they were inferior to the Italian and German forces. In discipline they at least equalled the Germans. And in fighting morale they were beyond comparison superior to the 'compulsory volunteers' sent by Mussolini.

From Germany and Italy, war material, including bombers and fighter planes, was being supplied to the Nationalists as lavishly as required, though at the outset the Nationalists often underestimated their requirements.

As a result of the British Government's warning, the French refused to sell the arms for which the Republic had already contracted. But, by roundabout financial arrangements with the Mexican Government, and chaotic purchases from private arms dealers, during the first couple of weeks of the war arms were still being shipped, sporadically and inadequately, to the Republic across the French frontier.

Britain's bold move

In the first week of August the British Government moved to block this supply. The French Foreign Minister was officially warned that if France failed to prohibit the export to Spain of all war material, Britain would thenceforth consider itself absolved from its obligation under the Treaty of Locarno to come to the aid of France in the event of war with Germany.

Overleaf: Franco's troops in action; inset: future Prime Minister Attlee shows solidarity with Republicans (while Britain blocked their arms); Communist poster

FELICIA
BROWNE

COMMUNIST
DIES
FIGHTING FOR
LIBERTY IN SPAIN ....

TOWER HILL IMPROVE
TO BE DEMOLISHED TO C
OPEN SPACE FOR PUB

On 8 August the French Government issued its prohibition.

It was a boldly decisive step forward by the British Government in the development of its general European policy. Nobody from then on could fairly accuse it of duplicity. It had spelled out, directly to the French and indirectly to all other governments concerned, the fact that if Hitler chose to make French aid, however passive, to the Spanish Republic an occasion for war against France, Britain would not move to deter him. And this meant, in effect, that whatever the sympathies of the French Popular Front Government might be with the anti-Fascist cause in Spain, it was inhibited from translating these sympathies into action, since such action could result in a full-scale German attack upon an isolated France. In such circumstances the only moderating factor would, in future, be such influence as might be exercised by the German General Staff which was still unwilling to commit the newly armed German forces to full-scale war.

The Fascist and pro-German forces in France were decisively strengthened. As a shattering blow to the Spanish Republicans in their resistance to the Spanish Fascists, and a major extension of Hitler's power to control events, the British decision was naturally welcome to them. At the same time they could, and loudly did, proclaim that this was one more example of that British perfidy against which they had always warned the French. Any policy based on the notion of Anglo-French solidarity against Germany was fraudulent and disastrous.

It could reasonably be pointed out that the British policy was not accurately to be described as perfidious, since it was simply the logical development of the British policy which had been shaping ever since Hitler came to power. But this was not an argument that could be successfully used against the propaganda of the French Right.

From August 1936 onwards, the road to Vichy was clearly mapped. French impotence had been recognized; the capitulation of France had begun. The political posturings and manoeuvres of the four intervening years were no more than a charade.

In agreement with Britain, the French Government had in the same week proposed that France, Britain, Germany, Italy and Russia all sign a Non-Intervention Agreement, in accordance with which all would pledge themselves not to give military aid and comfort to either side in Spain. The German and Italian Governments hesitated until they had been assured by their military experts that the flow of men and war material to the Nationalists could continue and increase unchecked. The Russians hesitated while they vehemently disputed among themselves the question whether and to what extent they could, if they joined the Agreement, mitigate its effects by evading its provisions. It was decided that the most fruitful course would be to sit in on the proposed Non-Intervention Committee where differences between the Powers might be exploited, and at the same time hasten the organization of their own intervention.

The Nationalists, calculating that non-intervention must work overwhelmingly in their favour, urged the German and Italian Governments to hasten the establishment of the Committee.

On 9 September the Non-Intervention Committee, composed of the representatives of twenty-four European countries, met for the first time in London. Prince Bismarck, who, along with Ribbentrop, was German representative on the Committee, correctly summed up its functions: 'It is not,' he reported, 'so much a question of taking actual steps immediately, as of pacifying the aroused feelings of the Leftist parties . . . by the very establishment of such a committee.'

War of attrition

The advantage to the Nationalists consisted in the fact that whereas the Germans and Italians had unimpeded access to the Spanish territories controlled by the Nationalists, the Russian shipments had to run the Italian blockade of the Mediterranean. Michael Koltsov, leading foreign correspondent of *Pravda* and Stalin's unofficial personal representative in Spain, gloomily remarked one day on the docks at Valencia: 'There are enough of our tanks on the floor of that damned great lake to have retaken Manchuria from the Japanese.'

Membership of the Non-Intervention Committee afforded the Russians some diplomatic advantages. But so far as Russian military aid was concerned it made no difference one way or the other.

The effect of the Non-Intervention Committee, except for the hoodwinking of 'the Leftist parties' envisaged by Bismarck, was simply to legalize the situation created by the action of the British and French Governments in banning transport of arms across the French frontier to the Republic.

As the conflict developed into a war of attrition, for which neither side had been prepared, the easy flow of war material to the Nationalists compared with the very rough passage of Russian arms became an increasingly important and, in the end, decisive factor.

There were intervals when, under pressure partly from 'Leftists', partly from non-Fascist Rightists, who saw a Nationalist victory simply as a victory for Germany and a menace to France, the French frontier was reopened to allow supplies of arms to reach the Republic overland. At the end of 1938, despite large Nationalist gains, a position had been reached in which influential leaders on both sides were prepared to recognize a stalemate. Secret conversations for a negotiated peace were conducted.

But the stalemate was broken when the Nationalists, who still demanded total victory, finally surrendered to the Germans a vast area of control over the rich mineral resources of Spain. For the Germans, control, present and for the future, of the Spanish mines had been all along a principal objective. For months, the more genuinely nationalist among the Nationalists had resisted and haggled over this sale of the basic national resources to foreign interests. The choice now was seen, rightly or wrongly, as being between that sale and a negotiated peace. The mineral rights agreement was made. A massive new injection of German military aid followed.

This, wrote Professor Hugh Thomas, was the most important act of foreign intervention in the course of the Spanish Civil War. 'It enabled Franco to mount a new offensive almost immediately and so strike the Republic when they had exhausted their supplies. Had it not been for this aid (itself the consequence of the German realization that after Munich nothing they did in the Spanish War would cause Britain and France to go to war over any of its implications), a compromise peace, despite all Franco's protestations, might have been inevitable.'

The new offensive was successful. Catalonia fell to the Nationalists. At the end of March the Nationalists entered Madrid.

One of the first casualties of civil war is the man-in-the-street. He disappears along with the innocent bystander. What Anglo-Saxon newspapers call Mr and Mrs Average Citizen are no longer at home when the enquiring reporters call.

During the war, such enquirers were endlessly seeking material for articles on How the Ordinary Spaniard Lives, or how he, or she, sees the war. The enquiries presupposed a state of affairs which no longer existed. There were no neutrals, no onlookers. And nobody was out of danger for long— either by direct enemy attack or by lethal activities behind the lines.

Observers noted that because of the drain of manpower to the front, and the partial blockade, many people were hungry. But it was hard to calculate which people were simply as hungry as they had always been, and which, through more equitable distribution of supplies, were actually eating better than they ever had before.

There was fear. But, as British people learned later during the blitz, fear does not exclude hope; and the danger which produces the fear produces the elation of a danger faced in common with hundreds of thousands of others. These phenomena cannot be measured like kilos of bread or litres of milk. But in Spain at that time took place a vivid demonstration of the reality of what had often seemed nearly meaningless clichés.

The sense that for the first time in western Europe the working class had a chance of victory was as real as the flow of adrenalin in the blood. It had supplied the elan of the first days and weeks when the workers stormed the barracks, and their militias fought in the Sierras. That was not remarkable. Remarkable was that it persisted in the towns, and in villages far from the front, right through the grimly dreary prolongation of the war. Above all in the villages, there was a sense not only of participation but of power.

This fact raised an enormous question mark over Republican policy: a question mark which at the time was meaningful, and ever since has been merely one of the large Ifs of history. Suppose the working class, factory workers and peasantry, had divided itself from its bourgeois Republican allies, seized total power, established Soviets, proclaimed a Socialist state. Would the resultant injection of adrenalin have compensated the perils attaching to that policy? The argument was at the heart of the many bitter controversies within the Republican Government, and in particular between the Communists and sections of their Socialist and Anarchist allies.

The Communists held that maintenance of the broad Popular Front was essential for reasons of internal and external policy. They believed that the vast resources of energy required to create out of nothing, and to sustain throughout long campaigns, a modern army could not successfully be employed at the same time in the total overthrow of the bourgeois state, and all that that implied. As for how fast, after a successful conclusion of the war, it would be possible to move towards socialism, they considered the question as unrealistic, speculative, and frivolously doctrinaire. They held that if the general direction of an historical process under particular conditions may be roughly calculated, its pace never can be. The unknown factors are too numerous, and that kind of prophesying becomes no more useful than examination of the entrails of birds for auspices.

The external effects of socialist revolution in Spain were less easily calculable. It was argued that the bourgeois public in Britain and France believed the Republicans to be a pack of Reds anyway, so that to turn this myth into reality would lose no valuable goodwill. It was not difficult to demonstrate that this was a coarse distortion of the facts. The extent of bourgeois goodwill towards the 'democratic Republic' was immense. The question was: How to rate its practical value? How high, for instance, should be rated the possibility that popular anti-Fascist feeling in Britain could bring about either a change of government at Westminster or a change of existing governmental policy?

In this writer's experience, Spaniards at every political and social level pitifully overrated this possibility. They allowed themselves to think wishfully. They were all, in varying degrees, prisoners of their own hopes and their own propaganda. They positively believed in 'international democratic solidarity'. In reality, what they chiefly shared with the democratic people of Britain and France was a disastrous underestimate of the power, intelligence and determination of the ruling class. Russian workers had made the same intelligible error in 1917-18 They supposed that once the Russian working class had shown the way out of the horror and ruin of the war, the working classes of central and western Europe, above all of Germany, would enthusiastically follow. It was a non-event which ineluctably changed the shape and direction of the Russian revolution. The effects on Spanish Republican policies were not less profound.

9 Britain 1936

Sharpening antagonisms

Spain had moved in on British political life in 1936, and for two years camped there; establishing, so to speak, squatters' rights, and obdurately refusing to be evicted.

Viewed from the plinth of the Nelson column, with multitudes seething in Trafalgar Square; viewed from hundreds of platforms, loud-speaker vans, and soap-boxes between Swansea and Aberdeen; viewed from Transport House and Downing Street, the war in the Peninsula could be seen as dominating or contumaciously obtruding upon every other issue.

But this enormous obtrusion was complex in character. Some of its most profound effects were not immediately obvious.

Immediate and obvious were its deepening of existing divisions between Left and Right, and its creation of political opinions, and hence divisions of opinion, where opinions seemed hardly to have existed before.

At the outset it certainly sharpened class antagonisms as the political Right was displayed in open sympathy with the enemies of the Republic. But, with prolongation of the war, a point was reached where the nationalist or patriotic elements in the intellectual and emotional make-up of influential people on the Right began to jostle for precedence over their class allegiance. The tendency was exemplified by Winston Churchill. In the first months of the war he was passionately hostile to the Republic. When in October 1936, Lord Robert Cecil tried to introduce him to Azcarate, Republican Ambassador in London, Churchill made an ugly scene. He muttered, 'Blood! Blood! Blood!' and refused, ostentatiously, to shake hands. He wrote and spoke in a similar sense. In December 1938, he and numerous other leading Conservatives had at length come to see in a victory for Franco, Mussolini, and Hitler a serious menace to British interests. Accepting an invitation to dinner at the Soviet Embassy, he there met Azcarate for the second time and held friendly and sympathetic conversation with him.

The confrontation of Left and Right was enforced by the Spanish War and sharply clarified by it. The shape of the confrontation was blurred and its effects blunted by the Labour Party, which for the first crucial months supported the policy of the Conservative Government and, when it shifted to opposition, was effectively trammelled by its insistence on considering anti-Communism as its first priority.

But, simultaneously with this confrontation a different sort of division, less easily defined but at least equally significant, was being created.

This was the division between what may very loosely be described as the politicians and the non-politicals.

When orators and leader-writers of the Left declared: 'the people of England whole-heartedly support the legitimate Government of Republican Spain', they exaggerated. When orators and leader-writers of the Right declared 'the people of England stand aghast at the prospect of the horrors of atheistic Bolshevism being extended by the forces of Madrid to the whole Peninsula', they exaggerated.

What they said was true in the sense that the extent, vigour and duration of the political feelings and activities motivated by the Spanish War were unlike anything previously seen in Britain. Awareness of political realities was at a new height, and affected hundreds of thousands, perhaps millions,

Previous pages: Pride and poverty. Women protest against indignity of means test, 1936

who—through apathy, ignorance, or, above all, a frustrated conviction of their own impotence to 'do anything' about anything much—had been quiescent in thought and action. They had been non-political and they had become political.

But, though man is rightly defined as, in the broadest sense, a political animal, there are very few moments in the life of a society when an overall majority of its members can be described as politically active or even politically aware. It is improbable that more than a minority of the citizens of Jerusalem bestirred themselves on the first Good Friday to find out who was being taken out to Golgotha by the Roman soldiers, and why. It is certain that in Petrograd, on the day the Bolsheviks seized power at the Smolny Institute, the majority of people ate their dinners as little aware of what was really happening as were the citizens of Dublin on the day of the Easter Rising in 1916.

How silent the majority?

This is the Silent Majority of which President Nixon once spoke.

Its existence is in general not only assumed but welcomed by those in power. It may not actively support the ruling policies, but it will be too much preoccupied with its own affairs to impede them.

As the Spanish War visibly politicized Britain, it was in the interests of the Government and the whole of what would now be called the Establishment to encourage maximum silence on the part of as many people as possible on the matters then at issue. At the beginning of the war the pro-Government newspapers and orators had not realized this. They positively sought to excite, rather than divert, public opinion by stories equating the Republican leaders with Bolsheviks and supporters of the Republic with Communists, of whom there were at the time about 30,000 in the whole of Spain. They assumed that the 'menace of Communism' would be as electrifying as it had been twenty odd years earlier. They used much verbiage—again with the mistaken object of exciting rather than soothing opinion —concerning 'Red atrocities'; notably burning of churches, murder of priests by savage villagers, and the violent rape of nuns. (Parenthetically, one may note that in a country very numerously populated by Protestants and pagans, it was still taken for granted that a majority of people would consider the violent rape of a nun to be somehow more disgusting than the violent rape of any other woman.)

It had been hoped and expected by the British enemies of the Republic that the victory of the forces led by Franco would be swift. Since a majority of people prefer to side with victors, and dislike association with the weak, such a victory would have been useful as demonstrating that the Republicans were not only Red rapists, but incompetent and cowardly.

With no swift victory, and no end of the war in sight; with the final outcome becoming, indeed, dubious; the tone of Conservative propaganda in Britain changed significantly. Emphasis was now laid on the theme that the bloody schemozzle beyond the Pyrenees was not Britain's affair. It was insisted, as was insisted still more shrilly by Chamberlain a couple of years later in reference to Czechoslovakia, that Spain was a far-away country of

which we knew little. And, as the conflict internationalized itself, and the roles of Mussolini and Hitler could not be concealed, another card—the card played so successfully against the League and ideas of collective security—was used again: the Fear card. It was used, often effectively, to turn the tables on those who, particularly in the political entourage of Winston Churchill, pointed to the dangers of international war inherent in the successes of the Fascist and Nazi dictators. This, it was declared by government spokesmen, so far from calling for some counter-activity by Britain, demanded the opposite, otherwise war could result. 'Keep Britain out' was the slogan. Once again it was possible to brigade, along with the genuine and high-principled pacifists, everyone for whom war had become the ultimate, all-embracing evil and disaster; the end, as they used to say in those days, 'of everything'. That belief deeply tinged the whole thinking of the thirties; so deeply that many people by their sincere abhorrence of the First World War and its consequences facilitated the outbreak of the Second World War. And to them, of course, were added all those affected by very natural funk. The Government and its spokesmen desisted from attempts to excite all such people: instead it exhorted them in suitably varied tones to keep their noses clean, and their hair on; to eschew involvement in foreign quarrels; to cultivate, more assiduously than ever, their gardens.

And the gardens, not only literally but figuratively speaking, were in fact becoming a little bit better worth tending.

Below the 'poverty line'—unemployed and families. Inset: unemployed demonstration; below: bitter message on coffin lid

Busy in the garden

At this point it is essential to bear in mind the remarks of John Hilton, Professor of Industrial Relations at Cambridge, in his Halley Stewart lectures of 1938. He was probably the best-informed man alive on the conditions and customs of the mass of British people at the time. He stated: 'I have been coming to the view since I began these investigations that as regards social conditions and business practice affecting the common people of this land of ours, no one knows anything about anything that really matters.'

Still, a few facts about life in the British garden during the late thirties are known, though how and in what sense they 'really mattered' must remain undecided.

Between 1930 and 1936 consumer prices had fallen by 7.4 per cent. The average of real wages had, in the same period, risen by 5.7 per cent. And the new buying power thus available was above that average in the newer industries and trades, remaining below it in the older industries.

Even so, two-thirds of wage earners and salary earners were getting less than £2 10s. weekly. That was eleven and a half million people. Eight million families had no savings; most of them lived on some form of credit, including hire-purchase which more or less precariously financed the sale of around two-thirds of all mass-produced goods.

Numerous social studies showed that despite the little lift in the real wage, despite the housing boom, huge sections of the working class lived somewhere on or just below the poverty line. The most reliable guide to the situation was provided by the Seebohm Rowntree survey of York in 1935-6. Rowntree took as his basic standard of measurement the figure of £2 3s. 6d. per week as the minimum required for the satisfaction of the minimum human needs of a man, his wife, and three children. (That was for needs other than rent.) That was the income line below which what was defined as absolute poverty began.

On this basis, Rowntree (most compactly summarized by Professor Mowat):

'found 31.1 per cent of the working population, and 17.7 per cent of the total population, to be below the poverty line (14.2 per cent of the working population being in abject poverty with an income of under £1 3s. 6d. per week). Over half the working class children under one were under the poverty line, and this same proportion of working-class people would, so Rowntree calculated, be in poverty at some time in their lives—usually twice, in childhood and old age, and a quarter at a third period in middle life (25-44) when the burden of a family was greatest . . . The causes of poverty were not difficult to find. Of the people in York below the poverty line, 28.6 per cent were doomed because the head of the family was unemployed; but another 32.8 per cent were doomed although the head of the family was in regular employment, but at earnings inadequate for the family's needs . . . 14.7 per cent were poor because old: the poverty of old age was found to be more acute than that due to any other single cause.'

A survey made in Bristol, a city rated as prosperous, 'ascribed unemployment as the cause of poverty in 32.1 per cent of the families in poverty, insufficient wages as the cause in 21.5 per cent of the families, old age in 15 per cent, sickness in 9 per cent. The first two causes explained 80 per cent

186

of all the poverty affecting children. The size of a family contributed to its poverty: 24.8 per cent of all families with three children were in poverty, 51.5 per cent of all families with four children or more.'

For a majority of people, the business of simply keeping above the level of destitution was a sufficiently absorbing preoccupation.

There were gayer aspects of the garden, though the average family had to think harshly before deciding which to spend cash on.

Clergymen, social critics, and foreign observers viewed with undisguised apprehension the fact that the British, always noted for gambling, now gambled more than ever. By 1936 around six million were paying an average of three shillings weekly for their entries to the football pools. The promoters handled £800,000 weekly. People anxious to cool the political temperature often wrote or said, with quiet satisfaction, that the British Working Man was a lot more interested in the football results than in the result of the Battle of Guadalajara. And the tone of regular and pervasive assertions to this effect was such that absorption in the football pools was presented as essentially a sensible, almost virtuous, and particularly British state.

In the thinking of these enthusiasts there seemed to be no room for many hundreds of thousands of people who paid their three shillings, filled in their forecasts, and were still interested in the Battle of Guadalajara.

In the office of every mass-circulation newspaper there was a conscious or subconscious belief that cultivating the garden, doing the pools, packing the stands at football games, pinning up film stars, spending Saturday night at the Palais (a new Palais de Danse was opening somewhere almost every week, and doing good and cheerful business), were all necessarily de-politicizing activities. Every journalistic supporter of the Establishment held that belief more or less fervently. And it was by instinct rather than direction from on high that editors and sub-editors felt uneasy when the war news was so sensational that it must be allowed to exert fully its up-setting, politicizing influence.

Breezes of Skegness

Under an Act of 1938, eleven million workers became entitled to one week's holiday with pay in each year. This was seen as a large improvement in the condition of the working class. And, judged by the factors of Comparison and Expectation it was. There had been no paid holiday for most. Now there was a week. The arguments showing that to be desirable might some day be successfully used to extend the paid holidays. The first Butlin Camp had, foresightedly, already opened in 1937. Much fun was had there. It was also in heavy demand by sociologists as an example, and indeed a symbol, of the heart's desire of the working class and its gradual satisfaction. Inevitably many words were written to the effect that the British Working Man was more interested in taking his family to Skegness than in the fate of Madrid. It was taken for granted by such writers and speakers that a week at Butlin's was depoliticizing in tendency; more so than an afternoon's spree on the Brighton *Skylark*.

The supposed consequences of the general introduction of holidays with

The British on holiday: beauty competition at holiday camp;
inset: typical diversions

pay involved the kind of miscalculations which, as a result of the huge gap in Britain between the educational and social conditioning of the governing class and the rest, were so regularly made, then and since. The workers, as could be clearly seen, had 'never had it so good'. In the sixties it was widely assumed by the governing class that having the money for a down payment on a television set, with the prospect of a colour-set looming up, was enough to stiffen the conservatism of millions; enough, certainly, to distract attention from upsetting political controversy. In the thirties every new amenity or distraction available to members of the working class was similarly assessed. Many assessors, not much in touch with working-class opinion, were sincerely surprised to hear that many workers could not see anything much more amazing in the fact of the worker drawing pay during his holiday than the fact of a Treasury official or a company director doing the same thing. It need not inhibit him from reflecting, as he romped on the sands at Skegness, that the Treasury officials and the company directors and Generalbloodylissimo Franco were all a lot of bastards.

It was necessarily the policy of the Government to maintain and so far as possible extend apathy and indifference concerning the war in Spain.

For achievement of this purpose there were many favourable factors in the situation. There was the basic fact that the greater part of so many people's time and attention was taken up with remaining above the poverty line. There were the widened interests and distractions offered by the rise in real wages. There was the fact that the housing boom, though it had not achieved all the ideological advantages foreshadowed by the *Daily Telegraph*, had, to an undefinable but certainly important extent, somewhat fostered an inward-looking, family-oriented view of life. There was the low level of general education, and in particular the primitive level of political education in England—rather lower than in Scotland and in Wales.

Yet the task of preserving indifference was, as government supporters often admitted, unexpectedly difficult. They had not foreseen the depth, intensity and durability of the popular indignation aroused by the Right's attack on the Spanish Republic; the degree to which not only the working class but sections of the middle class would identify their interests as workers and citizens of a democracy with those of the Spanish Republicans; the alarm and disgust with which even Conservatives and members of the upper class viewed the advantages accruing to Hitler and Mussolini. The passion roused in the country was certainly as intense, and far more enduring than was the brief, furious storm over the Hoare-Laval Pact on Abyssinia.

But the analogy immediately discloses the extent of the Government's success during the years of the Spanish War. In 1935, the Foreign Secretary had been forced to resign, and the Prime Minister reduced to humiliating apologies. The policy of the Government towards the Spanish Republic was of far greater import and significance than its behaviour in 1935. Yet during the Spanish War no member of the Government was forced to resign on the charge of having aided and abetted aggression, assisted in the destruction of a democratic regime, impaired British security in the Mediterranean and so on and so forth. On the contrary, the only change occurring on the high echelons of the Establishment was the political castration of the vigorously

190

anti-German Sir Robert Vansittart. He was removed from his position as permanent head of the Foreign Office to a position of distinguished impotence as Diplomatic Adviser to the Government which had repeatedly made clear that it had no intention of taking any advice he might give it.

Telling the people
The success of the Government, which baffled many native and foreign observers, was in part due to its own ability and political understanding. Its members, and their supporters at all levels of the national press, displayed —after their first ill-advised attempt to excite terror at the spectre of a Red menace in Spain—a clear intuitive understanding of the direction their propaganda must take if it were to be successful. They played with skill upon ignorance, insular traditions, and fear. Their propaganda was flexible, and often subtle: far more subtle than any the French Government was able to develop. Charged with the 'betrayal of democracy' they would state first that there was difficulty in determining to what precise extent the constitutional position in Spain could be described, in the strict British sense of the word, as wholly democratic. It would even, on occasion, audaciously use allegations by the Spanish Trotskyists and their British sympathizers that, under Communist influence, the Army of the Republic had become unduly disciplinarian, authoritarian; not a truly democratic people's army such as would properly engage the sympathy of democratically-minded Britons.

Alternatively, and sometimes simultaneously, the violence offered to democracy in Spain could be much deplored; one could wish that it were not happening; but was it, one must ask oneself, any business of British people? Was it not in the end more sensible to let ill alone and Spaniards be Spaniards?

But then it was charged that the Spaniards were not being allowed to be Spaniards and settle matters among themselves. If it had been so, the rebellion would by now have collapsed for lack of mass support and hence of manpower. It was surviving because of the arms supplied by Germany and Italy, and the resultant strengthening of the economic and strategic position of the dictators was a menace to Britain itself. To such charges of betrayal and cowardice the Government replied by a straightforward appeal to the latent cowardice of everyone within hearing: to thwart the dictators was to risk war. Did the people of Birmingham wish to expose themselves and their children to the fate of the women and children of Madrid, horribly recorded by the newsreels? Better keep Britain out.

Labour's ban
Indispensable, however, for the Government's success was the policy of the Labour Party. This was the factor which created the strange contrast between the successful public agitation against the Hoare-Laval Pact, and the failure of the deeper and more sustained opposition to the Government's policy towards Spain.

The Labour Party leadership had joined wholeheartedly in the short but effectively sharp attack on Sir Samuel Hoare. In so doing it took its place in a long line of attack extending from the Communist Party to the Liberals and including many battalions of Conservative voters. In the ranks, too, were a then unprecedented number of the normally indifferent or apathetic. The Government was forced into disorderly retreat.

For the attack upon the Government the same elements were available; in one respect they were far more numerous, for as the war progressed and its consequences became more evident, the number of citizens jolted out of apathy and indifference into angry resistance was enormously greater. But in this case the agitation was visibly led by the Communists. In partiticular, the Communists were responsible for the creation and leadership of the British contingents of the International Brigade. The volunteers for the Brigades personified and dramatized powerful emotions and instincts among masses of ordinarily unpolitical British people; they evoked a response, most unwelcome and alarming to the Government. It was a demonstration that the cynicism and apathy supposedly so characteristic of the thirties were not universally pervasive.

The popular offensive against the Government was baulked by the Labour Party. In the first crucial months of the war, the Labour Party positively supported the Government's policy. By October, it had changed position and now officially opposed the Government on the Spanish question. But the change itself, given the state of parties in the House of Commons, could have only minimal effect. The potential danger to the Government lay in the possible mobilization of a united public opinion such as had overthrown Sir Samuel Hoare.

The danger was visible. Non-politicals were being stirred. The silence of the Silent Majority was being broken. Tory M.P.s were joining with Independents, left-wing men, and Communists in the attack. Important groups within the Labour Party itself—notably the Socialist League led by Sir Stafford Cripps—were collaborating fully with the Communists in what was called the Unity Campaign.

The Labour Party leadership reacted to the Unity Campaign, and all other enterprises of the kind, exactly as it had reacted to the campaign on behalf of the unemployed. Then, it had issued what was generally known as the Black Circular, prohibiting association with the Communist Party or with a list of organizations scheduled as being inspired, controlled, or directed by the Communist Party. Now it issued a parallel circular entitled 'Party Loyalty'. It expelled the Socialist League from the Labour Party, and threatened similar action against any other groups that might co-operate with the Communists. The Socialist League thereupon dissolved itself, with intent thus to leave its members free to campaign as individuals on behalf of the Republic without thereby risking expulsion from the Labour Party. The Labour Party then announced that it would expel individuals detected publicly doing that thing.

Confusion on the Left

Although the Labour Party ban was often defied or evaded, it was on the whole successful in preventing united effort to defeat government policies, or in disrupting unity where it had existed at the outset.

It could not in the nature of things prevent Liberals, left-wing Conservatives, or Churchillian Conservatives co-operating with the Communists. But upon the crucial mass of the normally unpolitical it had a chilling, confusing, and dismaying effect. To many of them the Communists appeared as the first politicals they had encountered who were demonstrably prepared to go off and get killed in foreign parts for the sake of the cause they said they believed in. Now the leaders of the largest opposition party in the country indicated that it could be polluting to touch such people even with a barge-pole. It was in the highest degree discouraging to find the movement these non-politicals sought to associate with riven by what to them was a secondary and viciously disruptive vendetta. It tended to confirm them in their previous, comfortable opinion that politics was a dirty game, and sensible, sincere people had best keep out of it.

The state of mind thus produced in the country was in a high degree satisfactory to the Government. In terms of the immediate political situation, a threatening popular offensive against it had been dispersed, and its impact dulled.

In the longer view, the defeat of the mass opposition in Britain and of the Republic in Spain had secured results which promised well for the successful pursuit of the Government's basic policy. The activists of all parties had been defeated and politically discredited, in the sense that political failure can always be represented as discreditable to the defeated. They had declared it possible to mobilize forces sufficient to 'throw the rascals out'. For no matter what reason, it had not been possible. The people who had declared it possible were mistaken; they had misled those who had believed them. They were unsound.

The Labour Party, while retaining the traditional loyalty of its least militant members, had lost credibility as a Party prepared sincerely to lead the working class, and large sections of the middle class, in a joint effort to overthrow the Government which, officially, it opposed.

Most reassuring of all was the extension and intensifying of frustration, cynicism and *je m'en foutisme*. No danger was to be apprehended from those whose hearts sang with the songster 'I'll play my ukulele as the ship goes down'. Still less was to be feared from those who no longer bothered to inquire whether the ship was likely to sink or not, because they knew what the captain's answer would be, and had abandoned any thought of taking over the bridge or the engine-room. With the course shaped for Munich, the fewer questions asked by the crew and the lubberly passengers, the better.

10 The Politics of Sex

1937 *Nobody saved the King*

As the little moment between the crisis and the catastrophe slipped by, the tragedy of Europe was briefly interrupted by a farce from which, brief though it was, no element of ripe sex appeal, high-life scandal, tear-jerking sentimentality, and grotesque religiosity had been omitted. It was as though some planetary producer, having at his disposal a glittering cast of dedicated stars, including many renowned character actors and clowns, had seized the chance to put on a show in which, as in some gigantic spoof and send-up of a traditional morality play, or *Antony and Cleopatra* enacted on the dodgems, the Heart and Soul of Britain, together with a never-before-seen medley of Beliefs and Traditions, Manners and Customs, Ideas—some guaranteed nearly new, others exhumed from the graveyard at great expense and reanimated for the duration of this run only—Native Superstitions and Taboos, Thoughts high and low, would present to the watching world a unique Spectacle of Britain, almost certainly for the last time on any stage.

The bare bones of the plot hardly do justice to the lavish and illuminating production, which had—as many enthusiastic critics pointed out—its valuably educational side, too.

King George V died on 20 January 1936, and was succeeded by Edward VIII, then forty-one years of age. As Prince of Wales, he had been cast, by the press, as Prince Charming. He was ritually said to have won all hearts by his democratic manner. And he did have a genuine popularity, with jocose undertones. For public purposes he remained a boyish young man well into middle age, getting sometimes a little older, sometimes a little younger, according to what his duties required him to be chatting, talking, or pronouncing about.

The principal boy

By the generality of the grandees, the heavy swells of the plutocratic aristocracy and their entourage, he was jibed at, bitten in the back and derided. He reciprocated their feelings with a greater candour than they as a rule cared to put on their social record. The marked Cockney accent acquired from his old nurse in which he uttered his blunt comments on what he saw as a museum of antiques was sneeringly parodied. It was said that his family had been so glad to rid itself at last of the heavy German accent of Edward VII that they had never bothered about differences between English accents.

Papa-Doc

The heavy swells merged at many points with the more strictly political Establishment. The politicals also distrusted the new King. He did not, they noticed, seem to know his place. His place, ideally, was one where he would stand ever ready to envelop, when called upon so to do, the policies of the Conservative Government and the Higher Management in the prestige, the emotional appeal, and the supposed political partiality of the Monarchy. He could not, at forty-one, be expected to offer those sage counsels for which his father had been renowned. But it was announced that he would mature with age and above all, with growing realization of the immense responsibilities attaching to his position.

196

Previous pages: All for love and a crown well lost—Edward and his bride in Paris after the Abdication

In the meantime Baldwin, Prime Minister, by general accord second to none in his mastery of political intrigue, guile, disguise, bluff and chicanery, offered his services as mentor, family physician and a substitute father.

But there was scant time for sage counsels to hasten maturity. The Establishment was sensitively aware that the foundations of its structure were precarious. It was beset by fears of incalculable social earthquakes. The very silence of the Silent Majority, though welcome, could be menacing. Outbursts such as had defeated the attack on the unemployed early in 1935, and compelled the resignation of Sir Samuel Hoare, caused apprehension as to what the so-called 'secret people' might be silently thinking. The invention of the Silver Jubilee had been an admission that the Government, despite its seemingly comfortable parliamentary majority, felt the need— usually not felt except in times of obvious emergency—to play the royal card for all it might be worth.

In such a situation it was more than ever desirable that the King should know his place; should not speak before being asked to do so. With these requirements the middle-aged young man on the throne was not fitted to comply. His faulty education, his normal state of extreme nervous tension, the natural repugnance occasioned by so many of the heavy swells and by the gnarled and slippery politicals, and an unregulated human sympathy with those he saw to be hard done by, combined to produce occasional outbursts and interventions of an upsetting character. At one point he fatally roused the rage and fear of the Establishment by visiting South Wales, observing the condition of the workers there, and declaring that something had to be done about it and that he would see that it was done.

Contradictorily, he also felt, and expressed, strong sympathies for Hitler and the Nazi Party. British Leftists, whose eyes had dimmed with tears of pleased excitement when the King spoke up for the South Wales workers, found his pro-Nazism paradoxical. It was not so. In the light of his class background, his wretched education and his family connections, his attitude was no more unnatural than that of his princely German relatives, who brought him good news from the New Germany.

The Government, unwavering in its support and encouragement of Hitler, was none the less annoyed and embarrassed by the blatant pro-Nazism of the King. It was indiscreet at a time when discretion in the matter was most desirable. And over and above that, it was another instance of Edward speaking out of turn. It was not so much what he said that was objectionable but the fact that he said it at all without prior consultation with the father substitute.

As early as Whitsun 1935, Channon had noted in his Diary:

'Much gossip about the Prince of Wales' alleged Nazi leanings; he is alleged to have been influenced by Emerald [Lady Cunard] (who is rather *éprise* with Ribbentrop) through Mrs Simpson. The Coopers are furious, being fanatically pro-French and anti-German. He [the Prince] has just made an extraordinary speech to the British Legion, advocating friendship with Germany; it is only a gesture, but a gesture that may be taken seriously in Germany and elsewhere. If only the Chancelleries of Europe knew that his speech was the result of Emerald Cunard's intrigues, themselves inspired by Herr Ribbentrop's dimple!'

Mr and Mrs S.

Enter the Loved One. Mrs Wallis Simpson. The divorcée from Baltimore, in her richly rewarding role as An American Lady at the Court of St James's, seemed the result of an improbable but brilliant collaboration between Somerset Maugham at the time he wrote *Our Betters*, P. G. Wodehouse, and Henry James. Some critics thought the character of her husband, Ernest, too crude a caricature of the *mari complaisant*. But his almost silent appearances on the stage raised many a laugh. One may mention the brief scene where the King, Wallis Simpson, Ernest, Winston Churchill, and the Channons are found standing after dinner at Lady Cunard's. The men are dressed like old-fashioned waiters with white ties but black waistcoats; this is correct because the Court is still in mourning for George V.

The King is talking to the Loved One. 'There was a pause . . .when the King wanted some more Vichy water and couldn't find the bottle-opener. Wallis said, "Ask Ernest for his." "Ernest" apparently wears one on his key chain, so the Royal bottle was finally opened.'

Prince Charming had had a normal number of mistresses: sufficient certainly to calm the nervous spasms of those who feared he might cause embarrassment by preferring homosexuality like so many of his Oxford contemporaries and his German cousins. As things were, it was assumed that at least his sex life was not going to prove troublesome. Little did they know.

Channon, however, referring to an earlier mistress notes that 'it was ——

Righteousness: Mr Stanley Baldwin

The popular prince: with Lloyd George in W

who first "modernized" and Americanized him, making him over-democratic, casual and a little common. Hers is the true blame for the drama.'

Himself American by birth, and married to a Guinness, Channon was well-placed to detect signs of 'Americanization', and to gauge their effects upon the British upper sort. His highly observant eye unerringly discerned the social uneasiness, and the serious political hostility certain to be aroused by indications of 'over-democratization'.

The political hostility, resulting in treasonable thoughts and mutters, was evident for months before Love, Sex, Moral Indignation and the Old Time Religion were suddenly given the centre of the stage, bringing the audience to its feet in a brief frenzy of cheers and cat-calls.

The government men and the heavy swells resented the fact that the King had many friends who seemed a little independent, and more than a little contemptuous of themselves. The coterie down at Fort Belvedere was thought to be endlessly up to something: probably up to no good. Many of the friends could reasonably be described by the censorious as riff-raff. There was also Bedaux, another stock character: American tycoon and a snob, natural admirer of Hitler, and famous as inventor of the Bedaux System for regulation of industrial work. It was declared to be a big forward step in 'modernization', and as such appealed to the King. More specifically, it was a time-and-motion device to produce more work for the same pay, and as such often resisted in England by strike action.

Ernest Simpson, the ex-husband

Lord Louis

While affecting to be shocked by the riff-raff, the King's most serious enemies were more truly discommoded by what they considered the alarming, even sinister, presence at Fort Belvedere of Lord Louis Mountbatten. They had grounds for uneasiness. Mountbatten was among the few genuinely influential men at the top of the Establishment who seemed to understand the true significance of the Government's German policy and to be ready to point out its consequences. He was probably the only person known to the King, the Prime Minister, and the Heavy Swells who was familiar with the writings of Marx. Being of what was called—approvingly or opprobriously— a 'dashing' disposition, he could understand the King's emotional extravagances, and his 'modernized' tendencies. Of central European ancestry, born a Battenberg, he could view the English scene with unusual clarity. His combination of earnestness with political flair and agility rendered him formidable and horrifying to those who rightly feared that he was giving dangerous coherence to the King's bad thoughts about Papa-Doc, and inspiring new ideas inimical to Hitler. Furthermore his wife was beautiful, intelligent, well-educated, of Jewish extraction, with socialist sympathies, and a millionairess. The government men, the strategists at *The Times*, and the dimpled Ribbentrop unquestionably had cause for alarm.

A whispering campaign against the Fort Belvedere lot was set in motion. Unbridled licence about summed up what went on there: licence often tantamount to orgy. The King and Mrs Simpson were reported seen pruning roses in their pyjamas. There were boos from the dress-circle for a sketch in which an emissary of Papa-Doc arrived to find the King, Mrs Simpson, loose Society women, Lord Louis and others frivolling round a table littered with the most secret of official documents, these documents themselves being scandalously defiled and ringed with the moist marks of cocktail glasses.

Early in the year Channon and others had still assumed that sooner or later the King would 'drop' Mrs Simpson as he had other mistresses. And inasmuch as they were sensibly married women their association with the Prince of Wales had presented no political dangers.

But on 10 May 'Emerald came to lunch and regaled us with stories of the royal racket. It appears that the King is Mrs Simpson's absolute slave, and will go nowhere where she is not invited, and she, clever woman, with her high-pitched voice, chic clothes, moles and sense of humour is behaving well. She encourages the King to meet people of importance and to be polite: above all, she makes him happy. The Empire ought to be grateful.'

The enslavement caused the King to cock a notable snook at his critics by going cruising that summer with Mrs Simpson on the yacht *Nahlin*.

For the world's press outside Britain that trip under azure Adriatic skies, with sun-kissed beaches and beamy moons, was a bonanza, a peacheroo with trimmings, a gift on a plate and enthusiastically accepted as such. Love, *l'amour* and royal *Liebe* oozed across headlines from San Francisco to Berlin. The girl from Maryland had it made. Her mother complained that 'the way they're playing up this Royalty-commoner angle, you'd think our family came from the wrong side of the tracks or something.'

200

Instructive interlude, illustrating British mass media's attitude to the public, free communication, etc.

While the politically fateful doings of the British monarch were being chronicled, examined, assessed in the newspapers of half the world, it was not thought proper for British newspapers or radio to allude to the matter. Nor was the explosive news allowed to be imported. At the offices of, for example, Rolls Ltd, distributors of *Time* magazine, the staff was kept busy with scissors snipping out of each issue paragraphs, columns or pictures referring to the King and Mrs Simpson, before the issue could reach the bookstalls. Informed that they might be infringing laws prohibiting the sale as new of damaged products, all concerned took refuge behind the libel laws. The national newspapers generally excused their behaviour on the same ground. It was a notable example of the use, particularly in the thirties, of the libel laws as a form of disguised censorship. Further pressed on the matter, the editors spoke of their 'heavy responsibility' in so delicate an affair of State. Again, there was no need for censorship from above: editorial instinct could be trusted to avoid any rocking of the boat until the proper time.

Agonized appraisal

Back to Downing Street where we find Papa-Doc and associates facing dramatic dilemma: They now know (i) that Mrs Simpson is due to get her divorce from Ernest at a Court at Ipswich on 27 October and (ii) that, incredible though it may seem, the King seriously proposes to marry her after six months when the decree *nisi* becomes absolute.

If the King marries an American, twice divorced, so and so many million people—but the question is How many million? and there is no way of taking a poll in advance—are going to be outraged on more or less religious grounds. The traditionalists, everyone who deplores the trend to what was later called 'permissiveness', are going to be profoundly, dangerously shocked. Dangerously, because these are the very people, backbone of the Conservative Party, if not of the Nation as a Whole, who have to be depended on to keep the Establishment structure from crumbling. Dangerously, too, because it will produce a potentially fatal division between these conservatory forces and the Monarchy, of which the image is equally indispensable to the Establishment. Such a division has not been allowed to appear since the beginning of the second half of Queen Victoria's reign, when, for a brief, vigorously forgotten period, overt hostility to the Monarch, and even Republican tendencies, became respectable in England.

On the other hand, equally grisly spectres loom. Suppose we tell the King 'No'. If he caves in, well and good. But suppose he cocks a snook at us? Tells us in some common and vulgar phrase to put our governmental ban where the monkey put the nuts? There follows a confrontation between us and the Monarch. We may win, and topple the King. But in so doing are we not going to be compelled to topple with him a whole mystique of monarchy, and in destroying this contumacious King destroy the occult, talismanic power of the very abracadabra whose potency we acknowledged when we laid on the Silver Jubilee?

Baldwin, whose growing senility has been much remarked in the House of

Commons, votes to risk the confrontation. Most of his colleagues cannot believe that the King will do otherwise than back down. 'Men have died from time to time, and worms have eaten them, but not for love.' Quite frankly, which of those present would sacrifice power, vast popular acclaim, and enormous wealth for *love*? Neville Chamberlain? Viscount Swinton? Sam Hoare, who, after public humiliation as Foreign Secretary, had successfully devoted himself to creeping back to the Cabinet as First Lord of the Admiralty? Leslie Hore-Belisha, indefatigable political climber? After all, this Simpson woman's not the only girl in the world. Other fish in the sea. And if, as 'Chips' Channon keeps telling people, the King's thoroughly 'uxorious' is there a reason he can't marry some nice English girl, virginal for all anyone knows to the contrary, like Lady Roe or the Honourable Uxoria Roe, or even a properly vetted common if he insists?

The Ipswich Court granted the decree *nisi*. The British press recorded it with no more prominence than it would have given the matter had Ernest been any other well-known stockbroker whose marriage had gone on the rocks. The Americans thought it more newsworthy. 'King's Moll Reno'd in Wolsey's Home Town' was one of the headlines used.

Like many others, 'Chips' Channon was 'appalled' by the impression the King's behaviour was making upon informed people. He told Prince Paul, Regent of Yugoslavia, that 'the House of Commons openly talked of abdication etc. We discussed all the eligible princesses in Europe, and tried to agree on one whose charms we could urge on the King, but we could find none; perhaps he had better marry Wallis and be done with it.'

Factor X

Ministers equally anxious to urge upon the King any one of bevies of well-born beauties, were dismayed to learn that among the multiple ingredients of the King's deep love of Mrs Simpson, there might be a factor which none of them had reckoned with in their crude calculations: a factor which British inhibitions in the thirties made almost impossible to discuss in public—or even appear to take seriously. Romantic love was bad enough in the circumstances: romantic plus passionately sexual love and fixation was still less seemly.

Some of the closest friends and well-wishers of the King and Mrs Simpson asserted at the time that beyond all the sentimental and sometimes malicious talk of infatuation and obsession was a central, simple and perfectly normal physical fact. They said that Mrs Simpson happened to be the first woman with whom the King could obtain complete normal sexual satisfaction. Owing to the taboos of the period it was impossible for this central fact to be discussed or even mentioned in the newspapers without a resultant falsification of the whole situation. But reports of this fact did percolate to the mass of the people and brought to the King much sympathy from honest people. Anyone who was round the factory floors at that time can testify that this picture of the situation evoked much warmhearted understanding among working people.

To the under-sexed, to the sexually undemanding, and to those whose sex experience was limited to an extent more normal in the thirties than in

202

permissive later years, the importance of this factor was unintelligible. As a result they saw the King's feelings towards Mrs Simpson as being in some way unhealthy or abnormal: they often spoke as though he were afflicted by some kind of lunacy; whereas, in reality, nothing could have been, in terms of satisfactory happiness, more solidly, earthily sensible.

It was noticeable that as the King's problems became, despite the newspaper silence, public property, this factor was widely understood, and discussed with jovial approval and enjoyment by 'the man in the street'—more particularly by men and women in the factories and working class pubs and clubs where inhibitions were in general less operative than among middle class citizens. The King, it was felt, had struck lucky. And you couldn't, they said, blame a man for hanging on to that sort of good fortune. The graffiti on lavatory walls which sought to demonstrate the factor in question with clinical clarity were deemed offensive by the prim, but in reality expressed for the most part an exuberant human bonhomie, being sometimes accompanied by captions testifying to respectful envy.

Similarly, those critics who were either ignorant of this aspect of the facts of life, or censorious of anyone treating them as of more than trivial importance, displayed what later would be called male chauvinism, except that it was displayed as often by women as by men. They concocted an image of Mrs Simpson as a kind of evil Circe, a sex object diverting the King from the path of moral rectitude and duty.

In his dealings with the King before the Simpson divorce, Baldwin, whose faculties, despite an enforced rest cure during the summer, were duller than they used to be, seemed under the impression that what he had to deal with was essentially an impetuous, though unaccountably enduring, whim: a phase. If the commonsensical arguments—power, grandeur, popular esteem, and money—could be put simply and clearly by an older man who wished him well, the King would see reason. There would be no crisis. And, concurrently, the King would have made most valuable acknowledgement of his essential subservience to Baldwin and the Government.

Dear Sir . . . or else

But on 16 November, we see Papa-Doc in sterner mood. A sombre figure at raffish Fort Belvedere, he now threatens and seeks to extort. He denounces what he describes as the King's 'association' with the foreign divorcée. He demands that the King sign (now Baldwin is solicitor with document) a declaration binding himself never, never to marry her. If he refuses? The Cabinet will resign. Baldwin reports the interview in the strictest confidence to each individual member of the Cabinet: it is not a matter which can yet be the subject of a formal Cabinet meeting.

As had been safe to assume, members of the Cabinet hurry off to tell the news, in confidence, to their intimates. Hore-Belisha reports to Lady Cunard. Lady Cunard reports to Channon. Who wrote it down on the 22nd:

'Baldwin gave the King three weeks in which to make up his mind. The King is alleged to have been defiant. He intends, so Belisha believes, to speed up the Simpson divorce, and in about three weeks to marry her in the Chapel at Windsor. Immediately afterwards he will broadcast to the nation that he has devoted his life and his energies

LET THE KING
KNOW YOU ARE
WITH HIM

MRS. SIMPSO
IN FRANC
EVENING
STANDAR

Romance of the century? The lovers in France (top left) and Germany (top right). The loyal British public (far left) were bombarded with headlines (left), unfolding a never-to-be repeated, never-to-be forgotten drama in high places

to the welfare of the Commonwealth and that it is his intention to continue to do so, and that he, in marrying the woman of his choice, has only claimed the privilege allowed even to the very humblest of his subjects. A bombshell; Leslie thinks that the Conservatives will resign and that the premiership will be hawked about to anyone who will take it, and that Winston Churchill will summon a party meeting, create a new party, and rule the country! . . . I tried to dampen Emerald's excitement by telling her that Leslie Belisha is an imaginative Jew, that his mentality is a Hollywood one, but she believes it—and so, in a way, do I. The King is insane about Wallis, insane.'

As early as 14 October, at least one British publication, *The Week*, had reported plans to explode 'a social bomb under the King. The ideal method envisaged by those planting the bomb would be for a reference to be made from the pulpit to "the very different standards of conduct set to his subjects by the late King".'

On 1 December, Blunt, Bishop of Bradford, addressed a diocesan conference with remarks on those lines. Everyone concerned pretended that the sermon had come as a complete surprise: was simply an unplanned outburst of indignant Christian feeling.

The bomb had the explosive effect 'envisaged'. The British public was at length informed that its King and its Prime Minister were battling out the last round of a political championship fight, and a knockout could be expected any day.

For eight days the citizens of the democracy had the opportunity to examine and express their wishes in relation to what was now billed as the gravest constitutional crisis imaginable. Characteristically, it was not thought at all necessary to explain to the citizens why they, as distinct from the citizens of the United States and of Europe, had been kept in the dark for so long. They must simply face up to the fact that as of now the future of the Monarchy was at stake, the Constitution was at stake, Christian principles were at stake, the Moral Fabric of Society was at stake. Like candidates at some grotesquely devised examination, they were told to 'discuss this question giving reasons for your conclusions: you have the full time—more than a week'. The resultant performance was a kind of Black Jubilee, a Festival of Britain organized by Barnum.

The great charade

To the commonsense of the man in the street it was apparent that nothing he could say or do could appreciably alter the course of events. That was no reason why he should not noisily enjoy the gaudy game of make-believe. Indeed, it was a good reason for enjoying it to the full: no serious responsibility was involved. British democracy, in its titular role as a *roi fainéant* trundled in a public procession while the Mayors of the Palace settled serious business elsewhere, made the most of the brief and breezy outing. Numerous exhibition bouts were staged, Love versus Duty being among the most popular. Lord Beaverbrook, with the *Daily Express* and Lord Rothermere with the *Daily Mail* were on Love's side. Dawson at *The Times* declared that 'if private inclination were to come into open conflict with public duty' inclination must not 'be allowed to prevail'. The religious note was emphatically struck. It was noted and used in evidence against him that for weeks past

206

there had been no mention in the Court Circular of the King attending Divine Service on Sunday, either in Windsor Chapel or anywhere else. Not only Church-goers and Chapel-goers, but thousands who customarily spent Sunday morning in bed with the *News of the World* could at once see that this set a bad example to other people. Regular church attendance, they opined, was a desirable discipline for people inclined to question the established order of things.

The religious controversy, enthusiastically joined by people whose indifference to what they called 'organized religion' was profound, instantly broadened into a lively round in the naturally interminable battle between the defenders of what they believed to be the traditional English way of life, meaning in particular sex life, and the early standard bearers of permissiveness. Indeed a high percentage of argumentative verbiage on this topic employed during the sixties and seventies is found to have been already expertly handled by both sides in the heat of *l'affaire* Simpson.

Bitter sex antagonisms and jealousies found release in disputes which might have been considered stale or vulgar had they not centred around the Highest in the Land. Did the King imagine that he could treat a loving woman as the plaything of an idle hour, casting her aside like a soiled glove in a cowardly attempt to save his royal bacon? On the other hand, did this American adventuress, having figured in two divorces, with doubtless a lot more to them than met the eye, think she could successfully thrust aside decent, unmarried English girls, and nobble our ex-Prince Charming? What sort of home life was she likely to provide for an Englishman?

Padding busily back and forth along the corridors of power, innumerable Walter Mittys gave a fillip to their egos by making believe that they were effectively influencing events. Finding it intolerable to believe that in such a situation they were playing no significant role, they preferred to believe that whatever role they chose to play must be significant.

On the political front, all parties tried to make a quick appraisal of how best to use the crisis for their own purposes. The Communists, mistaking the public mood, thought the general vague sympathy for the King could be usefully canalized as a force against Baldwin and the Government. To the objection that the King was a crypto-Nazi, or as near it as made no difference, they replied—in a manner too dryly logical to have much persuasive appeal— that the pro-German policy of the Government was more dangerous than the erratic inclinations of the King; that the King without the Government would be politically impotent; and that therefore, putting first things first, God Save the King must be the slogan. In these calculations they, like many others, mistook the public excitement over the spectacle for a sign that truly deep political emotions had been aroused. The public did not, for all the noise it made, take the entire dust-up quite seriously. Too many of the issues seemed like props carted in by stage hands from some other production in some other century. Alike to the politically alert and the cynical or apathetic, the performance of politicians, prelates, newspaper owners and pundits around Fort Belvedere, seemed unreal, or at least largely irrelevant to the realities of life and labour. Huge numbers of people would have sincerely declared at the height of the crisis that they were of course taking it seriously. The assertion was almost immediately disproved. Controversies which the mass of the people take seriously last longer than the inside of a fortnight before almost everyone agrees to call it a day. And it was noted that even before that brief period was over, a significant number of people who at the outset had been more or less vaguely in favour of the King, turned against him on the ground that he was taking too long to make up his mind whether to abdicate or resist: he was keeping people unreasonably in suspense; he should get it over with one way or another. Which way the drama ended had become of secondary importance: the essential was that the curtain come down in time for people to catch the last train home.

The Labour Party backed the Government. Not for the first or last time it explained this defence of a government which it theoretically wanted to upset on the ground that at some future date a Labour Government might find itself in conflict with a king and wish to assert the constitutional right of the Cabinet to overrule him. It was a signal affirmation of the official Labour Party doctrine that the constitutional and legal apparatus of the State is in the nature of an automobile which must never be damaged, whoever the incumbent driver, because one day a new driver might want to drive it in a new direction.

'With sobs and sighs . . .'

On 10 December the Speaker was able to announce to the House of Commons the King's decision to abdicate. 'His voice broke,' Channon recorded, 'and there were stifled sobs in the House . . . The Speaker was tearful, but very few others were, though Geoffrey Lloyd was in tears, and so I thought, was David Margesson' (Chief Conservative Whip and operator for Baldwin).

One of the few people in the country who supposed that the whole business had been truly serious and therefore must have truly serious consequences was Ribbentrop.

On the day Parliament passed the Abdication Act, he was lunching with J. C. C. Davidson, former Chairman of the Conservative Party and one of Baldwin's closest advisers. Davidson in his memoirs records that 'Ribbentrop thought I would agree that this was the end of Baldwin, that there would be shooting in the streets and that the King's Party would eventually restore Edward VIII to the throne. Indeed he said he had been extremely nervous of coming to lunch on a day like that.'

He talked, said Davidson, 'more nonsense than I had ever heard at Ambassadorial level'.

He had come fresh from communicating his views by telephone to Hitler. It was an outstanding, even grotesque, instance of how wrong Ribbentrop and Hitler could be about what seemed to be the obvious facts of life in England, and yet at some subliminal level get the essentials right. Ribbentrop, described by Channon as 'looking like the captain of someone's yacht', had done his political sums so badly that he was actually afraid to lunch with Baldwin's co-adjutor for fear of being shot in the streets by members of 'the King's Party'. It would have been reasonable to suppose that he must be too crassly ignorant to be of any use to his chief, or be taken seriously by

France provided an eventual haven

anybody else. How could this evident moron be an important piece on the board?

Yet he was.

Intelligent and informed men at the Foreign Office wrote him off as an offensive and thick-headed ignoramus. They simply could not take seriously his intimacies with powerful people—themselves often grotesque, but still powerful. It was a mistake.

It was easy to sneer at Lady Cunard; hardly anything, in fact, could be easier. But, if not as an intriguer, then as an organizer of situations in which intrigues could seriously take place, she was a factor to be reckoned with. It was hard for many intelligent people to believe that Lord Londonderry, heaviest of heavy swells, and his wife, for years the most blatantly wire-pulling and pressurizing political hostess in London, were of really serious importance on the British political scene in the fourth decade of the twentieth century. It was said that Lord Londonderry held major positions in the Cabinet, or was allowed close to the centre of government, 'only' because of his wife's influence and his enormous wealth. But the reason was irrelevant: he was there. And Ribbentrop was so close to him that, as Channon records, 'the arch-Hitler spy of Europe' was known to everybody as 'the Londonderry Herr'.

Ribbentrop had got it into his head, and informed Hitler, that there was a 'King's Party' which would take to shooting in the streets and make a *putsch* against Baldwin. To the Nazi leaders that was a natural sort of thing to happen. It was an hallucination.

But Ribbentrop, not at all disconcerted by his error on this point, continued to tell Hitler that the opinion in British high places—in and outside the Government—was running strongly in his favour. And that was no hallucination.

It was as though he had been permitted a preview of Mao Tse-tung's advice to guerrillas: how they must find and exploit conditions where they could swim like fish in the sea. In London Ribbentrop found sea-water of just the right temperature.

Lord Londonderry moved out of the limelight. But the 'Londonderry Air' remained London's signature tune during the last years of the thirties.

YOU'RE IN THE ARMY NOW.

11 Rearmament
1937-8 *Guns for sale*

Only the start of rearmament stopped the development of another depression, and the outbreak of the Second World War in 1939 put an end to large scale unemployment: war seemed the only means of preventing widespread unemployment.

This feature of the last years of the decade is emphasized by academics. And there were observers in the thirties who, lugubriously recalling the years before 1914, concluded that it was beginning to look as though war were a *sine qua non* of British prosperity.

This was a melodramatic view of the facts. But the facts were that by 1937 economists were seeing signs of another slump; in the last half of that year the unemployment figures began to rise, and between June 1937 and June 1938, before rearmament had time to exert an effective pull, had risen by half a million; and between 1936 and 1937 real wages fell approximately three per cent.

There was a confused notion among politically naïve people in Britain, derived from half-digested sermons from the Labour Party, that armaments somehow 'caused' wars. It was a belief entertained more or less vaguely in sectors otherwise almost wholly unpolitical. The fact that Britain was now putting in hand a programme of rearmament contributed much to the fatalistic sense of impending and inexorable calamity which, however much the country cultivated its garden, hung so heavily over the twenty months or so before the catastrophe was seen to be not only impending but imminent, and the subsequent twelve months before it actually occurred.

This general sense of inevitable disaster was a great deal more pervasive and had a greater effect upon opinion than either the demands for rearmament coming from the Churchillian Tories, or the criticisms of the Left, based on the ground that so long as the National Government remained in office the arms would be in the wrong hands and pointed in the wrong direction.

In April 1937, Neville Chamberlain, still Chancellor of the Exchequer, presented his last Budget.

In it he justified, in a sense contrary to that of the original sneer, the description of him as the kind of man to 'make a good Mayor of Birmingham in a bad year'. Instructed to find the money necessary for rearmament, he opined that the best way to do it was to collect it from the profits of those who had been making money out of rearmament and were going to make a lot more in the future.

He proposed an entirely new tax, for this specific purpose, to be called the National Defence Contribution. The name seemed well chosen, as spelling out to all concerned the patriotic purpose towards which the industrialists were going to contribute.

Possibly Chamberlain recalled another sneer at his family uttered during the Boer War when the Birmingham armament people were doing so well. Lloyd George had said, 'The more the Empire expands, the more the Chamberlains contract.' The National Defence Contribution would put a stop to such jibes at Birmingham men.

Chamberlain's argument was deemed by the industrialists and their friends in the House to be offensive and socialistic in tendency. He pointed out that rising profits over the past few years had been the result partly of general governmental assistance towards business recovery from the slump, partly to the beginnings of national rearmament: in any case, the source had been public money spent for the public weal. The Contribution would therefore take the form of a tax based either on the relationship between a given firm's profits and its capital, or on the firm's average profits during the years 1933-5.

Enterprising but private

The makers of steel, the ship-builders, the great gunsmiths, the aircraft manufacturers, were deeply shocked. Up and down the country, and above all at Westminster, their richly powerful pressure groups and lobbies went to work. On the Stock Exchange, where the certainty of increased rearmament, and large profits for all firms concerned in it, had raised the relevant share values, there was naturally a slump. Disappointed speculators joined in the outcry against Chamberlain. The lobbyists and the pressure groups openly or covertly suggested that in such conditions it was dubious whether the rearmament of the nation could be accomplished at all. To factory workers was conveyed the information that if the profits of the armament makers were to be taxed in that fashion, a laying-off of hands must be expected. The unemployed had been led to expect that rearmament would mean jobs. But if this sort of imposition was to be made upon profits, the jobless were going to be out of luck. And if the Contribution was going to slow down re-

armament and re-employment, was it not a positively unpatriotic and callous proposal?

Also, as many Conservatives averred, it was not the money that mattered, it was the principle of the thing. Tax collectors were to be given inquisitorial powers. And as a result of their intrusive assessments, private enterprise was to be penalized for its energy and initiative. Certainly the scandalously defenceless country needed arms: it should be prepared to pay industrialists a profit commensurate to the need.

Tory backbenchers threatened that if Chamberlain insisted on introducing the Contribution, they would prevent him succeeding Baldwin as Prime Minister.

Chamberlain was in the quite unaccustomed position of having to defend himself against the charge of being a socialist: a saboteur of the basic mechanics of the capitalist system. He stuck to his guns as long as there seemed any practical likelihood of getting the Defence Contribution accepted. But in this, and in this only, he resembled Hitler: he, like Hitler, had to accept that in seeking speedy and efficient rearmament, the profits of the industrialists and their bankers must be given first priority on the agenda. The proposed tax was withdrawn in favour of a flat tax of five per cent on business profits.

Ship-building programme—Britannia no longer assuredly ruled the waves

Rush to arms

The success of the housing boom in producing houses had an influence on the official, and the general Conservative approach to rearmament. In the matter of houses, enterprise, free and with the minimum of fetters or controls, had delivered the goods. With a minimum of controls, the steel industry and other armament industries might parallel the achievement. The inducements must be large: that was why the defeat of the National Defence Contribution proposal was of such importance. For it would have meant that from each increasing profit, tax money would be skimmed off. With a flat five per cent tax on profits there would be an entirely different situation.

If it was not precisely—in a later phrase—a 'licence to print money' it was a licence to make up your mind whether you wanted to print money or not.

If you decided that it was worth your while as a steel manufacturer to secure, say, a £5 million contract from the Government to help defend the country, you needed only the simplest sort of slide rule to work out your sums.

Assume that your profit on alternative civil contracts would be £500,000. Assume—it was in those days an entirely reasonable assumption—that your profit on the government contract would be £800,000. Five per cent of that is £40,000. So as a sound businessman, and one who realizes the necessity

of national rearmament, you are going to come to the aid of Government and country.

And naturally this assurance of a maximum five per cent tax on business profits made book-keeping easier. It also, as the phrase went, 'took the speculative element out of speculation'.

It eased the impact of costly mistakes and more than compensated for the vast wastage of resources which continuously occurred.

The creaky and erratic workings of the whole rearmament apparatus were inevitable when the ultimate purchaser was a government department, constantly apprehensive of being swindled if it were not meticulous, or denounced as strangling the national defences in red tape if it attempted to examine and evaluate too exactly. Observers of the proceedings, were constantly reminded of Kipling's question:

> Who shall doubt the secret hid
> Under Cheops' pyramid
> Is that the contractor did
>   Cheops out of several millions?
> Or that Joseph's sudden rise
> To Controller of Supplies
> Was a fraud of monstrous size
> Upon Pharaoh's swart civilians?

Complaints of inefficiency, waste and fraud sometimes trickled, sometimes poured in upon newspapers, M.P.s, and the relevant government departments. They came from technicians, supervisors, shop stewards, and often enough from disgusted executives. Some were investigated; some even effectively dealt with. But it was felt, reasonably enough, that by and large the system had to work that way: such phenomena must be accepted as the inevitable defects of its qualities.

Materially and, so to say, atmospherically, this mode of armament production, with its uncertainties, its unforeseen—and in the nature of such a thing unpredictable—delays and deficiencies, which, for valid security reasons, could never be fully exposed in public, profoundly affected public and private policies and attitudes.

It seemed to confirm absolutely the general view that Britain was 'not ready' for war. To this the critics and opponents of the Government's German policy could reply that in such a situation readiness is a relative term: the German High Command sincerely affirmed that Germany was not ready for war either. It was also argued that it was pointless and misleading to look at British unreadiness in isolation. The degree of comparative readiness could only be calculated in relation to the readiness and military strength of prospective allies, and the pressures they could collectively and severally exert. With that, military factors merged with the political and diplomatic shifts in the total situation.

And in this connection, a process of interaction between the pace of rearmament and diplomacy. The Treasury was continuously accused of impeding rearmament on grounds of economic principle. Nothing, or as little as possible, must be done to upset the normal operations of production and commerce. There could be no serious rationing of production and manpower for civilian purposes—even for the production of luxury goods—in the interests of armament manufacture. Nor must expenditure be such as to upset the ratio of government taxation to government borrowing. But another consideration played a decisive role: nothing must be done to suggest to Hitler that Britain, under cover of a conciliatory diplomacy, was really preparing seriously for war.

This determination to reassure Hitler as well as to appease him was an essential guide-line of British Government policy. Since Hitler, like other statesmen, took for granted maximum duplicity on the part of all other Governments, the only reassurance that could have any meaning was to prove the sincerity of Britain's friendly gestures towards him by strictly moderating the pace of rearmament. This inevitably affected the confidence of potential allies; but, on balance, the British Government considered this disadvantage to be more than compensated by carrying to Hitler the conviction of the British Government's benevolent support for his regime. This assessment of the advantages and disadvantages involved was logical, since co-operation with Hitler was the essence and objective of the Government's whole policy, while the organization of collective security was a deplorable second best.

In the final two years of mounting tension and increasingly desperate diplomatic manoeuvrings, it was nearly impossible for any leader of any political party in Britain to be fully aware that, obscured by the spectacular nature of weekly and monthly events, a fundamental shift in the basic position of Britain was taking place.

In the tightly meshed interaction of the Government's international and domestic policies; in particular its domestic policies as they affected on the material plane rearmament, and on another plane the morale of the British people, the initiative, the power to inaugurate and control decisive action, was slipping out of British hands.

Shifting balance

From the very start of the thirties it had been assumed, no less in Washington and Paris than in London, that in the long run, and at every truly crucial moment, Britain would prove the determining factor. And the assumption had been repeatedly justified. British policy had been decisive in the disintegration of the League of Nations. It had been decisive when the future of the German regime was in the balance at the time of the Rhineland crisis. It had been decisive in the first weeks of the Spanish War.

By hindsight it was easy for anyone a few years later to detect and examine the process by which each of these decisive and effective actions, each logically justifiable by reference to their ultimate objectives, had sometimes obviously, sometimes more subtly, eroded the power position which had made them possible.

But at the time it was not easy for those most concerned to admit, even to themselves, that the initiative was passing to Berlin on one hand and Moscow on the other, or to appreciate the meaning of that shift.

As Sainte-Beuve remarked of the post-revolutionary French aristocracy: 'It is hard to learn that one no longer governs the world.'

12 Fly, and Fly Again

1938-9 *The Munich crisis*

Plotted on the charts in Moscow, the policies of the British Government seemed more logical and more intelligible than to many of its impassioned domestic critics. The Russian leaders had grown up in the days when the West had appeared a monster of well-oiled efficiency in malign operation against the hurried improvisations of the Soviets. They themselves still operated now among the stresses, heaves and *tohu-bohu* of post-revolutionary Russia. They still behaved as though in the West the political telephone lines were always in perfect working order.

But they by no means shared the belief, pervasive on the British Left, that the aim of British Government policy was, so to speak, to tool up the Nazi regime and, at a convenient moment, fire off Hitler eastwards like a torpedo.

It was no secret to anyone that there were important people in and around the Government, in the City, and notably at the head of the oil industry, who did nurture that notion. And nobody questioned the basic hostility of the British ruling classes and of the Labour Party leadership to Communism and the Communist regime.

But in Moscow it was judged that the essential role of Britain was to maintain, and where possible strengthen, the existing social and economic order of central Europe, and wherever else in Europe it might be threatened.

In the nature of things this role of policeman for the system could not be passive. Europe could not stand still. Politically and economically it was desirable that the German Reich should master, in one form or another, the areas to the south and south-east. Translated into non-emotive terms, what Hitler called 'living space' for Germany could become what would now be called a Common Market or Economic Community, economically and politically dominated from Berlin, highly profitable to German finance and industry, profitable to the sub-controllers of resources and commerce in the south and south-east, and socially a strongly stabilizing influence.

It would confront the Soviet Union with an immensely powerful, economically and militarily coherent capitalist society on its borders. As such, its existence would, militarily and politically, constitute an enduring threat to the Communist regime, and a general rebuff to Communism.

Western critics described this development, and British assent to it, as the 'price' Hitler demanded. The British Government was ready to pay for peace in the West; it would 'turn Hitler eastward', and dissuade him from attacking Britain or making unacceptable colonial demands outside Europe.

The Russian observers formulated it differently. They did not see such an arrangement as involving a British sacrifice acceptable for the sake of peace in the West, and the refreshment of capitalism in the East.

Long-sightedly, it could be viewed as a mutually advantageous partnership between the British Empire and a German Empire in Europe. The conception was grandiose, but not at all fanciful, let alone chimerical. The Russians, who always paid attention to the continuities as well as the abrupt zigs, zags and leaps of history, noted that it was in essentials a revival of Anglo-German plans which had been far-advanced in discussion between Berlin and London in 1911 and 1912, and wrecked, buried, and nearly forgotten when contrary forces prevailed and brought about war instead.

220

Previous pages: Ill-met at Munich. Ribbentrop (left), Hitler, Chamberlain and interpreter; right: Daily Express *cartoon*

Glittering prospect

The two imperial powers, as Hitler repeatedly suggested in his writings and speeches, could not merely co-exist, but closely and actively co-operate in the organization and exploitation of the rich under-developed resources of great areas in the world. It was an aim which was naturally endorsed by the City. Thus would be achieved a concentration and consolidation of finance capital in London and Berlin which would have at its disposal a reservoir of raw materials and an apparatus of industrial production superior to those of the United States. The appeal of such an objective to the commonsense of capitalists could be reasonably appreciated in the Kremlin.

Molotov told de Gaulle that he once stood behind Stalin, who believed himself alone. 'With his two hands he covered large parts of the terrestrial globe that stood in his study; then, with one hand, Europe, and murmured, "It's small, Europe".'

The global, as distinct from the European, aspects, aspirations and necessities of British imperial policy seemed sometimes more clearly understood by Russian analysts than by Liberalistic or Labouristic economists in Britain. Contemplated from the Eurasian capital, the problem of the Indian section of that continent so largely occupied by the Soviet Union could be freshly evaluated by the Bolshevik leaders.

Until the early thirties, the idea of a German domination of the Balkans, threatening Soviet Ukraine, certainly, but Turkey too, would have had to be considered in London in the first place in relation to India. The imperilling of the 'route to India' would have been seen much as similar thrusts by Germany, dramatized by the 'Berlin-Baghdad railway', were seen before the First World War.

But in the thirties it became apparent that on this issue the imperial strategists, economic and military, of Britain, differed in their assessments. From the Russian point of view, the differences were of the highest import-

STEPPING STONES TO GLORY.

ance. If the maintenance of British power in India were to be given undisputed priority, then the essentials of the old calculation would be unchanged. Extension of a German sphere of influence towards the Middle East would be a danger hardly to be out-balanced by any compensatory advantages elsewhere. German, no less than Russian, control of south-east Europe must be combatted. The best hope for British policy must remain what it had been when the area of the lower Danube was shadowed by Austro-German power on the one side, Russian power on the other: namely, the continued Balkanization of the Balkans.

But the evidence indicated that by the mid-thirties the Higher Strategy in Britain already had India down in its balance sheets as an eventual write-off. Reluctantly, and later rather than sooner, British control would be broken. At that stage, the aim could be only to Balkanize, as it were, India: at least to the extent of splitting its control between two mutually hostile states. But, if that were accepted, then the disadvantages of a German-dominated south-east Europe weighed very little against the advantages of the imperial bargain in which this was to be only one element.

The long periphery

From the western end of the trunk line to Vladivostok, Mukden and Port Arthur of unhappy memory, the rough parallel between British policy in relation to Germany and American policy in relation to Japan was obtrusively evident.

For the Americans, to seem to avoid a dangerous, and expensive, confrontation with Japan was axiomatic. But there was an influential school of thought in Washington which did consider that to curb, where possible, the expansion of the Japanese military and economic empire must be a first priority. In late 1931, when the Japanese military advance into Manchuria began, the U.S. Government first refused League of Nations requests for an inquiry unless the Japanese agreed to it. Then it suggested joint Great Power gestures of censure. All League action, and any formal censuring of Japan, being then vetoed by the British Government, the U.S. Government, while suggesting to press and public that the resultant inaction in face of Japanese aggression was the fault solely of the British, made no further restraining move.

For there was an equally, and often more decisively influential school of American thought which considered that a more or less explosive expansion of Japanese power was inevitable: that Japanese economic aims could be satisfied by the exploitation of Manchuria: that Japan would thus police large areas of the Far East, and incidentally keep them safe for American business interests threatened by the anarchy of China: and finally, that the development of Japanese power in that area would constitute a permanently useful threat to the Soviet Union.

When Muscovites then approaching middle age were in their teens, these threats on the whole periphery of Eurasia, from Archangel to Poland, from the Ukraine and Baku to Harbin and eastern Siberia, had materialized in the wars of intervention. The interventions had failed. But for years peace at almost any price had been the inexorable rule of Soviet policy.

222

The Russians had been in no shape to resist being ignored when matters affecting their interests were decided among the Powers, and pushed, as the saying goes, around.

At great cost to their economy, industrial and military strength had been built up to the point where the Soviet Union was, to put it at the lowest, a power to be reckoned with: the reckoning being much affected by the varying abilities, and prejudices of military attachés, spies, and visiting industrial observers.

The new option

What may loosely be classified as the traditionalists, following what they saw as the road of minimum risk, opted for continuation of a policy of armament in isolation. Essentially they calculated that imperialist hostility to Communism would inevitably prove stronger than 'inter-imperialist rivalries'. It was thus an illusion to suppose that any valid, long-term co-operation or collective agreement with one or more of the capitalist states was a practical possibility.

The contrary opinion held that such views were part of a general hangover from the early post-revolutionary years and the wars of intervention. The most ferocious of imperialists could no longer imagine that the dismemberment and exploitation of Russia offered a simple solution to the problems of the capitalist world. Simultaneously, with the increase of Soviet strength, those inter-imperialist contradictions were becoming more acute. Reduced to their simplest possible terms—sometimes in pedantic formulations often favoured by the Bolsheviks—the decisive questions were:

Is there a point where those contradictions will become dominant; will, so to say, take over?

Specifically, is there a point at which the British Government must feel impelled in British national interests to resist German policies, even to the point of war? A moment at which the American Government must feel impelled in its own national interests to resist Japanese policies?

Answer: it is reasonable to assume that there is such a point; but nobody in Moscow, London or Washington knows where it is. It cannot be neatly marked in on a graph.

But they, over there in London, know just as well as do we here in Moscow that such a point may come. Therefore it is to be assumed that in the Government, or pressing close to the Government, and certainly in large sectors of influential opinion, there must be developing a demand that preparations be made for the moment when this Point X is reached: even a demand that Point X be defined in advance.

And if that be so, then it is not, after all, hallucinatory to suppose that somehow, some time—perhaps soon enough to contain the feared explosion— it may be possible for Britain, France and the Soviet Union to find a common interest in constructing a system of collective security.

In 1934, the victory over the traditionalists of 'those in Moscow who advocated Russian participation in seeking collective action', was proclaimed: the Soviet Union joined the League of Nations. What was personalized in the West as 'the Litvinov period' began. Litvinov was simultaneously an 'old Bolshevik', an intellectual, and long experienced in diplomacy, both underground and official. The fact that his wife was English, with good connections in British Left intellectual circles, was seen as an important 'fringe benefit'.

The key point
The advance into the novel and dangerous area of 'collective security' involved important reassessments of the military forces involved. And it was apparent that the key factor in the whole situation must be Czechoslovakia.

Precisely the same assessment was made in Berlin.

For years in remarks off the record, and later in public denunciations, Hitler had described Czechoslovakia as 'a dagger pointed at the heart of Germany'.

In the Top Secret directive issued in July 1937 by Field-Marshal von Blomberg to the three heads of the Armed Services, the 'elimination of Czechoslovakia' was stressed as the first, and indispensable, objective of German military action.

The Russians could also see Czechoslovakia as a dagger at the heart of Germany. By the middle of 1934, plans for Russo-Czech military collaboration were already agreed. The Franco-Soviet Pact was of major importance not only because it acquired an ally, however dubious, in the West, but— perhaps principally—because it was closely linked to the Franco-Czech Pact signed just before. The essential was that Czechoslovakia was geared into the Franco-Soviet system of military security: it was regarded by the Russians as the central feature of the whole structure.

It was so geographically. The two mountain ranges which met just south of Dresden formed a defensive line which heavy fortification could render as near invulnerable as any line could be: certainly less vulnerable than the Maginot line. As a base for counter-attack, or 'pre-emptive strike', Czechoslovakia was ideally situated in relation to Berlin and to the whole industrial complex of south-eastern Germany.

The Czech industrial potential was high, particularly in terms of the armament industry. The Skoda works, at least during the first years of German rearmament, were superior to Krupps.

The Russian military could evaluate the Czech alliance, in terms of direct strategic effectiveness, as being more immediately important than arrangements for collective action with France and Britain. Thus the existence of such an alliance could justify, against the traditionalists, the risks of sudden and dangerous involvement which had to be accepted by the partisans of collective security.

In 1937, Hitler was on record with the view that the threat from Japan to Siberia would paralyse Soviet action in Europe. A year later, as the Russo-Czech military collaboration developed, he had concluded that Russia must be expected to give military support to Czechoslovakia even if France reneged on its treaty.

The effects upon Russian military capacity of the bloody purging of the Red Army in the late thirties, involving the execution of an unrecorded
224

number of officers of all ranks, including the highest, were variously and contradictorily assessed inside and outside Russia.

The natural assumption in the West was that the results must, from a military viewpoint, be seen as entirely negative. A very large number of experienced officers had been violently removed, and the value of their training and abilities squandered. The effect upon the morale of the officer corps in general must be lowering indeed. At the best, it had to be regarded as an exceedingly dangerous swapping of horses in mid stream.

That Russian military men untouched by the purge, and highly-placed civilians, should insist that the results were positive, was equally natural and inevitable. They saw the purge first as proof that dangerous disaffection had existed in the Army, seriously weakening it as a reliable instrument of policy, and secondly as a means—the speediest possible means—of stopping the rot, of reorganizing and reanimating the Army: a blood-letting essential for improved health in the future. Russians took pleasure in recalling to British inquirers the well-remembered shooting of Admiral Byng 'pour encourager les autres'. They enquired whether the memoirs and other documents relating to the First World War did not show that if the British, French, Italians and Russians—not to mention the Germans and the Austrians—had 'liquidated' many of their generals before the outbreak of that war, many disastrous set-backs might have been avoided, many monstrous displays of incompetence prevented?

In Britain, the purge certainly led to a down-grading of Russia's military potential. On the other hand the Czechs, who were the most intimately concerned, were not at all deflected from their military arrangements with the Soviet Union which proceeded as though on the assumption that the savage shake-out had been entirely positive in its consequences.

Politically, the Czechs could rate these startling manifestations as advantageous. Even had it been assumed, as it was not generally at the time, that Tukhachevsky and many others were the victims of an elaborate frame-up, the political tendency emphasized was, from the Czech standpoint, positive. The affair had been conducted in such a way as to constitute a violent blow and warning to those elements which, considering pacts and alliances with the West as dangerous delusions, continued to believe that the salvation of Russia lay in a revival of the close military collaboration with Germany practised throughout the 1920s.

The collective advance

The 'collectivists' pursued their aims vigorously. In March 1936 Litvinov, at the meeting of the League of Nations Council following the German march into the Rhineland, took an initiative which sketched the shape of things to come: he proposed joint sanctions against Germany. In Taylor's words, already quoted, 'his advocacy was enough to damn the proposal'.

In Britain, partisans of collective security lamented what they described as a rebuff to the Soviet Union: they argued that it must undermine Russian confidence in the good faith of the Western Powers as alleged opponents of aggression; they opined that the Russians would be piqued, resentful. These appraisals were mistaken. The Russians had even less confidence in the

H   225 good faith of the West than the West had in the good faith of the Soviet Union. Pique and resentment were strictly private emotions; they were not likely to spill over into the deliberations of the Supreme Soviet and the High Command. More importantly, the supposed rebuff was not seen as such by the Russians.

By their actions immediately following the invasion of the Rhineland the British and French Governments had already made perfectly clear that no such action as the imposition of sanctions was going to be approved by them. From their point of view it was most undesirable that such a proposal be made at all.

In making it, the Russians considered they had achieved a double objective. They had forced the British and French into a public avowal that they were either unwilling to take action, or were not strong enough to do so. And, by forcing the issue in this fashion, they had begun the mobilization, so to speak, of the contrary, oppositional opinion within Britain and France— including not only opinion on the Left, but in Conservative circles. Each subsequent initiative of this kind from Moscow produced similar results. It powerfully increased the influence of those who more and more cogently urged that ideological hostility must not be given precedence over national self-interest. It emphasized the fact that if Germany were to be resisted at all, it was absurd, not to say criminal, to ignore or reject Soviet offers of collective action. And if it were argued by the Government leaders that there was no need or intention to resist Germany, then that answer brought nearer the moment when there would have to be an answer to the question: Is there ever to come a point where the inter-imperialist contradictions have to be treated, in the national interest, as dominant? Where a policy of resistance to Germany must take over?

These Russian initiatives were dangerous in the sense that any one of them might possibly have been treated by Hitler as an open act of diplomatic hostility, an 'intolerable provocation'. Relying on British, and hence French, passivity or even benevolence, he might have abruptly brought forward a direct attack upon Czechoslovakia and, consequently, upon Russia. But the Russians, in their relatively new role as the activists among the non-German powers, were confident that, given their alliance with the Czechs and the resultant strategic advantages, they could destroy Germany's war potential before Germany could destroy Russia's. They did not believe it would come to that. For they were well-informed of the condition of the German Army which, as was later shown by the German archives and the disclosures of the German generals, was in no shape to conduct a successful war at that time.

In a first drive to weaken the position of Czechoslovakia, Hitler, in March 1938, invaded and annexed Austria. The Russians proposed a Four Power meeting to concert measures to halt further aggression. Prime Minister Chamberlain rejected it. The 'contrary opinion' was expressed more loudly than before by the Churchillian Conservatives and—in a significant development—by the National Council of Labour, representing the Labour Party and the T.U.C. The National Council demanded that Britain unite with France and Russia in a common front against the aggressor. Chamberlain rejected the proposal, declaring that to accept it would divide Europe into two camps and 'inevitably plunge us into war'. In May, speaking to American journalists at the house of Lady Astor, by then popularly identified as the unofficial headquarters of the pro-German and anti-Russian forces, he made clear that Britain would not fight for Czechoslovakia 'in its present boundaries'. He looked forward to a Four Power Pact to preserve the peace of Europe. The adherents to the Pact were to be Britain, Germany, France and Italy. Not Russia.

The May crisis

A few days later, the Czechs, in conjunction with the Russians, again seized the initiative. In an over-confident demonstration of intent, German troops began to concentrate on the Czech frontier. The Czech Government, declaring that an attack was imminent, ordered partial mobilization of the Czech Army. The rapidity of this reaction convinced many in London, Paris and Berlin that the Czechs and Russians might be about to launch a 'preventive war' against Germany. Other reports led to the belief in the West that Hitler, overriding the advice of the General Staff, intended to risk a Blitzkrieg against Czechoslovakia. In either case, there would be a war: one in which Germany's chances of victory were no better than fifty-fifty.

The shock and alarm in London and Paris was near panic. The two Governments had no choice. The only way out was to warn Hitler first, that the French would come to the assistance of the Czechs if they were attacked, secondly that the British, in the light of such a conflagration, might well feel obligated to fulfil their commitments to France. The French reinforced their warning by direct assurances in Prague.

In the face of this first and—as things fell out—last demonstration of collective security in action, Hitler immediately went into reverse. The troop concentrations were dispersed. The Czech Ambassador in Berlin received denials of any offensive designs by Germany. More importantly, Czech and Russian military observers were able to report that the German preparations for immediate action had ceased.

Litvinov and the collectivists had proved that they held the initiative: the British and French Governments had been forced into a most unwelcome course of action, contrary to the whole line they had followed from the time of the military occupation of the Rhineland to the annexation of Austria.

It was not to be supposed that, as a result of this action, the British Government would be finally deflected from its essential policy.

On the contrary: it became necessary for it to accelerate and redouble its attempts to accommodate Hitler; to appease him.

(Here a semantic sidelight was thrown upon the scene. A few years earlier, Anthony Eden, British Foreign Secretary, had spoken of the 'appeasement' of Europe. He used the term in the first sense of the word 'appease', as given in the dictionary: 'To bring to peace, settle (strife, etc.); to calm (persons).' Chamberlain continued to use the word, indicative of a laudable endeavour. But by 1938 the word had assumed, and was universally seen to have assumed, its second dictionary meaning: 'To pacify (anger etc.) . . . To propitiate (him who is angry) . . . To pacify, by satisfying demands.)'

But now the 'inter-imperialist contradiction', and the consequent clash between what may be called the nationalists and the neo-imperialists in Britain became blatant.

The shift in Conservative opinion, already noted in the case of Winston Churchill between the beginning and the end of the Spanish War, was developing to an extent which could be seen as even threatening to the Government.

From this point on the political conflict within Britain reached a new intensity, a new virulence. For the first time the Chamberlain Government was on the defensive against serious attack. It was a change of situation which explains much of its behaviour in the ensuing months. Actions which were seen at the time as inexplicable, myopic to a barely credible degree, or even—by the conspiratorially minded—as the result of some secret treachery in high places, were in fact motivated by the need for haste: sometimes amounting to panic haste. It was essential, if a repetition of the crisis at the end of May and its immediate outcome were to be avoided, that the policy of 'appeasing' Hitler should show immediate results.

It was above all necessary to obliterate, both in Prague and in Berlin, the effects of the warning to Germany and the consequent reassurance to Czechoslovakia uttered from London in May. The method chosen was to recognize and espouse the cause of the Sudeten, the racially and linguistically German minority in north-western Czechoslovakia, resident in and behind the area of the Czech fortifications. To this end, the Chamberlain Government insisted, despite diplomatic resistance by the Czechoslovak Government and a French refusal to participate, on sending to Prague a mission headed by Lord Runciman which was to examine Sudeten grievances and demands, but in effect to give them, so to speak, international status.

The mission was denounced as a gross British interference in the internal affairs of an independent state. The denunciations were of course expected, and were not unwelcome; they helped to emphasize, in Berlin and Prague, the direction and objectives of British Government policy. Lord Runciman ostentatiously conferred not with representatives of the Czech Government but with those of the Sudeten, headed by Henlein, Gauleiter of the Nazi Party in the Sudeten area. At the same time, the British Government called upon the Czechs for concessions to the Sudeten, and Chamberlain notified Berlin that he was anxious to arrange a personal meeting with Hitler. During the same period, as an indication of the more positive elements of Anglo-German collaboration, news was leaked of conversations between a financial representative of the Reich, Helmuth Wohltat, on the one hand, and Sir Horace Wilson, Chamberlain's closest adviser, and R. S. Hudson, parliamentary·secretary to the Department of Overseas Trade. The details were kept vague. But it was given to be understood that what was under discussion was a huge loan — reportedly £1,000 million—to be raised in London for the purposes of facilitating Anglo-German co-operation in various fields, including the colonial field. (As a social 'stabilizer' it might have been a preview, in miniature, of the Marshall Plan.)

Speed-up

The political need of the Chamberlain Government for quick results inevitably increased Hitler's power of leverage. Events in the West were now being determined to a quickly increasing extent in Berlin and Moscow.

Parallel with the speed-up of appeasement by the Government's diplomatic exertions, on the home front the supporters and, in some cases instigators, of the policy intensified their campaign in a manner which seemed even to some of their adherents almost reckless, and certain to incur considerable public obloquy.

Obloquy was indeed incurred.

The emotions of the Tory nationalists were sharply expressed by a Churchillian, in personal controversy with a self-made American millionaire, a Nazi sympathizer of the Bedaux type, who had become naturalized and assumed a position in high British Society. 'I suppose,' said the Churchillian, 'I ought not to be surprised to see you betraying the interests of your adopted country in the supposed interests of your adopted class.'

The most influential of the British partisans of appeasement, in the later sense of the word, had been identified or, as it were, encapsulated as the Cliveden Set, Cliveden being the Thames Valley home of Lord and Lady Astor. Michael Astor wrote, many years later, that he had been unable to make up his mind whether the newsheet *The Week*, which originated the description, had 'discovered' the Cliveden Set or 'invented' it. Those who denounced the Cliveden Set referred also—recalling the Cagoulards, or hooded men, heading Fascist conspiracy in France—to the 'Cagoulords', meaning Lords Halifax, Londonderry, Lothian and Astor. The most obviously powerful of those so closely associated with Cliveden was Geoffrey Dawson, editor of *The Times*.

All those under attack at one time or another denied that there was such a Set or stated that if such existed they were not members of it. So far as that was concerned, the question was simply how anyone defined a 'set'. The denials were reminiscent of Thomas W. Lamont's denial of the existence of a Power Trust. There was no Trust—just people interested in the same objectives 'standing around in a co-operative frame of mind'. In any case, by 1938 the phrase 'Cliveden Set' had taken on a general, symbolic meaning: in popular language and in the press of the western world 'Clivedenite' was taken as a convenient classification of anyone rich or politically powerful who was active in furtherance of policies beneficial to Hitler.

Under whatever name, the people associated with Cliveden did constitute a highly influential group of political activists, exercising a close personal influence on the Prime Minister, and—through *The Times*—a very powerful influence on domestic and international policies. It was repeatedly said that foreign governments were too prone to assume that *The Times* was the official organ of the British Government. They may have been thus prone. But since the policies favoured at Cliveden, in Printing House Square, and in Downing Street were, during that period, barely distinguishable, the misapprehension was academic.

The activities of those described as 'Clivedenites' were by no means indefensible. (They were also frequently referred to with opprobrium as a

Fifth Column. But the original Fifth Column—the supporters of General Franco inside Republican Madrid—had clear, and in their own terms, justifiable personal and political reasons for their hostility to the Republic.

Chamberlain's close advisers and supporters saw the Hitler regime, and British collaboration with it, as indispensable in the preservation of the existing social structure. Even if the nature of the Nazi regime were deemed deplorable, the only alternatives these supporters could envisage were more deplorable still: the breakdown of the social order in Europe with Communism to follow. It was unreasonable to expect the very rich, and those closely associated with them, to do anything but exert themselves to the utmost to avert such a calamity. It was absurd to ask them to act in a manner favourable to the interests of proletarian revolution, or, indeed, of democracy if democracy, as in Spain, seemed to involve the erosion or displacement of the capitalist system of society.

They declared that to accommodate Hitler was the sole means of avoiding a disastrous war. It could be, and repeatedly was, pointed out to them—particularly in view of the object lesson offered by the events of May 1938—that collective security offered at least as good a chance of avoiding war as did the appeasement of Hitler. But collective security involved co-operation with the Soviet Union and, inevitably, the strengthening of Soviet power and influence. Here again, it was hardly reasonable to ask leading British capitalists readily to act in a manner favourable to the socialist state. And, however they may have been criticized in Britain, certainly nobody in Moscow was surprised at the spectacle of representatives of the ruling class acting in such accordance with the simplest text books of the class war.

On 7 September *The Times* at length spelled out the message to Czechoslovakia which had been implicit in the diplomatic manoeuvres, suggestions and pressures of the previous weeks. It urged the Czechoslovak Government to consider 'whether they should exclude altogether the project, which has found favour in some quarters, of making Czechoslovakia a more homogeneous state by the secession of that fringe of alien populations who are contiguous to the nation with which they are united by race.'

The verbiage, though thickly Pecksniffian, required no translation. The 'project' the Czechs were being called upon not to 'exclude altogether' was simply the abandonment of their strategic frontiers and their elaborate fortifications. It was a request that Czechoslovakia reduce itself to military impotence; an impotence as complete as that of Austria on the eve of the German invasion.

It was a logical request. It could be seen in London, as clearly as in Berlin and Moscow, that those natural and artificial defences were the key to the whole situation. Their abandonment was indispensable if the policy of Anglo-German collaboration were to succeed. It was Hitler's minimal demand.

On 13 September, Chamberlain telegraphed Hitler to request the personal meeting which had been planned since mid-August. Hitler instantly invited him to Berchtesgaden, where he arrived on 15 September. Back in London on the following day, he proposed to the Cabinet that in the name of 'self determination' for the Sudeten, Czechoslovakia should be compelled to cede the crucial frontier areas to Germany. Furthermore, Czechoslovakia must change the direction of her foreign policy by renouncing the Treaty with Russia. Having secured, against the opposition of some members, the agreement of the Cabinet, he saw on the 18th Daladier and Bonnet, French Premier and Foreign Minister. They agreed to the proposal on condition that the new, undefended frontier of Czechoslovakia be guaranteed by Britain and France. Chamberlain insisted that Germany must be added to the guarantors. He was able to report to the House of Commons that a solution had been found 'which would not automatically compel France to take action in accordance with her obligations'.

The way to Munich

The demand was formally presented in Prague on the following day—19 September—with a demand for an immediate reply, as Chamberlain proposed to report progress to Hitler on the 21st. President Beneš rejected the demands and offered to submit the matter to arbitration. He was informed that if this refusal were followed by a German attack, Britain and France would stand aside. Litvinov, at Geneva, pledged Russian support. Beneš intimated acceptance of the Anglo-French demands.

Flying to Godesberg on the 22nd, Chamberlain was informed by Hitler that the plan was no longer acceptable to Germany: it would take too long to complete. German troops must occupy the frontier areas immediately. Chamberlain, showing sharply increased awareness of oppositional opinion in Britain, declared that he had taken his political life in his hands in supporting Hitler's demands, he could not agree to a programme and timetable which would not be accepted by public opinion as carrying out the agreed principles in orderly fashion, not under threat of force. Hitler insisted. The Czechs mobilized to resist the threat of immediate occupation.

In London, Chamberlain was confronted with a notable stiffening of nationalist opposition to acceptance of Hitler's latest demands. The Labour Party was organizing protest meetings throughout Britain. The Conservative Party was more sharply divided than it had ever been on the German question. In the Cabinet only Chamberlain, Simon and Hoare were mildly or vigorously opposed by those who held that to accept Hitler's demands would be finally disastrous for British prestige, and perhaps for the existence of the Government. Although it was possible to suppose that a great section of the public was mesmerically paralysed by the fear of imminent war, there was certainly the possibility of a dangerous outburst of nationalist feeling. Even *The Times* now found Hitler's demands unacceptable. The *Daily Telegraph*, central organ of the Conservative Party, declared that Hitler was calling for 'an abject and humiliating capitulation'.

Chamberlain continued to communicate pleadingly with Hitler and to threaten the Czechs.

Hitler and his advisers were variously impressed by the change in British public opinion, or rather by the emergence of a public opinion not hitherto expressed, and above all by the mobilization of the British fleet. After bitter dissensions, and with a group of generals belatedly and clumsily plotting a *putsch* to overthrow Hitler in order to prevent a war which they believed

231

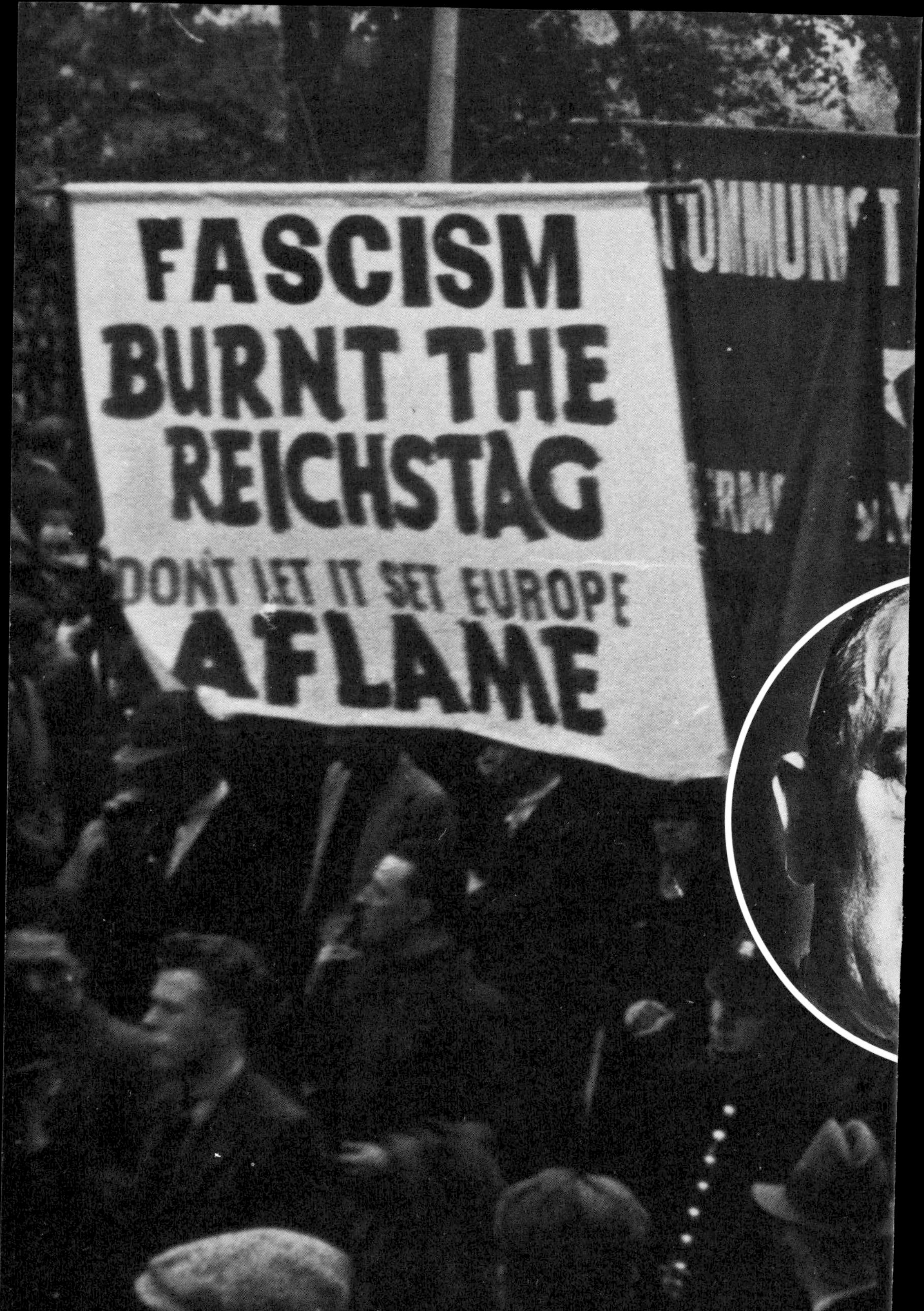
FASCISM
BURNT THE
REICHSTAG
DONT LET IT SET EUROPE
AFLAME

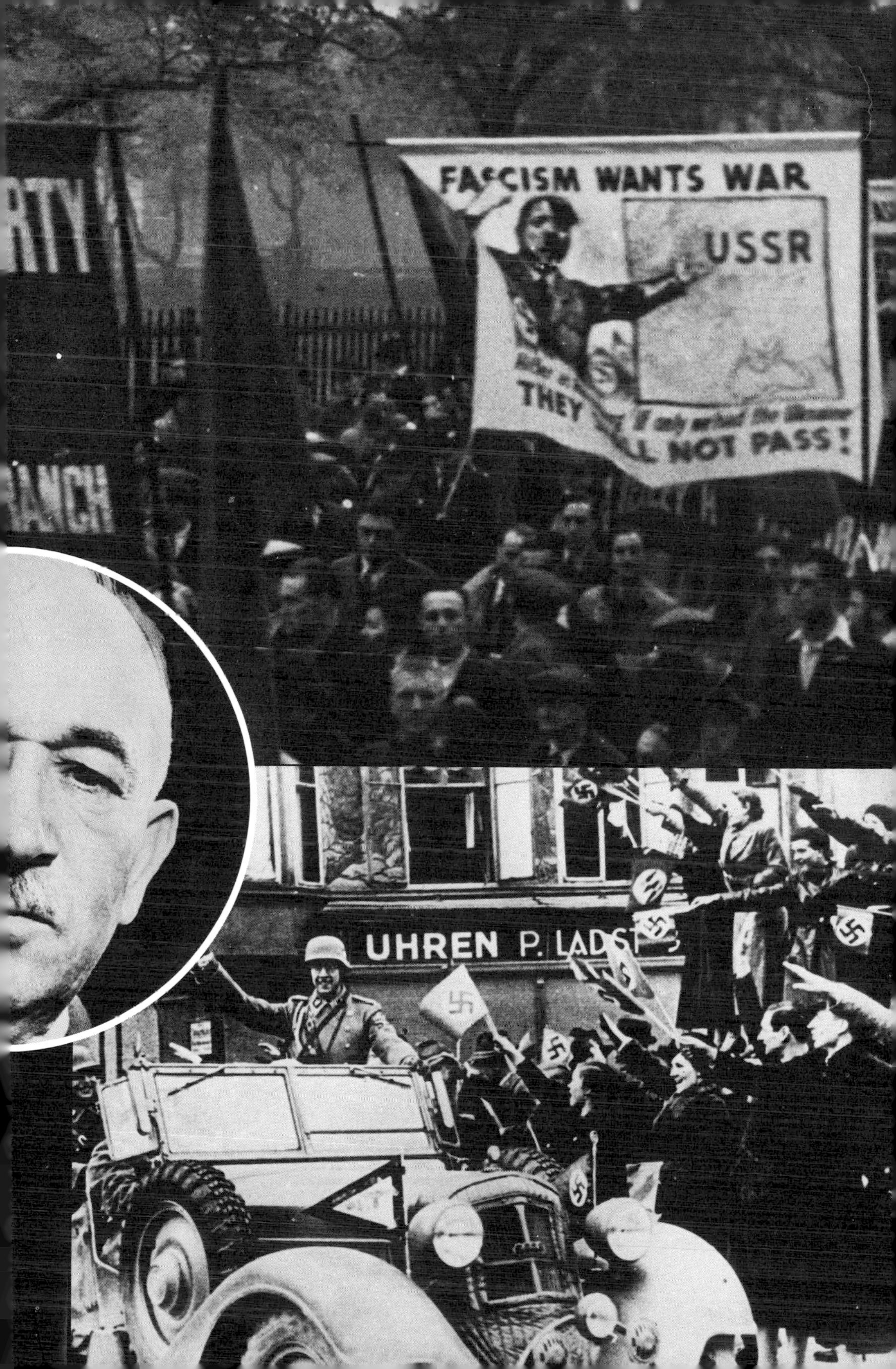
FASCISM WANTS WAR
USSR
THEY
NOT PASS!
UHREN

would be lost, Hitler, replying to a message from Chamberlain, asked him to continue to work to bring the Czechs to reason.

Chamberlain immediately answered that he was prepared to discuss the details of 'the transfer' with Hitler immediately. There need be no long delay. He believed he and Hitler could reach agreement within a week. He had also appealed to Mussolini to intervene with Hitler.

On 28 September he was able to announce to the House of Commons, which had been expecting to be told what was now inevitable, that he was to join Hitler, Mussolini and Daladier for a conference at Munich.

The third question

On the eve of the conference, the Russians made a final effort to carry to its logical conclusion the defensive-offensive policy whose central features were the alliance with Czechoslovakia and her special strategic position.

In consultation with the Czechs, advance squadrons of Soviet bomber and fighter planes positioned on the military airfields near Prague, and in north-eastern Bohemia. As increasingly threatening news came in from Berlin, London and Paris, President Beneš suddenly requested that the Soviet Minister come to see him immediately. At the moment when the summons was received, the Minister was in conference with Michael Koltsov, Foreign Editor of *Pravda* and known to be, in Prague as he had been in Spain, the direct personal agent of Stalin. (Hugh Thomas in his *Spanish Civil War* [published 1961] notes that in November 1936, when the Republican Government left the control and defence of Madrid to a *junta* under the leadership of General Miaja, Koltsov 'seemed for a while the chief inspiration of the *junta*'.) On the Minister's arrival at the Presidential Palace, Beneš said he had two questions to ask him: first, supposing the League of Nations called upon its members to carry out their obligations under the Covenant by joining in organized resistance to Hitler, would the Soviet Union participate in such action? Both Beneš and the Minister knew very well that there was no possibility of the League doing any such thing. However, the Minister replied somewhat impatiently that certainly the Soviet Union would respond to such a call to arms. Second question: suppose the League does nothing, but the British and the French Governments take action, would the Soviet Union do the same? The answer was, naturally, again 'Yes'. Reporting the scene to Koltsov a half-hour later, the Minister described how he and Beneš had sat for a while in silence. Then the Minister said: 'There is surely, is there not, a third question which you would like to put?' Again, the President and the Minister were both aware what that third question was: suppose neither the League, nor Britain nor France are prepared to fight on this issue, and suppose the Czech Government were now to appeal directly to Moscow, would the Soviet Union respond? The Minister was authorized to give, again, the answer 'Yes'.

The Minister described Beneš as sitting silent 'like a photograph of himself'. He did not ask the third question. The Minister returned gloomily to the Legation, where a lot of young high-ranking officers of the Red Air Force were sitting about, waiting for news.

In the course of the next couple of hours the Minister and Koltsov dis-

234

cussed the situation, at the Legation and by telephone with members of the Czech Cabinet, with Czech Army commanders and with Moscow. From their talks with the Czechs they gathered that no invitation to the Soviet Union would be given, the Treaty would not now be invoked. And a little later they learned that the presence of the Soviet planes on Czech airfields was no longer welcome: it could be considered a provocation to Hitler. They were not much surprised. There had always been a number of members of the Czech Government who, for sufficiently obvious reasons, were opposed to the idea of an armed resistance without the West, and with the Soviet Union as Czechoslovakia's sole ally. The reasons varied. Some had always regarded the treaties with East and West as of strictly deterrent value: If the deterrent failed, and the choice was between war and capitulation, then capitulation must be accepted as the only way of saving Czechoslovakia from a war which would ravage and destroy the country whatever its ultimate outcome. (This had for months been a principal argument advanced in Prague by British and French spokesmen.) There were others whose chief pre-occupation and fear centred on the political effects of a conflict in which Czechoslovakia would be solely dependent on the Russians. The Red Army would have to cross the narrow intervening Rumanian or Polish territories, and operate where necessary inside the country. They foresaw a permanent 'bolshevization' of Czechoslovakia.

The most determined and powerful advocate of resistance at all costs, who had all along reckoned that if war came it would be fought with the Soviet Union as sole ally, was the Army's Chief of Staff. His opinion had often been decisive at times when the Cabinet was divided and uncertain. But he had left the previous day for the Army Headquarters in the north-east. He had seen Koltsov just before he left. He had at that time taken it for granted that the decision—to resist, and call in the Russians—had been finally taken. Koltsov now tried to reach him by telephone, but failed.

It became necessary to inform the Air Force commanders that they would have to return to the airfields and await final orders to return to their bases in the Soviet Union.

Just as they were leaving the Legation, grumbling and cursing, there came an urgent call from the President to the Minister. It requested the Minister to get from Moscow an up-to-the-minute estimate of the time it would take to get a previously agreed Soviet force of Russian air power into position for immediate action from Czech bases. The Minister promised the information within an hour. Koltsov hurried out of the Minister's room to counter-mand the order to the Air Force men.

The information came from Moscow, the Minister rushed to the Palace. He returned in dejection. On arrival he had been told that his visit to the President was cancelled: the President was no longer interested in the information for which he had asked.

The game was up.

The Munich Agreement secured for Hitler the whole of his immediate objectives. The frontiers and fortifications were abandoned. The Czech-Soviet Treaty was abrogated. Soon afterwards Beneš resigned and went into exile. In March 1939 Hitler occupied Prague.

Those hours of indecision, and finally of decision, in Prague were an historical turning-point: a point, as soon appeared, of no return.

The final rejection of Soviet action in the imminent war was a crippling defeat for the 'collectivists', signalized a few months later by the dismissal of Litvinov and his replacement by Molotov. (Litvinov is reported to have told friends later that he had been in hourly expectation of arrest and probable execution, and had only been saved because Stalin recalled that Litvinov had saved him from being beaten up by British dockers during Stalin's only visit to London, during the 1907 Congress of the Russian Social-Democrats.) At about the same time Koltsov was dismissed, arrested and shot.

The collectivists had lost what was later described as 'credibility'. The principal material justification—the strategic position of Czechoslovakia—was gone. There remained the possibility of a developing collectivity with the West. The deep stirring and shift in British public opinion in the brief interval between Godesberg and Munich had been impressive. But it had not been decisive. And it was impossible to assume that it ever would be decisive in time: in time, that is to say, to make it credible to Hitler that he had only the choice between political retreat and a war on two fronts.

Throughout the spring and early summer of 1939 it was still assumed in Moscow that there existed the possibility that British public opinion, led by the Churchillian Conservatives who more and more urgently demanded close military collective action with the Soviet Union, would compel the Government to act in that sense. The possibility certainly existed: but it did not become a reality in time. Opinion in favour of collaboration with Russia was strong enough to get a military mission, of ostentatiously secondary status, sent to Moscow. It was not strong enough to persuade the Government to bring pressure upon Poland, now guaranteed British aid in case of German attack, to agree not to oppose the advance of the Red Army into Polish territory in the event of war.

The position of the collectivists was thus further eroded, and at last altogether eliminated. The alternative policy of armed isolation prevailed. It differed from earlier Russian isolationism in that it required, as compensation for the loss of the Czech barriers, the extension of Russian control over the Baltic States and eastern Poland. These were essentials of the Non-Aggression Pact signed, in August, between the Soviet Union and Germany. The removal of the Finnish fortifications west of Leningrad—known as the Mannerheim Line—was also considered essential in Moscow. It was achieved only as a result of the Russo-Finnish war in the winter of 1939-40. The fact that Britain and France, although by that time at war with Germany, organized an expeditionary force designed to cross northern Norway and Sweden and fight against the Russians, confirmed in Moscow the opinion that anti-Sovietism had all along been the decisive factor in British policy, overriding—even after the outbreak of war—the requirements of resistance to Germany.

London smog
In Britain, after a few weeks during which alarm and despondency over the

Previous pages: Germans enter Prague. Herr Hitler could no longer be described as a gentleman

Munich agreement were obscured by the enjoyment of a blessed release from the fear of instant war, the mood was dolorous indeed.

The political activists of the Left, though they continued agitation in favour of one more heave to achieve collective security against the Nazi menace, were half-numbed by the overwhelming victory of the policy of Chamberlain and 'the Cliveden Set'. They, too, had lost credibility. Only a minority of people can find enthusiasm for a cause which sustains, as the British Left had done, nothing but a series of disastrous defeats.

The nationalist Right, too, intensified its agitation, seeking to arouse patriotic feeling in a country seen as now in mortal danger. But the Right suffered also from its more or less spectacular failure to achieve any significant change in policy during the brief period since it seriously opposed the Chamberlain line.

The apathy and cynicism which had stood the Government in such good stead from the mid thirties onwards, were thickened and, it could seem, justified by the Munich Agreement. After the first few relieved and bewildered weeks, hardly anyone other than the most fervid supporters and admirers of the Prime Minister, together with some fanatical pro-Nazis and ultra-Conservatives who rejoiced in the isolation of the Soviet Union, supposed that the Agreement represented anything but a dangerous triumph for Hitler, achieved by means of a humiliating act of betrayal by Britain. If 'betrayal' were considered too emotive a word—What else could we have done?—there was still a commonsense awareness that the arrangement had been at the best sordid. A significant number of people normally considered, and considering themselves, unpolitical, were oppressed by a sense of guilt. It was an honourable and respectable reaction: but, like all feelings of irremediable guilt, debilitating to the muscles.

13 Terminal Year

1939 'We've lost the key of the bloody mortuary'

Strangest of all phenomena of that terminal year of the thirties was the behaviour of the Chamberlain group in the Cabinet. Several of their colleagues, and Conservative opponents, had the impression that these men were suffering from some morbid, collective paranoia, seemingly nearly pathological in character.

Detached observers, particularly American journalists and diplomats, found themselves repeating in bewilderment: they must be mad.

It was obvious to all reasonably informed people the day after Munich that within weeks, or at the most months, Hitler would invade and occupy Czechoslovakia as he had Austria. His aim was no secret.

It was clear, too, that the West now faced a very early choice between war and capitulation. Munich had changed all the terms of the equation. In Winston Churchill's summary:

'The subjugation of Czechoslovakia robbed the Allies of the Czech Army of twenty-one regular divisions, fifteen or sixteen second-line divisions already mobilized, and also their mountain fortress line, which in the days of Munich had required the deployment of thirty German divisions, or the main strength of the mobile and fully-trained German Army. According to Generals Halder and Jodl, there were but thirteen German divisions, of which only five were composed of first-line troops, left in the West at the time of the Munich arrangement. We certainly suffered a loss through the fall of Czechoslovakia equivalent to some thirty-five divisions. Besides this, the Skoda works, the second most important arsenal in central Europe, the production of which between August 1938 and September 1939 was in itself nearly equal to the actual output of British arms factories in that period, was made to change sides adversely . . . Finally, there is this staggering fact: that in the single year 1938 Hitler had annexed to the Reich and brought under his absolute rule . . . a total of over ten millions of subjects, toilers, and soldiers. Indeed the dread balance had turned in his favour.'

Chamberlain himself argued later that at Munich he had 'gained time'. The comparative figures affecting armaments, and manpower show that— except in a limited though vital sector of aircraft production—the time 'gained' profited only Hitler.

Yet, during the first months after Munich, the Chamberlain Government held it to be axiomatic that no serious acceleration of preparations for war must be made in Britain lest it provoke Hitler. Thus the initiative had passed so completely to him that he could to a serious degree control the pace and extent of British rearmament.

Early in March, Sir Samuel Hoare gave a special briefing to selected journalists on the immediate prospects in Europe. He devoted part of it to a derisive attack upon 'sensational journalists'—naming in particular Pertinax of the *Echo de Paris*, Madame Tabouis of *l'Oeuvre*, and the present writer—for predicting new crises, and reporting rumours that Hitler was on the verge of moving on Prague. He declared that on the contrary the situation was one of increasing calm and prosperity.

In view of the visible realities after Munich, this statement could be seen as one of those which justified the charge of lunacy. Most of Hoare's chosen listeners, however, gave their readers the essence of this off-the-record statement. *John Bull*, then a mass circulation weekly which had to start going to press a week or more before it appeared on the bookstalls, devoted

242

its entire leading article to Hoare's theme. It pointed out that this—the day of actual publication— was the day named by 'the fat boys' of Europe, seeking to make our flesh creep, as the day on which Hitler would march on Prague. Yet nothing, said the article, has happened. Indeed the situation in Europe was not only better, but much better.

On the afternoon of the day the paper appeared the German Army marched into Prague.

The episode was important for the light it threw upon both the Government and the supporting press. It seemed impossible to suppose that the Government was ignorant of the general situation, and of facts known to every informed journalist in Europe—though suppressed by many on advice from the various establishments that publication would disturb both the political atmosphere and the stock exchanges. Equally, it was hard to discern adequate reasons for deliberate lying. There were those who, given the cynicism, corruption and moral confusion of those 'condemned times', took for granted that members of the Government were engaged in a squalid manoeuvre to produce a sudden rise in share values for their personal profit. And it was true that so far as several members of the Government were concerned there was nothing in their record that ruled out this possibility: two of them at least had been involved in notable speculative scandals earlier in the decade.

The jolt

The annexation of Czechoslovakia, though so easily predictable, jolted British public opinion: the fact that it came as a jolt at all proving the depth of that morass of bewildered indifference and fatalism existing after Munich. Himself jolted by the stirring of public indignation, Chamberlain suddenly warned Hitler in a public speech that 'any attempt to dominate the world by force was one which the Democracies must resist'.

Philosophers, evaluating beliefs, used to say that 'we can be said to believe something when we are prepared to act as though it were true'.

By that standard neither Chamberlain nor his colleagues believed what he said. And the mass of people hardly behaved as though they believed it either.

The rearmament programme was gently accelerated, but with the strangling proviso that nothing must be done to upset or interfere with the operations of ordinary civilian production or business. Neither materials nor manpower must be controlled, let alone conscripted, in preparation for this strange war: a war, that is to say, which everyone was learning to think of as simultaneously inevitable and awful, and yet somehow not something that was really going to happen.

Chamberlain's reference to 'the Democracies' which were going to 'resist' was, to the normally unpolitical, and those who had become unpolitical through frustration, nearly meaningless. To the politically aware, and all who had even casually observed the character, the aims and the preoccupations of the Government, it was a very sick joke: a kind of music-hall impersonation in bad taste.

In the first armed confrontation between 'the Democracies' and their enemies, the war in Spain, the Government had thrown its whole weight into the balance against the Republic, and had ensured that France, too, should leave the Spanish democracy to its fate. Czechoslovakia had been a democracy. When, in May 1938, it had resisted Hitler's 'attempt to dominate by force', and had the support not only of the Soviet Union but, briefly, of Britain and France, its resistance had been successful. The British Government had at once set to work to ensure that no such resistance could be offered again.

To those who understood that the role of the British Government throughout the thirties was to police Europe on behalf of the existing social and economic system, and to resist democratic pressures tending dangerously to threaten it, the Government's policies had always seemed sufficiently intelligible. Seen as the necessary defence of a particular class structure, they could be logically explained.

Instant Democrat

But the Chamberlain Government did not thus explain itself to the citizens. Chamberlain's sudden dedication to the cause of the democracies sounded like the incantation of a spoiled priest superstitiously reciting the *Confiteor Dei* on his deathbed.

The outstanding fact was that in all the fateful years of the thirties, the citizens of the British democracy, where the ballot box was ostensibly democracy's guarantee, had been able to express themselves at a general election only twice. The first had been conducted in the midst of an officially stimulated panic, after the previously elected Government had been overthrown without benefit of Parliament. At the second, the Government had been re-elected on a pledge to support and strengthen the League of Nations, which it took immediate steps to dismantle.

Were it not a verifiable historical fact, it could seem incredible that Great Britain passed from 1931 to 1940 without a change of government. An occasional shuffle and reshuffle of the personalities in the pack was all that ever faintly registered reactions to the convulsions of Europe.

It could seem that in the role of policeman and conservationist which had been thrust upon it, the British people had lost the use of its democratic faculties: its muscles had atrophied through disuse.

Yet parallel with the frustrations, the frauds, and the resulting indifference, some democratic muscles were being tentatively flexed. In the first half of the decade, the unemployed, organized for the first time, had, by extra-parliamentary action, successfully fought off a massive attack upon their standard of living. Between 1935 and 1938, membership of trade unions had risen by nearly two and a quarter million. Equally important, the organization, activity and influence of shop stewards had profoundly affected conditions—economic and, in the broadest sense, political conditions and developments—on the factory floor. This was especially remarkable, indeed crucial, in the engineering industry. Branson and Heinemann note that 'it is significant that as the Amalgamated Engineering Union increased its organization in the mass production industries, it came to depend more and more on its shop stewards, official payments to whom in 1935-8 were nearly

The drama widens and the plot thickens: Hitler's new ally Stalin; and Japan (also Hitler's ally) in action against Russia in Manchuria

three times as great as they had been in the previous four years . . . The exchange of information between shop stewards' committees, and the organization of solidarity by one factory for another, became an important part of the effort to raise wages . . . Organizations of shop stewards came to play a key part in the industry.'

The militant shop stewards were a demonstration that within industry the muscles of democracy were not atrophying but developing.

It was among the shop stewards and the generality of skilled workers that awareness and suspicion of the real motives, aims and consequences of the Chamberlain policy was most acute. Politically educated, and with much tough experience of political and economic realities gained on the factory floor, they in general regarded governmental statements, assurances and explanations with absolute scepticism, treating them as either irrelevant or fraudulent. In this social stratum to believe otherwise was exceptional: though very numerous, the Tory Working Men were not much represented among the shop stewards. Thus a significant proportion of key workers—key in terms of their position in industrial relations and of their influence upon other workers—found it difficult to take seriously any governmental appeals on behalf of democracy threatened, freedom in peril. They took for granted that class considerations were responsible for the interminable refusal of the Government to join seriously with the Soviet Union in the organization of collective security.

Until the actual outbreak of war such sentiments were predominant. The Communists, carrying the logic of such conviction to an extreme conclusion which only a small minority chose to share with them, declared, after initial wavering, that the war was simply the outcome of inter-imperialist conflicts, and must be exposed as such. They quoted Dimitrov (hero of the Reichstag Fire Trial and Secretary of the Comintern): 'The working class will end this war after its own fashion, in its own interests, in the interests of all labouring mankind.'

It was an aspiration based on the mistaken belief that the German working class, though certainly as disgusted by the war as the British, was neither able nor, in general, at all willing to overthrow Hitler and destroy the Nazi regime.

On the other hand, those who supposed the Communists' behaviour was to be explained simply as an automatic 'following of the line of the Comintern' underestimated the extent to which total hostility to the Government, deep mistrust of any cause the Government seemed to sponsor, was at this time indigenous, so to speak, on British soil. The point was heavily emphasized later when, with the Soviet Union under attack and at last in alliance with Britain, the Communists, now supporting the war, were acknowledged, particularly by the Ministry of Labour, as having an effective importance in the factories out of all proportion to their numbers; it was recognized that Communist shop stewards had retained an influence which was both welcome for the moment, and disconcerting in regard to the future.

The foreign policy of the Chamberlain Government during the weeks and months after the invasion of Czechoslovakia sharply increased the confusion, demoralization and cynicism of large sections of the citizenry, and was

246

reassuring to hardly anyone. The only section of British public opinion which was encouraged was that which felt that any course of action was preferable to serious involvement with the Soviet Union.

Just over a fortnight after the occupation of Prague the Government took the step of guaranteeing Poland against agression. This action was spectacular in the contrast it presented with the refusal of the same Government —except during the brief interlude of May 1938 similarly to guarantee Czechoslovakia. Czechoslovakia had been a strong military and industrial state, with a strategic frontier which, by nature and fortification, was the most defensible in Europe. It had a long record of uncompromising resistance to German expansion. Poland had no such frontiers. Its Army, though the courage and patriotism of its personnel were highly praised, was, in terms of modern equipment and training, largely obsolete. Its Government, realistically enough, had always sought to maintain cordial relations with the Nazi regime and had shared, with Germany, the dismemberment of Czechoslovakia. The British offer of a guarantee had in fact been precipitated by the news that Poland was about to ally itself with Hitler.

There was one other outstanding point of difference between the two states: Czechoslovakia had been in close political and military alliance with the Soviet Union and a British guarantee would have involved joint military action, or the threat of it, with the Soviet Union. For sufficient political, social and nationalistic reasons no such links existed, or could exist, between Moscow and Warsaw.

There was at the time fierce Conservative and Opposition criticism of the fact that when the British Government did at length agree to military connections with the Russians, it sent an ostentatiously low-grade mission to Moscow.

But by the time the mission was sent, two facts were already clear to almost all observers: first, the Polish Government, for the social, political and nationalistic reasons already referred to, would not and could not agree to permit the free entry of the Red Army to Polish territory in the event of a German invasion from the west. In Czechoslovakia, the fears of the Czech bourgeois classes for the social structure of the state had, at the eleventh hour, sufficed to prevent President Beneš calling in the Red Army as Czechoslovakia's only ally. It had been touch and go. The politico-social balance of power within the country had been nearly even. No such balance existed in Poland. The political strength of anti-Communism and anti-Russianism was unquestionably overwhelming.

The British 'man in the street' was understandably amazed and indignant at the attitude of the Poles. It appeared to him incomprehensible and more or less impudently fraudulent that the Polish Government should involve Britain in a guarantee to Poland against German aggression while refusing the only military aid available in the shape of the Red Army.

But the Government was perfectly informed of the realities of the Polish position. It was well aware of them when it gave its guarantee.

Secondly: unless the Polish Government was prepared to do what everyone knew it was not prepared to do, it was military nonsense and a political impossibility for the Soviet Government to join in any sort of guarantee to

Poland. No informed military man supposed that the Polish Army could resist a German attack for more than a couple of weeks. If the Red Army were inhibited from crossing the Polish frontier in the first hours or days of the war, the result would be that the German Army would reach the Polish eastern frontier almost intact and would thus be several hundred miles further advanced towards Minsk and points east to Moscow. To accept such a prospect could and would be seen in Moscow as a deliberate betrayal of the interests of the Soviet Union.

There was, theoretically, the possibility that the British Government would exercise such pressure in Warsaw as to compel the Polish Government, however reluctantly, to enter into the necessary agreement with Moscow. Such a course was in fact urged upon Chamberlain from both sides of the House of Commons and upon the Military Mission in Moscow. The French Government did inform the Russians that so far as the French were concerned the Russians were to cross Poland to the counter-attack whether the Poles wanted them to or not. But the British Government would not and perhaps could not exert any such pressure in Warsaw as it had used, in a contrary sense, in Prague all through the previous summer.

It was therefore evident that the military talks in Moscow could serve no immediate or serious military purpose, and this was the conclusion drawn in Moscow and by a large body of British public opinion. For at that very late hour British public opinion was at least sufficiently stirred to force the Government into a serious effort to convince the public that something was happening which was not. Historian A. J. P. Taylor, writing of the projected Anglo-Soviet alliance, neatly sums up the most intelligible explanations of government policy:

'No alliance has been pursued less enthusiastically. The British Government acted as though they had all the time in the world. They held every Soviet formula up to the light and took days, sometimes weeks, to answer. Halifax was invited to Moscow. He declined the invitation, and Chamberlain denied in the House of Commons that it had been made. Eden offered to go to Moscow on special mission. Chamberlain turned the offer down. The British Government were mainly concerned to conciliate public opinion. As well, they hoped to give Hitler a vague fright. They did not at any time seek Soviet miliary aid in practical terms. Not only did they fear the consequences of Soviet victory and German defeat. They were hoping all along to strike a bargain with Hitler when the prospect of resistance had made him more moderate, and kept the door open for agreement. Like many people at that time, they imagined that Germany's real grievances were economic and therefore thought of proposing a sort of Anglo-German economic partnership: Germany to be predominant in eastern and south-eastern Europe; a colonial condominium for the exploitation of tropical Africa; and a British loan to Germany of £1,000 million to tide over the difficulties of disarmament.'

Efforts to arouse and sustain British enthusiasm for Poland were, so far as the mass of the population was concerned, a failure. And their nature and failure were themselves expressive of the social situation on the eve of war. It was not possible to present the Polish regime, dominated by military men, landowners, bankers and the Catholic Church, as being at all part of Us. To the popular view Colonel Beck and his colleagues looked to be the image not just of Them, but of Them preserved in some Ruritanian museum.

Attempts were made to emphasize their patriotism and gallantry. But when it came out that their gallantry was going to be displayed by deploying mounted lancers of pre-1914 type, against tanks, people felt sorry for them, but not reassured as to their efficacy in the role of military allies. Poland was represented as essentially small, and helpless. A glance at the map showed it to be fairly large as countries go, and the news of its helplessness was dismaying or bewildering. Why would they not accept aid from nearby Russia rather than far-off England?

It is risky to assume that normally intelligent people, in a position to be well-informed, in fact proceeded in culpable ignorance of realities. Yet in the particular instance of the Anglo-Russian negotiations, it seems possible that the British Government was in part unaware of political developments in Moscow, or refused to consider seriously the information available.

Ever since Munich the 'collectivists', sometimes called the 'war party', had been in serious trouble in Moscow. That day in Prague, already des-cribed, when unilateral Russian aid was rejected, had been seen by many of their critics as decisive: the 'collectivists', the advocates of maximum de-fensive/offensive action against Germany, had, it was argued, demonstrably miscalculated. The natural and intelligible fear in the capitalist-bourgeois states, of Communism, and the bolshevization of Europe, would always inhibit them, even when, as in Prague in 1938, the alternative was total surrender, from effective alliance with the Soviet Union, as against the nightmare of extending Communist power, the dream of Hitler's expansion south-eastwards, would always prevail.

Koltsov, in the late evening of that crucial day in Prague, spent some hours sketching for the present writer a map of the unpleasant political possibilities now opened. He was under no illusions as to the exposed nature of the position in which the collectivists would now immediately find them-selves. Within a few hours he himself was due to be reporting to Stalin. And it was already evident that what had for several years been the big gun in the battery of the collectivists' arguments—the military argument—had been spiked.

Until a few hours before, it had been possible to envisage a series of violent and perhaps paralysing Soviet-Czech attacks upon nearby Berlin, and the still closer industrial areas of Saxony and Silesia, carried out within an hour of the expected announcement of agreement in Munich. The Russians were sure that the Czech Army would prove itself equal, if not absolutely superior, to any force the Germans could mobilize immediately. The strategic defence line in the Sudetenland would be impregnable at least for several weeks.

It was largely on the basis of such calculations that Stalin and a majority of those in power had backed 'collectivism' to win. But those calculations had suddenly been rendered obsolete. And Koltsov, illustrating his pre-view with Yiddish proverbs and macabre Russian stories in the colourful manner of Odysseus, had some grim precognition.

What some might see as his acute extra-sensory perception of things to come, and others as an inexorable Marxist analysis by a man who knew intimately all the players in the Moscow drama, including Stalin, enabled

Koltsov to tell what turned out to be a notably accurate story of what might, and, the way things looked, probably would happen.

Signals showing the progress of the controversy in Moscow were soon clearly visible to anyone who wanted to see them. Stalin made a speech in which he warned the West not to expect the Soviet Union to pull its chesnuts out of the fire for it. It was a warning to all those who confusedly supposed that because Nazism was the most grave and immediate threat to the Soviet Union, the Communists, however reluctantly, must always support the West against Hitler, however much Soviet aid might be disregarded and Soviet proposals rebuffed.

Molotov, no collectivist, replaced Litvinov. Koltsov himself was dismissed, arrested, and soon after shot.

By the late spring the collectivist policy was in retreat though not quite decisively defeated. But already the arguments of the isolationists appeared increasingly unanswerable. All the news from London seemed to indicate that the British Government had no intention of making serious military arrangements with the Soviet Union. It would not lift a finger to persuade the Poles to make such arrangements possible. It seemed almost ostentatiously to hope for the success of an ingenious manoeuvre by which Russia would involve itself in war with Germany without the possibility of being able to advance across Poland to encounter the Germans at least half way. On the other hand, if the West were left to pull its own chestnuts out of the fire, the Russians could avert the possibility—the probability indeed—of a German attack across Poland which would develop into a bi-later al Russo-German war, while the British and the French remained passive behind the Maginot Line and the North Sea. Part of the price which Germany would in the circumstances have to pay would be a Russian occupation of eastern Poland.

It is just possible to suppose that had the British Government, in the early summer, taken the facts of the internal struggle in Moscow fully into account, it might at the last moment have reversed its policy on Poland and insisted on passage for the Red Army. Possible, but unlikely, and in any case it did not do so.

At the end of August the final victory of the isolationists was signalized by the signature of the German-Soviet Pact.

The biggest aspidistra

Among a great mass of people, particularly unorganized workers and members of the vast lower class, there prevailed during those last months before the catastrophe a mood of ironic, self-ridiculing resignation.

It is dangerous to describe any historical situation as having been unique, unprecedented. Too many similarities and parallels recur. Also, if it be asserted of any period within living memory that 'people' felt this or that, numberless people will come forward to testify that they personally felt quite otherwise.

Even so, the psychological condition of Britain in the summer of 1939 presented some features unusual in a country on the eve of war. Some of them were unusual only in the sense of unprecedented, for the reason that the general public had never before approached a war in time of radio, nor in time of such general literacy.

This circumstance was responsible for many notable split-levels of emotion and understanding. Thus in a couple of months the public had to be assured that Poland was a great freedom-loving state, full of military ardour. It would have been, at that date, nearly treasonable for the media to have said anything else. The result was that people could, and did, in the course of the same day, and in accordance with the nature or mood of their companions, seriously discuss this mythical entity—Poland—and even, for the moment, seriously believe in it, and yet remark variously that (a) they had no clear idea where Poland actually was, (b) did not suppose that this bunch of Johnny-come-latelies amounted to anything worth bothering about, (c) that things must be in a poor way if we were relying on Poles, (d) that it was pretty steep to ask British people to upset their whole lives for the sake of these Poles.

On a more general level, other sets of quite contradictory beliefs were entertained by the same people almost simultaneously. It was accepted, perhaps more widely than ever before, that the Government, the political leaders and the media were all telling packs of lies. One had, people told one another, simply stopped paying attention to them. At the same time more people listened more intently to the radio than ever before.

The point upon which consensus was probably broadest was belief that if and when the war came, everyone, nearly everyone, or anyway 75 per cent of living being, would be wiped out within six weeks, six days, or six hours. This kind of estimate did, as is now known, have the expert endorsement of the Committee on Imperial Defence. That was the shape of things to come— and the phrase, from Wells's book and the resultant film, was already a worn cliché, but not yet worn out.

For many people this conception of a general wipe-out had the qualities of a death wish. There were, naturally, pathologically suicidal types in whom the death-wish existed in the literal sense. But in many millions of what are loosely called normal people, this wish lurked, consciously or subconsciously, as a form of relief: relief that all the botherations and uncertainties, the argument and strife, the worry, worry, worry of the past years in which those damned international politics had come barging into the living-room, the kitchen and the bedroom, would at least be abruptly ended and superseded by restful oblivion.

If it were true that millions of people had begun to think it at least probable that sudden death for the majority and conditions of primitive barbarism for the survivors were just around the corner, that there never would be another Merry Christmas, it might have been expected that there would be on the one hand some upsurge of religious emotion, and on the other outbreaks of license—the traditional last dance on the edge of the volcano.

Neither, on any notable scale, came to pass. And this in itself was of a piece with the general mood of apathetic, sometimes cynical, sometimes humorous resignation.

As so often happens, the 'secret people', the taciturn majority, seemed to display an awareness of their true situation more realistic than any shown by their ostensible leaders. In those months, there could be obtained a kind of preview of attitudes and reactions which were later often supposed to have made their appearance only long after the war, with the visible dismantling of the Empire and the decline of Britain from the status of a First Class Power.

Hardly definable, the mood was of the kind expressed by Gracie Fields in her threnody for the Biggest Aspidistra in the World:

> The Borough Council told us we'd have to cut it down,
> It interfered with aeroplanes that fly above the town.
> So we sold it to a woodyard for a lousy half-a-crown,
> The biggest—biggest—biggest aspidistra in the world.

The mental, emotional and above all material confusion of the country on the very eve of war was such that it could be said that the only organization immediately ready to meet the emergency was the Family Planning Association, organizer of birth control clinics and appliances. In the first week of September, the Government took the step of commandeering, for use in the aircraft factories, all available supplies of the rayon rubber used in the manufacture of condoms. Scouring London and Manchester, the F.P.A. discovered a huge quantity of the material in a warehouse. It had been ordered from the London Rubber Company by the proprietors of a new luxury hotel which had been about to open in Paris when war intervened. The rubber was to be used as decorative yet waterproof covering for the floors of the luxurious bathrooms. The material was thus richly patterned with coloured designs of birds, bees and flowers.

The energetic chiefs of the F.P.A. took over the entire stock and had it tailored, so to speak, to its own requirements. These ornate condoms were distributed in many thousands. According to a statement by an official of the F.P.A. in February 1972, a few of them are still preserved in the homes of citizens here and there as souvenirs of the last days of peace.

The general mood was finally dramatized on 3 September with Chamberlain's plaintive announcement that, contrary to his hopes and expectations, Britain was at war with Germany. It was, he said, a sad blow to him personally. He at that moment supremely personified all that was meant by Them as distinct from Us.

When the first air-raid sirens sounded as he finished speaking there was grim fear in the streets. When the warning proved to be a false alarm, it seemed fitting and quite unsurprising that the war should start on a phoney note.

But at the moment when the siren went off, and the warning was taken to be the real thing, people in responsible positions up and down the country had a grisly consciousness of how little, despite all the expectations, all the warning signals, had been done to prepare for the horrible reality.

In that first minute of war, as the siren sounded, the chief of one of London's principal A.R.P. centres was called on the telephone by one of London's principal hospitals.

'What are we supposed to do?' shouted the voice from the hospital. 'We've lost the key of the bloody mortuary.'

Waiting . . . for what?

Index

Photo Acknowledgements

Associated Press, 2, 17, 42, 43, 55, 91, 93
Barratts, 82, 93
Butlins, 67
Conway Picture Library, 3, 36, 47, 48, 53, 54, 61, 62, 66, 68, 72, 75-77, 86, 92
Fox Photos, 4, 8, 9, 12, 18, 19, 28, 33, 34, 41, 59, 60, 64, 65, 78, 84

John Hillelson Agency/David Seymour photograph, 57
Keystone Press, 10, 15, 21, 22, 39, 40, 46, 51, 52, 56, 63, 69, 70, 71, 79, 80, 88, 89, 90
London Express, 45, 81, 85
Mander and Mitchenson, 26, 27
National Film Archive, 30, 31

Popperfoto, 7, 11, 13, 16, 58, 87
Prudential Assurance, 14
Radio Times Hulton Picture Library, 6, 20, 24, 29, 38, 73
Sport & General, 35, 49, 74, 83
Syndication International, 32
United Press International, 50
Woolworths, 23, 25